THE
REGENCY
UNDERWORLD

In memory of M.A. MacC.

THE
REGENCY
UNDERWORLD

DONALD A. LOW

SUTTON PUBLISHING

This book was first published in 1982 by
J.M. Dent & Sons Ltd

This edition first published in 2005 by
Sutton Publishing Limited · Phoenix Mill
Thrupp · Stroud · Gloucestershire · GL5 2BU

British Library Cataloguing in Publication Data
A catalogue record for this book is available from the British
Library.

ISBN 0 7509 4047 6

Typeset in 11/13.5pt Iowan.
Typesetting and origination by
Sutton Publishing Limited.
Printed and bound in Great Britain by
J.H. Haynes & Co. Ltd, Sparkford.

CONTENTS

SIGHTS AND SOUNDS OF REGENCY LONDON

The Regency is associated, to a greater degree possibly than any other period in English history, with social poise and distinguished cultural achievements. Jane Austen's England: the words call to mind an ideal of elegance and moral alertness typified not only by the shrewdly observed, eminently proper novels of Jane Austen and Sir Walter Scott, but by Constable's tranquil Suffolk landscapes, patrician portraits by Lawrence and Raeburn, the dignified colonnades of John Nash's Regent Street, and an unparalleled national heritage of fine country houses. This was the time which produced the poetry of Wordsworth and of Keats, deeply imprinted with the beauty of the English countryside. It was a period, too, of lovely dresses which flowed with the natural line of Grecian taste, of carefully groomed horses and light, skilfully designed phaetons and landaus. Brighton Pavilion, seeming to float magically on air, symbolizes the pursuit of ideal beauty which is so characteristic of the Regency. Abroad, the Navy and the Army – which were to most people synonymous with Nelson and Wellington – brought victory and heightened self-confidence to complement the outstanding artistic achievements at home.

The brilliance of this extraordinary flowering of cultural life makes it easy to overlook a very different facet of early nineteenth-century Britain. For alongside the world of *Pride and Prejudice* and the Nature poets there existed a pulsating, undisciplined urban underworld of young thieves, body-snatchers and gamblers. Pleasure-seekers and criminals alike were enjoying a final fling before the coming of the Metropolitan Police in 1829. Gambling and drinking were endemic in upper- and lower-class society, fraud in the middle classes. Historians have often neglected this other world in favour of the high culture of the period, or the movement for political reform. But the life of the streets of Regency Britain is colourful, fascinating and varied; and, at least as far as social history is concerned, the Police Act of 1829 and the Anatomy Act of 1831 tell us just as much about the first thirty years of the nineteenth century as the Reform Act of 1832.

This book covers the period 1800 to 1830. 'Regency' is thus used in its extended sense to include the actual reign of the fourth George, described by Thackeray as 'the Magnificent', as well as his regency of 1811–20 and the decade before that. (The influence of George's personal example on the code of behaviour of his less respectable subjects is readily apparent; he helped to set the tone of the age, especially with regard to gambling and womanizing, but also by making popular such 'new' pursuits as horse-racing.) 'Underworld' is defined by *Chambers Twentieth-Century Dictionary* as

the world beneath the heavens: the world, or a region, beneath the earth: the place of departed souls: the part of the world hidden below the horizon: the antipodes: a submerged, hidden, or secret region or sphere of life, especially one given to crime, profligacy, or intrigue.

While the activities of the resurrection-men make it necessary to keep in mind the second of these definitions, 'a region beneath the earth', it is the last part of the dictionary definition which applies directly to the entire subject. What calls for investigation is the submerged, hidden or secret life of the times, the delinquent or 'other' Regency. Crime and profligacy and intrigue all have a place in the story. So also, paradoxically, has the love of display and of *brio* which is so characteristic of the period. Guilty secrets and an ostentatious way of living often went together.

Essentially, the underworld explored in these pages is that of London. In the early nineteenth century the old rhyme still held good:

> Derbyshire for lead, Devonshire for tin,
> Wiltshire for plovers' eggs, Middlesex for sin.

The English provinces were of course by no means wholly given over to rural innocence, and Dublin and Glasgow certainly witnessed occasional acts of spectacular lawlessness; but in this period, as in most others, London surpassed the rest of the British Isles in crime and vice. All the leading gambling 'hells' were concentrated in the capital, which harboured every variety of law-breaker from young children trained by criminal parents to steal handkerchieves to the hardened veterans – in reality, only a few years older – of Newgate and the 'hulks', or prison ships.

Physically, late Georgian London was a boisterous, noisy, confusing mixture of city, town and village, a strange amalgam of old and new. Its two ancient citadels, Westminster and the city, the former technically outside the original London, were separated from each other by a densely populated area of startling contrasts: on the one hand, fine squares and dignified thoroughfares – like Bond Street, all glitter and poise, as elegant as anywhere in Europe, with magnificent shops and houses – and on the other warrens of narrow, evil-smelling and badly lit alleyways in which a stranger might lose anything from his pocketbook to his life. One moment the vista might be of noble colonnades, bow-windows and gleaming door-knockers, the kind of prospect being developed northwards along the length of what is now Regent Street by the leading architect of the day, John Nash. The next, if you chanced to take a careless turning, it was to find yourself among gin-shops, pawnbrokers and broken-down dwellings of such squalor that they literally oozed filth.

This pattern of stark contrast between prosperous and mean streets within a stone's throw of each other was repeated many times across London from Tothill Fields to Rotherhithe, reflecting dramatic differences in welfare and lifestyle between rich and poor. Frequently, too, there were public buildings of note in the midst of seamy districts. Drury Lane and Covent Garden theatres, for instance, were situated in a notoriously bad part of London, the haunt of murderers and escaped convicts, as well as of women on the game. Closeness to the river, in their case and in many others, brought insecurity and ill repute. The new London Dock, and further east the West India and East India Docks, were symbols both of the wealth and of the criminality of London, solid, imposing places, protected by high walls and by their own specially recruited police against river thieves. They had to be, for the Ratcliffe Highway which ran through Shadwell had almost as bad a reputation as the Thames itself. Seamen in Shadwell went on wild drinking bouts along with the prostitutes of the district, orgies which lasted for as long as their joint ingenuity could supply them with the means to drink. South of the river, where Bermondsey shaded into the Borough, there were equally riotous public houses and 'dangerous' classes of citizen. It was here that the 'Boys of the Borough', London's most successful resurrection-men, had their daytime lairs.

The sheer size of London, and the rate at which it was expanding, encouraged both crime and its concealment. In 1801 the population was just under a million, more than eleven times that of any other British city. The figure went up astonishingly to one and a quarter million by 1820, and then again by 20 per cent in the next ten years. Now it is true that in the years 1821 to 1831 Liverpool, Manchester, Birmingham and Leeds all had increases of population of 40 per cent or more. But these cities lacked London's centuries-old criminal underworld tradition; their incomers drifted to poverty and unemployment often enough, but not to 'rookeries' (criminal districts) and 'flash-houses' (pubs frequented by criminals) like those of St Giles and

Whitechapel: petty offences flourished rather than really ambitious law-breaking. In London, on the other hand, there was every encouragement to commit crime. In his *Treatise on the Police and Crimes of the Metropolis*, published while Peel's Police Bill was before Parliament in 1829, John Wade wrote:

> Here there is no curiosity about neighbours – every one is engrossed in his own pursuit, and neither knows nor cares about any human beings except the circle to which he has been introduced and with which he is connected by ties of business, pleasure, or profit. It is from this circumstance London affords so many facilities for the concealment of criminality. The metropolis is like an immense forest, in the innumerable avenues of which offenders may always find retreat and shelter.

'Ties of business, pleasure, or profit': as the mercantile centre of Britain, and a thriving international port, London offered rich pickings to thieves of all kinds. But it had also acquired a reputation of another sort, as an exciting place for those in pursuit of worldly pleasure. Theatres and mistresses belonged to town, just as cracksmen and receivers did. The rakish ne'er-do-well and the professional criminal alike had scope in the capital, where every form of self-indulgence was provided for. And because dicing, whoring and gin-drinking were all activities which tended to land indiscreet Regency bucks on the fringes of the underworld, the thieves from the streets preyed upon the high-born rakes. Nothing about the early nineteenth-century underworld is more fascinating than its internal networks and lines of connection from one sphere of pleasure or corruption to another. The prostitutes who haunted Drury Lane and Covent Garden theatres sought the protection of gentlemen from the clubs of St James's – where large fortunes were won and lost at roulette and hazard – and yet they had dealings, too, with pawnbrokers in the backstreets adjoining Petticoat Lane. Thus stolen pocketbooks and watches made their way to Rat's Castle in the 'Holy Land' and other rookeries. There were clear demarcation lines within the criminal population, no less than between the rich and the poor. But while the city contained many different sub-cultures, each with its own colourings, the essential unity within diversity of its complex underworld is indisputable.

A visitor's first impression was usually of London as a bustling, crowded city and a great centre of trade. Britain controlled many of the world's key sea-routes, which meant that trading vessels were constantly coming and going and discharging valuable cargoes. Near the river, the view at any time was likely to be dominated by the masts of sailing ships moored in the Thames or preparing to set off downstream after unloading goods. In *Don Juan* Byron offers a glimpse of such a characteristic London scene:

> A mighty mass of brick and smoke and shipping,
>   Dirty and dusky, but as wide as eye
> Could reach, with here and there a sail just skipping
>   In sight, then lost amidst the forestry
> Of masts, a wilderness of steeples peeping
>   On tiptoe through their sea coal canopy,
> A huge, dun cupola, like a foolscap crown
>   On a fool's head – and there is London town!

Two clues in Byron's description help to make clear why so much theft went on near the Thames. There was always plenty to steal in the vicinity of the river, whether from ships, small craft or wharves; and the overhanging 'dun' pall of sea-coal smoke made it easy for thieves, even when caught in the act, to elude recognition and capture.

Inadequate lighting and a murky atmosphere had much to do, similarly, with the astonishing amount of casual theft elsewhere in London. In 1807 thirteen gas lamps were installed on the south side of Pall Mall, and five years later the Gas Light and Coke Company established its first gasworks in Great Peter Street, Westminster. But the process of lighting the common streets of London – as distinct from the main streets of the West End and the City – took more than twenty years to complete. During that period, although the technical innovation of gas naturally impressed city-dwellers and tourists alike, the actual supply of light was uneven and inadequate, and any improvements which were made were not enough to keep pace with the increase in population of the underworld. Many a young thief gave the slip to the officers of Bow Street by running down a sidestreet or passageway into impenetrable darkness. Prostitutes and others with dubious business to conduct simply moved out of the circle of gaslight into the surrounding shadows.

Early nineteenth-century London is brought vividly to life in Robert Southey's *Letters from England* (1807), which purports to be a selection of the letters sent home by an anonymous Spaniard travelling in England. This device enabled Southey both to convey surface impressions which Britons often took for granted, and to express unusually frank criticisms of their social customs. *Letters from England* is full of London sights and sounds. We read, for instance, of the constant movement in the streets, and of the splendid appearance of shops in the centre of town:

> when I reached Cheapside the crowd completely astonished me. On each side of the way were two uninterrupted streams of people, one going east, the other west. At first I thought some extraordinary occasion must have collected such a concourse; but I soon perceived it was only the usual course of business . . . the rapidity with which they moved was as remarkable as their numbers. It was easy to perceive that the English calculate the value of time. . . . The carriages were numerous in proportion, and were driven with answerable velocity.
>
> If possible, I was still more astonished at the opulence and splendour of the shops: drapers, stationers, confectioners, pastry-cooks, seal-cutters, silver-smiths,

book-sellers, print-sellers, hosiers, fruiterers, china-sellers – one close to another without intermission, a shop to every house, street after street, and mile after mile . . .

Southey's London is a city where even 'a dead wall, a vacant house, or a temporary scaffolding' is covered with printed bills; advertising is everywhere. So too is noise. He describes the typical street-cries and sounds of one night and morning . . .

Here was the watchman, whose business it is, not merely to guard the streets and take charge of the public security, but to inform the good people of London every half hour of the state of the weather. . . . A strange custom this, to pay men for telling them what the weather is every hour during the night, till they get so accustomed to the noise, that they sleep on and cannot hear what is said.

Besides this regular annoyance, there is another cause of disturbance. The inhabitants of this great city seem to be divided into two distinct casts, – the Solar and the Lunar races, – those who live by day, and those who live by night, antipodes to each other, the one rising just as the others go to bed. The clatter of the night coaches had scarcely ceased, before that of the morning carts began. The dustman with his bell, and his chant of dust-ho! succeeded to the watchman; then came the porter-house boy for the pewter-pots which had been set out for supper the preceding night; the milkman next, and so on, a succession of cries, each in a different tune . . .

Elsewhere he writes about ballad-sellers loudly peddling news of murders and the last dying confessions of wrong-doers in Newgate, about troublesome quack-doctors who went up to strangers in the street to talk volubly about their 'never-failing pills', and about noisy newspaper and post boys. London was no place for anyone seeking peace and quiet.

Southey's contrast between 'those who live by day' and 'those who live by night' had a solid basis in fact, and not one exclusively related to law-abiding citizens on early dustcart or milk rounds. It was by night that the worst house burglaries took place, along with the nastiest murders, and the graveyard trafficking in corpses for resale to surgeons. Women of the streets and their 'flash' companions were very much creatures of darkness, as were convicts on the run and men who had come back from Botany Bay swearing vengeance against the magistrates and law officers who had sent them there. In short, the guilty and the outcasts of society chose to appear during the hours when London's safety was entrusted to the curious makeshift army of watchmen, who held few terrors for them.

Southey also draws attention to another division in London, even more significant than that between 'Solars' and 'Lunars' – the marked differences in social and economic status between the inhabitants of the eastern and western parts of town.

London is more remarkable for the distribution of its inhabitants than any city on the continent. It is at once the greatest port in the kingdom, or in the world, a city of merchants and tradesmen, and the seat of government, where the men of rank and fashion are to be found; and though all these are united together by continuous streets, there is an imaginary line of demarcation which divides them from each other. A nobleman would not be found by any accident to live in that part which is properly called the City, unless he should be confined for treason or sedition in Newgate or the Tower. This is the Eastern side; and I observed, whenever a person says that he lives at the West End of the Town, there is some degree of consequence connected with the situation: For instance, my tailor lives at the West End of the Town, and consequently he is supposed to make my coat in a better style of fashion: and this opinion is carried so far among the ladies, that if a cap was known to have come from the City, it would be given to my lady's woman, who would give it to the cook, and she perhaps would think it prudent not to inquire into its pedigree. A transit from the City to the West End of the town is the last step of the successful trader, when he throws off his *exuviae* and emerges from his chrysalis state into the butterfly world of high life.

There is ample testimony to the essential truth of this analysis of social mobility and of the dynamic leading the ambitious and successful westward within London. The pattern could apply equally to those whose origins lay in other parts of the East End than the City proper, as is witnessed by the career of William Crockford, a Billingsgate fishmonger who became the patron of West End gamblers. Even if much hypocrisy, and even more snobbery, lay behind it, the 'imaginary line' of demarcation was strongly felt by many Londoners.

The year after *Letters from England* appeared, an ambitious print-seller called Rudolph Ackermann began to publish from his shop in the Strand a very different but no less truthful and revealing work, *The Microcosm of London*. This consisted of aquatint plates, 104 in all, of most of the main public buildings and sights, with descriptions to match. The plates were the joint work of A.C. Pugin, a skilled topographical artist, and of the caricaturist Thomas Rowlandson – a genial gambler, nearly always short of cash – who added human figures to enliven the views. Ackermann's main aim was to create an accurate and impressive visual record of London as a great capital city. The emphasis in *The Microcosm of London* is therefore very much on grandeur, imposing façades, and whatever conveyed an impression of dignity and wealth. These things went down well with the public he had in mind, and the series of plates sold quickly.

Thanks largely, however, to the irreverent genius of Rowlandson, the life of another, much less respectable London kept breaking in. Billingsgate Market, for example, became something more than a topographically exact representation of the riverside trading area where fish were bought and sold. As handled by Rowlandson, it is a scene of anarchic energy: as you look at his cleverly drawn crowd of porters, fish-sellers, and costermongers, you can almost hear their shouts and feel their elbows being driven into your sides. In the background, true to the life of the times, someone who has stolen fish is being pursued hotfoot, and violence is about to break out. There is nothing polite, either, about the spectators Rowlandson draws in front of the pillory at Charing Cross. Women stand arguing noisily, children crawl beneath the legs of the grown-ups, while the inmates of two stage-coaches, held up by the press of people, unashamedly crane their heads for a better view of the men in pillory at the centre of the scene. Rowlandson knew his London, just as Southey did. He was familiar with the traditional English love of a vindictive spectacle, whether pillory or hanging, and thoroughly understood the bold humours of the mob. (He has another drawing in which a young pickpocket goes to work at the very moment when a man and woman wait on the gallows.) Social control, in his eyes, existed only precariously: just beneath the surface were greed and anger and lust. Time and again he drew gross, self-indulgent figures, pot-bellied magistrates and aldermen, blowsy prostitutes, watchmen who quite clearly cared more about their own comfort than about safe-guarding London's citizens during the hours of darkness. He even dared to hint at the reputation for lewdness of a certain Old Bailey judge. One plate shows an attractive female prisoner being advised during her trial on an unspecified charge, 'Hold up your head, young woman, and look at his lordship' Her best hope, it seems, lay in that direction.

Rowlandson saw much evidence of hypocrisy and of a grasping spirit in the more strictly fashionable of the places which Ackermann asked him to illustrate. Like Hogarth before him, he seemed impelled towards broadly inclusive social satire, and his work suggests that very often the have-nots of Regency London – impertinent, unruly, inclined to make off in haste with whatever they could snatch – were simply imitating the example of their superiors. 'A

Masquerade at the Pantheon in Oxford Street' shows the classes mixing, and makes the point that one group is as bad as the other: the plate is accompanied by an explanation,

> It is composed, as these scenes usually are, of a motley crowd of peers and pickpockets, honourables and dishonourables, Jew brokers and demireps [women of doubtful reputation], quidnuncs [gossips] and quack doctors.

Christie's auction room struck Rowlandson as grotesque, a setting for the most extraordinary behaviour, where well-heeled squires competed to own objects that they did not begin to understand. At the 'Showing of Pictures in the Royal Academy', it was much the same. Ladies with social aspirations preened themselves haughtily, while their husbands ogled paintings of nudes in a forthright manner. 'Connoisseurs', the artist seems to imply, are no better than costermongers.

What Rowlandson captures, above all, is the Londoner's appetite for life, gusto and cheekiness. When he draws a group of spectators at Sadler's Wells, he notices the fact that they are paying more attention to each other than to the aquatic spectacle which is taking place on stage. This characteristic piece of observation matches exactly what can be learned from other sources. People went to the theatres of London at this time expecting to have the freedom to make their own entertainment when the performance of the players failed to hold their interest. Many brought food, and ate quite openly. Talking went on almost continuously – the fact that a large part of the audience was seated a long way from the stage did nothing to aid concentration – and it was common for fights to break out during the 'after-piece' or minor supporting play, when those in the cheaper seats grew bored or had had too much to drink. There would be frequent catcalls, wolf-whistles, and outbursts of beery communal singing. Regency theatre, after all, was the unrestrained and undisciplined forerunner of Victorian music hall. Most people on an evening out were seeking participation, not passive amusement. When they were not watching the actors, or observing the explicit sexual byplay taking place in the pit and boxes between men about town and the 'fashionable impures' who haunted the theatres nightly, they shouted themselves hoarse.

While we have, then, a number of sources providing information about the appearance of early nineteenth-century London and illustrating some aspects at least of its 'hidden life', documents which communicate a convincing idea of what it felt like actually to belong to outcast society – whether permanently or for a short time only – are very scarce. Part of the value of Thomas De Quincey's *Confessions of an English Opium-Eater* (1821) lies here.

Like many others since, De Quincey in his youth found his way to Piccadilly and Soho where, virtually penniless, he was reduced to the condition of a homeless waif seeking somewhere to sleep and the barest means of survival. In his *Confessions* he describes his association with a young prostitute called Ann, as vulnerable and unsure of herself as he was, with whom he formed a brief but deeply felt relationship of mutual protection. Whether or not Ann really existed or was merely a figment of his imagination, the description he gives of Ann's life and her background undoubtedly contains much general truth derived from his own observations.

Being myself at that time of necessity peripatetic, or a walker of the street, I naturally fell in more frequently with those female peripatetics who are technically called street-walkers. Many of these women had occasionally taken my part against watchmen who wished to drive me off the steps of houses where I was sitting. But [there is] one amongst them, the one on whose account I have at all introduced this subject . . . For many weeks I had walked at nights with this poor friendless girl up and down Oxford-street, or had rested with her on steps and under the shelter of porticos. She could not be so old as myself: she told me, indeed, that she had not completed her sixteenth year. By such questions as my interest about her prompted, I had gradually drawn forth her simple history. Hers was a case of usual occurrence (as I have since had reason to think), and one in which, if London beneficence had better adapted its arrangements to meet it, the power of the law might oftener be interposed to protect, and to avenge. But the stream of London charity flows in a channel which, though deep and mighty, is yet noiseless and underground; not obvious or readily accessible to poor houseless wanderers: and it cannot be denied that the outside air and frame-work of London society is harsh, cruel, and repulsive . . .

Before long, De Quincey tells us, Ann and he were parted, never to meet again. His final thoughts on leaving London were, unsurprisingly, of its harshness towards the young and essentially innocent who became its victims. Too many girls like Ann and young men like himself had been left without hope in that uncaring city:

So then, Oxford-street, stony-hearted stepmother! thou that listenest to the sighs of orphans, and drinkest the tears of children, at length I was dismissed from thee: the time was come at last that I no more should pace in anguish thy never-ending terraces; no more should dream, and wake in captivity to the pangs of hunger. Successors, too many, to myself and Ann, have, doubtless, since trodden in our footsteps, – inheritors of our calamities: other orphans than Ann have sighed: tears have been shed by other children: and thou, Oxford-street, has since, doubtless, echoed to the groans of innumerable hearts.

Here, perhaps, the anonymous underworld finds a human identity and a voice.

PREFACE TO THE SECOND EDITION

A society's underworld has its own vitality which overlaps and interconnects with the respectability and correctness present in day-to-day experience. In most large cities there is a seamy side to daily living which not only encourages crime but also its concealment. Much of this book concentrates on London society during the Regency, where immorality and respectability went hand in hand and anticipated the confusion and hypocrisy of the Victorian period.

The Regency took its tone from the larger-than-life figure of the Prince of Wales. His authority as second best was suspect. As Prince Regent, he did not give orthodox leadership. Shockingly extravagant, grossly fat, addicted to gambling, a womanizer with a preference for mistresses older than himself, he married Caroline of Brunswick so that his father would increase his allowance – such was the common view of him during the Regency and subsequent spell as king. One man alone, however, did not generate all the negatives of the time. The age bred a lively underworld of scandal, criminality, gambling and personal notoriety. Embezzlement and fraud flourished then as now. The war against France caused further instability and led to the breakdown of law and order.

The Parliamentary Committee of the Police set up by Peel in 1823 commented that it was 'difficult to reconcile an effective system of police, with the perfect freedom of action and exemption of interference, which are the great privileges and blessings of society in this country'. But Robert Peel knew that 'the long-term containment of the underworld depended upon preventive police'. Preventive policing has not however decreased juvenile theft which, often drug related, is again on the increase. Who could have foreseen that today, despite prison reform, we would have the return of the 'hulks' or convict ships common in the Regency? There is now more openness about the Metropolitan Police Force, including corruption, than ever before. In modern society age, title, power or privilege do not guarantee exemption from public accountability.

Medical history continues to fascinate. It was only in the eighteenth century that surgeons succeeded in establishing themselves as a separate professional group from barbers. To surgeons, human bodies provided by the bodysnatchers were a source of information and a means to improve their operating skills. To the rest of society, the 'sack-'em-up' boys, the resurrectionists, who provided corpses for dissection, induced anxiety and fear. As the boundaries of medical research are pushed back ever further and into the realms of genetic biology, the public appetite for detail relating to medical science remains. Today, as in the Regency, the need for surgeons to advance operating techniques is just as vital but thankfully the technology of the late twentieth century provides a less gruesome alternative to the resurrectionists.

Gambling in Britain, which now has a National Lottery, is flourishing as it did during the Regency and is available to all without going to 'gambling hells' or clubs. Criminals still exploit the get-rich-quick opportunities which present themselves. Larger-than-life figures continue to dominate and feature in scandal. If I were to write *The Regency Underworld* again I would include more about the role of women, more about racial tensions in nineteenth-century Britain and more of the undemocratic effects of building speculation on the environment of London. Characterized by *joie de vivre*, hedonism and dreams of freedom the Regency was indeed different, a breathing space for the nation before it became enveloped in respectability.

DONALD A. LOW

ACKNOWLEDGEMENTS

In the course of writing this book, I have received practical encouragement from busy individuals who have been generous with their time. All errors are strictly my own. I particularly wish to thank Dr P. J. Giddings, Warden of Sherwood Hall, University of Reading, whose thoughtfulness enabled migrant Scots to spend two summers very pleasantly where we wanted to be; and Emeritus Professor H. H. Lamb of the University of East Anglia, who took the trouble to reply in detail to what must have seemed a distinctly odd question about the possible effects of weather on criminal behaviour in early nineteenth-century London. Jocelyn Burton was once again a thoroughly helpful editor. The staff of the British Library and of the British Museum, of the Museum of London, and of the Mary Evans Picture Library, Blackheath, made the choosing of illustrations a pleasure. Above all, my wife Sheona has inspired, shared, and lightened the project, and it is to her, and to Chris and Kirsty, that *The Regency Underworld* properly belongs.

I would like to thank Una Wills of the Picture Library of the Museum of London for her help in providing a large selection of prints from which a final choice was made. Christopher Feeney, for his suggestion of an enlarged edition, and Nick Wright, both of Sutton Publishing, are also due thanks. Dr Suzanne Gilbert of Stirling University English Department helped me with an up-to-date list of books on the Regency but special thanks go to Anne Bennett for 'looking after the book' in a friendly and positive manner.

ONE

OF ROOKERIES AND THIEF-TAKERS

Most early nineteenth-century Londoners were intensely proud of their city. Shopkeepers or noblemen, those who lived in London took pride in the ancient capital of the land they knew to be the home of freedom. London might be dirty, crowded and unhealthy, bursting at the seams under the pressure of continually expanding trade and population, but this growth was in itself witness to the importance of the city as the commercial hub of a mighty nation and empire. From all over Europe diplomats came to the Court of St James's, and the entire world sent ships to the Thames.

With this London pride, however, there went a less certain mood, tinged with apprehension and fear. Crime in the metropolis had reached epidemic proportions, and there seemed little prospect of bringing it under control: every kind of criminal offence known to man appeared to be committed in and around town, from petty theft to armed assault and murder. In particular, property was safe nowhere. A man could scarcely walk down a main thoroughfare at midday without running the risk of being robbed of his handkerchief, pocket-book or watch. A stallholder in any of the great markets – the Fleet, Smithfield or Covent Garden – might have his goods taken from under his nose at any moment. Forgery was rife, and house-breaking so common that it was no longer possible to go away for any length of time without taking elaborate precautions.

The well-to-do London citizen was also likely to be aware, sharply or vaguely according to his experience, that a great deal of gaming and whoring took place in certain parts of town, and that those who consorted with gamblers or prostitutes ran the risk of becoming the victims of blackmail, as well as of assault and theft. Anti-semitic feeling was strong, and for the injudicious gambler there was no greater fear than that he might fall into the hands of Jewish moneylenders, many of whom frequented the doubtful environs of Rosemary Lane in Whitechapel.

It is undeniable that the early nineteenth-century underworld has been neglected by historians. Far more has been written about Hogarth's London, and the excesses of the first era of cheap gin, than about this period. In a sense, this is understandable, for it was the eighteenth century that saw the unprecedented increase in violence on the streets of the capital which laid the foundations of social reforms not implemented until much later. But the years 1800 and 1830 deserve to be seen as vitally significant, too, as a bridge between old and new. On the one hand, they revived and gave a final intensity to the riotousness and hedonism of the old London: 'the Regency', it has been observed, 'is where the eighteenth century dies'. On the other, the proliferation of crime, especially theft, in these years led to major changes in the way in which London was governed, among which pride of place must be given to the introduction of the Metropolitan Police. It could indeed be said that the early nineteenth-century underworld brought the 'peelers', professional officers of the law, with their top hats and truncheons, upon itself. Elderly watchmen with lamps were no match for the denizens of the rookeries.

As I have suggested, much which culminated during the Regency had its origins considerably earlier: the mid-eighteenth century saw the growth of the underworld, and London's most alcoholic period ever. 'Gin Lane' was no myth, but sordid reality. The astonishingly lax laws which permitted the manufacture and sale of very cheap gin to the populace were directly responsible for a great deal of human misery, squalor and crime. In 1750 there was said to be one public house to every fifteen houses in the City of London, one to every eight in Westminster, one to every five in Holborn and more than one to every four in St Giles. (Incidentally, this distribution closely relates to the main centres of criminal activity.) More than half of the wheat sold in the London markets was converted into alcohol. Nor was it very different in outlying districts. Two years later Smollett reported that 'the suburbs of the metropolis abounded with an incredible number of public houses, which continually resounded with the noise of riot and intemperance'. These public houses, brandy- and geneva-shops, were in his view 'the seminaries of drunkenness, debauchery, extravagance, and every vice incident to human nature'. It was a simple matter in such an age for enterprising criminals who kept relatively sober to turn the drunken youths of the town into apprentice thieves – just as it was easy to start serving-girls on the path to prostitution. And so it was in this period that the underworld of the capital began to be systematically 'farmed' and organized. Gangland bosses have existed in every century; but not until the eighteenth century did they and their sisters in crime, the brothel-keepers, become truly formidable in their power and influence in England.

This was in large part because the likelihood of being caught was so low: London's criminals had proved much quicker in adjusting to change than had the forces of law and order, which still largely consisted, as in centuries past, of broken-down old men, the watchmen of the parish, acting on the orders of unpaid local magistrates. Methods of law enforcement were cumbersome, slow and very rough and ready, and scarcely any provision was made for the passing of vital information from one parish to another; in this sense, the operation of English justice was literally parochial. As a result, even the most conscientiously administered parishes were vulnerable to really determined criminals, whose habit it was to steal in one part of London and lie low in another. Moreover, much depended in this uneven contest upon the magistrates' alertness, dedication and social conscience. Many of them were indeed hard-working and honest, and they did their best to run the system, such as it was, so that their own parish should not get a worse name than others. But by no means all observed either the spirit or the letter of the law. Too often a network of contacts existed whereby justice could be thwarted: if a corrupt magistrate did not himself risk dealing directly with a criminal who wished to buy off a charge, then he had at his beck and call a murky and bedraggled army of practised intermediaries – unscrupulous parish beadles, prison turnkeys and the like. These corrupt magistrates, or 'trading justices', who were always expecting something – cash, liquor, or favours from a pretty girl – brought discredit on the whole antiquated machinery of the law as the eighteenth century wore on. Hogarth's contempt for thieves and drunkards was not as great as his anger at the venality of magistrates who yielded to the temptations placed in their way.

Hogarth was joined in his attack on corruption by Henry Fielding, whose *Inquiry into the Causes of the Late Increase of Robbers* (1751) ranged over many topics, from the scandalous drinking habits of the age to the inefficiency of its measures to combat highwaymen. In 1749 Fielding had been appointed as salaried chief magistrate for Westminster, succeeding a notorious trading justice: he knew what he was talking about. With the same energy and strong imagination which he had already brought to the writing of fiction, Fielding set himself to identify the main social forces which had led, within a single generation, to a dramatic upsurge of every kind of illegal activity. Much of the blame must be ascribed, he argued, to 'the vast torrent of luxury' which made people indulge in too frequent and too expensive amusements, drunkenness and gaming. A large part of London's population lacked the education to cope with such pursuits, and once exposed to an essentially licentious style of living, simply did not know how to stop. In his official capacity as magistrate, Fielding tirelessly exerted himself in the cause of justice. No puritan, he nevertheless saw to it that serious scandal did not interfere with the discharge of his duties. Often these were humble enough, as the *Covent Garden Journal* shows:

several wretches being apprehended the night before by Mr Welch, were brought before Mr Fielding and Mr Errington: when one who was in a dreadful condition from the itch was recommended to the overseers; another, who appeared guilty of no crime but poverty, had money given her to enable her to follow her trade in the market . . .

Beggars, paupers and vagrants, as well as professional law-breakers and hardened murderers, processed before the novelist turned magistrate.

The house in Bow Street where Henry Fielding worked quickly established itself as the natural centre of law enforcement, not only for Westminster but for a wider area of the capital. Fielding's blind half-brother, John, who succeeded him in 1754, carried on the tradition until 1780. Lacking Henry's exceptional intelligence, Sir John was nevertheless able and tenacious, very much a product of the eighteenth century in combining the zeal of a social reformer with an easy-going personal morality; it was said that young women had reason to look out when their path crossed that of the Bow Street Justice. As the years went by, the staff at Bow Street grew, and came to include specialist thief-takers, known from their fleetness of foot as Bow Street 'Runners'. Employed to catch the most daring and successful criminals – it was already recognized that watchmen were hopelessly unsuited for such work – they soon came to be held in awe by the general public, if not by the community of thieves. The best-known Bow Street Runners were often hired by private citizens, as well as by banks, to protect or to restore valuable property.

The response made by the Fieldings and by Bow Street to the strong and continuing challenge from the criminal underworld was decidedly ahead of the sluggish main drift of eighteenth-century thought and legislation. A pattern had by now imposed itself upon this area of British life. Nothing was done until crisis, near-disaster or fear amounting to panic provided a spur for action, and then there was a flurry of discussion and, occasionally, minor changes in practice. From time to time Parliament debated law-and-order issues, but almost always the outcome was either a perpetuation of the status quo – as if the process of talking about social problems was enough in itself to make these problems disappear – or parliamentary statutes so restricted in their application as to be practically negligible. No government dared to tackle the single outstandingly glaring defect of the policing system in operation, namely its lack of co-ordinated control. Vested interests, combined with inertia, were too powerful. So the underworld continued to flourish, outpacing the means whereby London struggled to keep it at bay.

All this is borne out by the story of the Gordon Riots and their aftermath. For nearly a week in the summer of 1780 the streets of London were abandoned to mob violence, including an orgy of window-smashing, theft and casual assault. Ostensibly the Riots were directed against the proposed emancipation of Roman Catholics, but the slogan 'No Popery' became an excuse for every kind of lawless act. It took the personal intervention of the King, the vigorous presence of the Army, and sheer exhaustion to bring them to an end. (By a cruel irony, Sir John Fielding lay dying while looters burned his own and Henry's papers at Bow Street and the city blazed on all sides.) The seriousness of the Gordon Riots caused politicians to realize belatedly that provision for the policing of London was totally inadequate. Accordingly, in 1785, Pitt's Solicitor-General, Sir Archibald MacDonald, introduced a Bill designed to bring the control of the entire metropolitan area, including the City, under a single police authority. But in the City, memories of the Gordon Riots proved short, and those of ancient civic privileges correspondingly long. One alderman commented that, 'if a torch had been applied to the buildings it could not have created greater alarm'. Faced with such implacable opposition, Pitt was forced to drop his Bill.

To be fair, the City had a point. Its methods of controlling crime might not be very effective, but most observers agreed that they were infinitely superior to the haphazard and piecemeal arrangements for policing in the surrounding parishes. This difference in approach dated from as far back as the thirteenth century – when of course very little of the rest of London existed. At the time of the Statute of Westminster, drawn up 'to abate the power of felons' in England, the City was granted its own statute, dividing the area into twenty-four wards, each with six watchmen supervised by an alderman. The City's independence in local government was proudly, sometimes fiercely, guarded down the centuries. The Court of Common Council passed an Act in 1663, for instance, providing for the employment of one thousand watchmen or bellmen during the hours of darkness. These watchmen came to be known as 'charleys' because they were instituted in the reign of Charles II. A further Act in 1737 established a complementary system of day police. True enough, the charleys were objects of mirth. As T.A. Critchley has written:

> for the most part they were contemptible, dissolute, and drunken buffoons who shuffled along the darkened streets after sunset with their long staves and dim lanterns, calling out the time and the state of the weather, and thus warned the criminal of their approach, while attracting to themselves the attention of ruffians and practical jokers . . .

but at least there was a consistent and uniform, if mediocre, level of policing within the City, and the compact, well defined physical area to be patrolled made for a certain degree of success on the part of those entrusted with upholding the law.

Elsewhere in London, near chaos ruled – mainly because, in contrast to the City, the parishes lacked unity and central control. When most of the population of London had been concentrated within a small area, this had not mattered. It was possible then to operate with moderate success the system of individual civic obligation on which paving, lighting, cleansing, and patrolling of the outlying parishes all nominally depended. That time, however, was past. The City alone enjoyed a common standard of administration, but only about one-tenth of the people of the metropolis now lived in the City. The rest, numbering about one million – approximately a tenth of the entire population of England and Wales – inhabited a kind of twilit administrative no-man's-land made up of over ninety parishes or precincts situated within the three counties of Middlesex, Surrey and Kent. Each parish vestry was held responsible for the conduct of its own affairs. Local trusts existed to look after such matters as cleansing; and some idea of the hopeless confusion which reigned may be gained from the fact that in the single parish of Lambeth there were no fewer than nine separate trusts concerned with lighting alone. A few energetic individuals brought before Parliament proposals relating to the administration of affairs in their parish: otherwise, inertia prevailed. Policing was undoubtedly the least satisfactory area of all – though sanitation also left nearly everything to be desired – as well as being the area where co-operation across parish boundaries was most urgently needed. Some 40 per cent of such regular patrols as there were for the entire area of London operated strictly within the confines of the City.

It was no accident that the most notorious of London's rookeries were located outside the City yet close enough to it for thieves to be able to steal from the centres of wealth and business there. For example, the Spitalfields–Whitechapel area on the north-eastern boundary of the City lay conveniently beyond the jurisdiction of the City's day and night patrols, yet adjacent to streets where messengers to the Bank of England and the Royal Exchange might be waylaid. It was part of the training of young thieves to learn the quickest escape routes from Houndsditch and Leadenhall Street into the seamy purlieus of Petticoat Lane, and to master every line of access into the warren of courts and alleys between Grave Lane and Wentworth Street. (When the way was blocked, they could make for the smaller rookery of Rosemary Lane off Tower Hill.) On the west side of the City, Fleet Street was close enough to the dingy sidestreets of Drury Lane and Covent Garden for any thief worth his salt to give pursuers the slip, and from there it was but a short step to sure sanctuary in the cellars and lodging houses of St Giles: Buckeridge Street, Church Lane and Bainbridge Street never saw City officers. Another rookery which was close to the City yet beyond its control lay to the north of Holborn Hill. Field Lane had a very bad reputation as a distribution point for receivers, many of whom had their pawnshops or other obscure places of trade a few hundred yards away, in or near Shoe Lane and Saffron Hill. And yet another 'known resort of thieves and prostitutes' was situated a little to the east in St Luke's parish, Clerkenwell, where Whitecross Street, Bunhill Row and Grub Street provided ready refuge for law-breakers, as did Golden Lane.

To the south of the City was the river: in this direction also the pattern was repeated. The Borough of Southwark had already gained notoriety in Elizabethan times as an area exempt from City authority. For a long period the Mint had conferred immunity from process of debt, and the district had remained infamous as a favourite resort for criminals. Jonathan Wild, underworld boss of the early eighteenth century, had kept his horses in Red Cross Street. Apprentice thieves still drank at Wild's pub there and honoured his memory. Hardly more salubrious were the gin-shops of Tooley Street in Bermondsey, beloved of seafaring men, where many riverside robberies were planned and concealed.

In fact, the City was ringed by thieves' kitchens, surrounded by ill-lit and unpatrolled criminal areas, into which those who stole were drilled from childhood to make their safe exits. The City of Westminster – although unlike the City of London, it had never been allowed to elect a Lord Mayor or a Court of Aldermen – also stood out as better protected than the other metropolitan parishes, having in Bow Street the only recognized place of anti-criminal activity in London. Given the self-sufficiency and indifference of the City of London it was inevitable that those who sought a reform of policing methods should look to Westminster for a model and example. (Not that Westminster did not have its own persistent trouble spots, including a rookery to the south-west of Westminster Abbey. As many 'cracksmen' and their molls were to be seen in Tothill Fields as anywhere in London, this being home territory for a large number of those thieves and prostitutes who chose their victims at the west end of town, in Pall Mall and St James's.)

The rejection of Pitt's London and Westminster Police Bill in 1785 was a signal to the leaders of the underworld to step up their attacks on the inadequately protected propertied classes. The Runners of Bow Street had never been so busy, and those who avoided serious injury were able to earn large sums. Sir John Fielding had at one time introduced a Bow Street highway patrol: this had fallen into disuse, but Fielding's successor, Sir Sampson Wright, found it essential to revive the unit. More than this, in 1790 he was obliged to create an armed foot patrol to tour the streets of the metropolis from dusk until midnight. This went some little way to deal with an alarming increase in the incidence of robbery with violence, an increase which politicians viewed with growing alarm in case it should be a portent of the presence in London of a revolutionary movement like that in Paris.

Wright's response to the mounting crime-rate did not, however, go far enough to safeguard with any real efficiency the welfare of the citizens of London. The prevailing mood continued to be one of unease and anxiety. Prompted by its own sense of insecurity, in 1792 the Government sponsored a private member's Bill which proposed the establishment of seven new Public Offices on the lines started by Henry Fielding at Bow Street. Henry Dundas, the Home Secretary, pointed out in the House that pickpockets in particular had become so numerous and so audacious that no person could walk the streets in safety. Even this modest Bill did not go unopposed, however, although it was deliberately framed to leave untouched the self-government of the City. Fears that 'police' were synonymous with spies, that the idea smacked of

France and the *gendarmerie,* and similar prejudices were very strong. Significantly, too, the Bill was criticized as likely to do 'a great deal of mischief' by William Mainwaring, a Middlesex MP and a notably corrupt Chairman of Quarter Sessions, who detected in it a threat to his patronage as an old-style 'trading justice'. However, a majority of MPs lent their backing to the Middlesex Justices' Bill, which duly became law.

Its scope was very restricted, although it seemed revolutionary at the time. Each of the seven new offices was to be manned by three stipendiary magistrates, appointed by the Crown at an annual salary of £400. Every Office would have its own force of salaried constables – limited in number to six – with responsibilities corresponding to the routine duties of the Bow Street Runners. Perhaps the most significant feature of the new legislation was that all the offices were to be provided and equipped by the Home Secretary, who would assume overall responsibility for their administration. Thus his Department would become a clearing-house for information relating to the prevention and detection of crime throughout London. The locations for the Offices were carefully chosen to provide a strategically situated network of 'police' centres. Westminster was to have two offices, at Great Marlborough Street and Queen Square; Middlesex, with its dense concentration of population, was allocated sites at Hatton Garden (Holborn), Worship Street (Finsbury Square), Lambeth Street (Whitechapel) and High Street (Shadwell); and the remaining station was to be in Surrey, at Union Street in Southwark.

Although it marked an advance on the previous absence of all central planning, the Middlesex Justices' Bill was but a shadow of the Bill which Pitt had tried to have passed seven years before. Clearly, almost everything would depend upon the quality of the first set of men recruited to the paid and arduous magistracy – unlike magistrates elsewhere, the personnel at the Public Offices were to work regular hours from ten until three, and then attend again in the evening. As it turned out, the selection made in the first year was a very mixed one. It included three clergymen, two starch-dealers, three barristers, two former MPs, a former Lord Mayor of London and the Poet Laureate. Most owed their position to the patronage of highly placed acquaintances rather than to any special skill or experience in the kind of work to which they now found themselves committed; and for some, at least, exposure to the raw diet of nightly crime in London came as a rude shock. But there were some remarkable individuals among them, and one man of such exceptional calibre as to be a kind of genius.

This was Patrick Colquhoun, a Scotsman who had twice served as Lord Provost of Glasgow, and who had come south to seek new worlds to conquer. Colquhoun was in his mid-forties, bursting with ideas, ambition and energy. His life up to this point reads like a kind of blueprint for the career of a practical man of the Scottish Enlightenment, which he was. His father died while he was still in his teens, and he decided to leave his native Dumbartonshire and try his luck in North America. He prospered as a trader in Virginia, then returned to Scotland, where he rapidly established a successful business in Glasgow. Not only did he rise within a few years to the leading position in local government in the West of Scotland; he founded the Glasgow Chamber of Commerce, earning the description 'Father of Glasgow' during the phenomenally rapid growth of economic activity there in the 1780s. His business interests frequently took him to Manchester and to London; and he also had connections with Ostend and with other trading towns on the Continent.

Colquhoun's horizon had never been limited to mercantile affairs alone, however. He was already a determined planner and thinker about social problems. The publicity over the Middlesex Justices' Act attracted him, and he became leading magistrate at the Worship Street Office. There he at once threw himself wholeheartedly into what he undoubtedly judged to be a necessary war against crime. While his colleagues in other Offices contented themselves with carrying out their stated duties, Colquhoun in his spare time set up soup kitchens to feed the indigent, kept a register of known receivers, explored to the best of his ability connections between crime and vagrancy, and made early contact with Jeremy Bentham, the most original and penetrating social theorist in London. The fruits of this hectic activity were given to the world in the course of the next eight years.

Most significant – and controversial – of all his writings was his *Treatise on the Police of the Metropolis*, which reached a fifth edition in 1797, when he transferred from Worship Street to the Office at Queen Square. This was no mere pamphlet, although it provoked the writing of pamphlets by others, but instead a weighty volume containing easily the most detailed and comprehensive analysis which had ever been made of the state of crime in the capital. Colquhoun pointed to the existence of problems on a massive scale, and backed up his argument at every stage with impressive statistics – though he did not show the sources of his figures. London, he claimed, had become 'the receptacle of the idle and depraved of almost every country, and certainly from every quarter of the dominion of the Crown'. Drawing a sharp distinction between poverty, which he saw as an unavoidable and indeed necessary feature of society, and the more severe condition of indigence, which always produced a 'disposition to moral and criminal offences', he put forward various ideas for the control of pauperism and the prevention of crime. His most radical proposal was for a centrally organized body of police. It was no longer good enough to rely on the efforts of a few individuals in scattered parishes, or even on the new Offices like his own in Queen Square, Westminster. Coordination was needed:

A *Centre-point* is wanted to connect the whole together, so as to invigorate and strengthen every part, by a superintending Establishment, under the immediate controul of the Secretary of State for the Home Department.

A tangle of local arrangements seriously hindered law enforcement, as did the aloof attitude of the City. But Colquhoun's proposal was original in another way also. Until this time, the function of the police had been seen in

Britain solely as that of bringing criminals to justice; the usual, and disparaging, phrase was 'thief-catchers'. Colquhoun, however, wanted to place the emphasis instead on the prevention and detection of crime. Characteristically, he insisted on the need to clarify and define roles. 'Police in this country', he asserted,

> may be considered as a *New Science*; the properties of which consist not in the Judicial Powers which lead to *Punishment*, and which belong to Magistrates alone; but in the *Prevention and Detection of Crimes*; and in those other Functions which relate to internal Regulations for the well ordering and comfort of Civil Society.

Had Colquhoun's case rested on nothing but theory, it might have been quietly ignored. Instead, he created intense public interest by proceeding to give details about the criminal and 'dangerous' classes in Britain, and particularly in London where, he stated, no fewer than 115,000 persons were engaged in criminal pursuits. Of these, half were prostitutes or 'lewd and immoral women', 8,500 were 'cheats, swindlers, and gamblers', and another 8,000 were 'thieves, pilferers and embezzlers'. The passage in which he enumerated the different categories within the underworld is worth quoting in full, because it helped to establish the terms of the argument about crime and policing which was to take place in Britain during the next thirty years. (It is also characteristic of the period in its ethnic prejudice.)

ESTIMATES OF PERSONS WHO ARE SUPPOSED TO SUPPORT THEMSELVES IN AND NEAR THE METROPOLIS BY PURSUITS EITHER CRIMINAL – ILLEGAL – OR IMMORAL.

1. Professed Thieves, Burglars, Highway Robbers, Pickpockets and River Pirates, who are completely corrupted; – many of whom have finished their education in the Hulks, and some at Botany Bay:

N.B. There will be a considerable increase of this class on the return of Peace, now estimated at about: 2,000

2. Professed and known Receivers of Stolen Goods (of whom 8 or 10 are opulent): 60

3. Coiners, Colourers, Dealers, Venders, Buyers, and Utterers of base Money, including counterfeit Foreign and East India Coin: 3,000

4. Thieves, Pilferers, and Embezzlers who live partly by depredation, and partly by their own occasional labour: 8,000

5. River Pilferers, viz. Fraudulent *Lumpers, Scuffle-hunters, Mudlarks, Lightermen, Riggers, Artificers* and *Labourers* in the Docks and Arsenals: 2,500

6. Itinerant Jews, wandering from street to street, holding out temptations to pilfer and steal, and Jew Boys crying Bad Shillings, who purchase articles stolen by Servants, Stable Boys, etc: generally paying in Bad Money: 2,000

7. Receivers of Stolen Goods, from petty Pilferers, at Old Iron Shops, Store Shops, Rug and Thrumb Shops, and Shops for Second-hand Apparel, including some fraudulent Hostlers, small Butchers and Pawn-brokers: 4,000

8. A class of suspicious Characters, who live partly by pilfering and passing Base Money – ostensibly Costard Mongers, Ass Drivers, Dustmen, Chimney Sweepers, Rabbit Sellers, Fish and Fruit Sellers, Flash Coachmen, Bear Baiters, Dog Keepers (but in fact Dog Stealers), etc. etc. 1,000

9. Persons in the character of menial Servants, Journeymen, Warehouse Porters, and under-Clerks, who are entrusted with property, and who defraud their employers in a little way, under circumstances where they generally elude detection: 3,000

10. A class of Swindlers, Cheats, and low Gamblers, composed of idle and dissolute Characters, who have abandoned every honest pursuit, and who live chiefly by fraudulent transactions in the Lottery; as *Morocco Men, Ruffians, Bludgeon Men, Clerks*, and *Assistants*

during the season; who at other times assume the trade of *Duffers, Hawkers and Pedlars, Horse Dealers, Gamblers* with E. O. Tables at Fairs, *Utterers* of Base Money, *Horse Stealers*, etc.   7,440

11. Various other classes of Cheats, not included in the above: 1,000

12. Fraudulent and dissolute Publicans who are connected with Criminal People, and who, to accommodate their companions in iniquity, allow their houses to be rendez-vous for Thieves, Swindlers, and Dealers in Base Money: 1,000

13. A class of inferior Officers belonging to the Customs and Excise, including what are called Supernumeraries and Glutmen; many of whom connive at pillage as well as Frauds committed on the Revenue, and share in the plunder to a very considerable extent, principally from their inability to support themselves on the pittance allowed them in name of salary: 1,000

14. A numerous class of Persons who keep Chandler's Shops for the sale of provisions, tea, and other necessaries to the poor. The total number is estimated at *ten thousand* in the Metropolis, a certain proportion of whom, as well as small Butchers and others, are known to cheat their customers (especially those to whom they give a little credit) by false weights, for which, excepting in the parish of Mary-le-bone, there is no proper check: 3,500

15. Servants, male and female, Porters, Hostlers, Stable Boys, and Post Boys, etc. out of place principally for ill behaviour and loss of character, whose means of living must excite suspicion at all times, about: 10,000

16. Persons called *Black Legs*, and others proselytized to the passion of Gaming, or pursuing it as a trade, who are in the constant habit of frequenting houses opened for the express purposes of play: 2,000

17. Spendthrifts – Rakes – Giddy Young Men inexperienced and in the pursuit of criminal pleasures – Profligate, loose, and dissolute Characters, vitiated

themselves, and in the daily practice of seducing others to intemperance, lewdness, debauchery, gambling, and excess: estimated at: 3,000
18. Foreigners who live chiefly by gambling: 500
19. Bawds who keep Houses of ill Fame, Brothels, Lodging-Houses for Prostitutes: 2,000
20. Unfortunate Females of all descriptions, who support themselves chiefly or wholly by prostitution: 50,000
21. Strangers out of work who have wandered up to London in search of employment, and without recommendation, generally in consequence of some misdemeanour committed in the Country; at all times above: 1,000
22. Strolling Minstrels, Ballad Singers, Show-Men, Trumpeters, and Gipsies: 1,500
23. Grubbers, Gin-drinking and dissolute Women, and destitute Boys and Girls, wandering and prowling about in the streets and by-places after Chips, Nails, Old Metals, Broken Glass, Paper, Twine, etc., etc., who are constantly on the watch to pilfer when an opportunity offers: 2,000
24. Common Beggars and Vagrants asking alms, supposing one to every two streets: 3,000

                                   Total   115,000

Understandably perhaps, some Londoners concluded that Colquhoun, with his passion for classification and obviously strict sense of morality, was simply a crank. His estimate that there might be 50,000 women living at least partly by prostitution in London was mind-boggling – although for a time the figure was not directly challenged. Colquhoun based this calculation upon his experience as a magistrate, and made it clear that he included 'all parts of the town': at one time, he suggested, nearly half of the number of women in question would have been employed 'as Menial Servants, or seduced in very early life', and only 5,000 out of the total would be above that social rank, with 'well educated' prostitutes numbering no more than 2,000. Many readers suspected exaggeration, but they had no means of disproving the statistics, and the thesis advanced in the book was recognized as both sensational and important. The *Treatise* made its impact by disturbing the social conscience of the capital, and also by building up a formidably minute case for the existence of a continual and powerful threat to property from the criminal classes. There were elaborate tables to show how much money went missing annually as a result of different kinds of crime. Colquhoun pointed out that, if anything, he had understated these figures, since he had left out of the reckoning many forms of 'delinquency'. Among those which he did itemize, small thefts accounted for the largest sum, £710,000, while thefts upon the rivers and quays and in the dockyards on the Thames came to almost half a million pounds. Substantial amounts disappeared through burglaries, highway robberies and various forms of swindling. The sum which most closely touched the man in the street, though, was the estimate of the total yearly loss to the law-abiding community – a staggering two million pounds.

The *Treatise* contained, in its author's own phrase, 'a shocking catalogue of Human Depravity'. And the public responded appropriately. Many years later, Robert Southey was to pay tribute in the *Quarterly Review* to the pioneering contribution made by the book. As he saw it, Colquhoun had provided a kind of anatomy of the underworld which had been totally lacking before. 'No inhabitant of this great town', he wrote,

> could be ignorant that its vast population was mixed up with swindlers and pick-pockets, thieves, vagrants, beggars, and prostitutes; but Mr Colquhoun enabled us to trace them to their lurking places: – he gave to each class a 'local habitation'; he brought them to our view in groups amounting to thousands, and their pilfering and plunder to millions.

And Southey made it plain that in his judgment the *Treatise* was essentially accurate. It dealt with 'that part only of the wickedness of the community which is cognizable by human laws: how large a portion then remains untold!'

But in 1797 Colquhoun was ahead of his time, just as Henry Fielding (whom he intensely admired) had been in his *Inquiry* of 1751. Only those who had suffered theft themselves, or who were in some way committed to reform, were ready to accept his ideas for preventive police, public prosecutors and other agents of social control which we now take for granted. The root objection to police was a widespread conviction – often an unexamined prejudice – that the freedom of the individual citizen was put at risk by any such institution. The centuries-old practice of the British people had been to trust to local communities to guard themselves, through a system of Constable and Watch. This method of dealing with crime was known to be imperfect, and in some circles it was completely discredited; but the instinct of many, nevertheless, was to patch it up and hope that all would somehow be well. Suspicion of Colquhoun, the statistical moralist, and his kind was very real. He seemed thoroughly un-English (he was in fact very Scottish); and it certainly did not help his case that he actually went out of his way to commend the police system which had been developed in France, nor that his *Treatise* was translated into French while the war was at its height, and extravagantly praised by the national enemy.

All kinds of pretexts could be found for not going along with Colquhoun; but behind the controversy and the distrust with which his ideas were received was a sharp ideological conflict – nothing less than a head-on clash between two opposed views of the best means of preserving the traditional liberty of Britons. To Colquhoun, it seemed crystal-clear that the right way to achieve this end was to introduce police, who were not at all inimical to 'the comfort, the happiness, and the true liberty and security of the People'. His critics, on the other hand, argued that any regular system of police would inevitably destroy the very freedom it was nominally designed to protect. For instance, an anonymous pamphleteer of 1800 who referred to himself as 'a Citizen of London, but no Magistrate' described Colquhoun's scheme as an engine of despotism and inquisition; while Sir Richard Phillips made out that Colquhoun had 'written a large book to prove the incompetence of the police of London to its purposes'. According to Phillips, London was a law-abiding city, and the charleys had their place:

A few old men, armed with a staff, a rattle and a lantern, called watchmen, are the only guard through the night against depredation; and a few magistrates and police officers the only persons whose employment it is to detect and punish depredators; yet we venture to assert that no city, in proportion to its trade, luxury and population, is so free from danger to those who pass the streets at all hours, or from depredation, open or concealed, on property.

Such writers pooh-poohed the suggestion that anything like two million pounds went astray each year. In their eyes Colquhoun was untruthful, insulting and unpatriotic.

The government paid lip-service only to Colquhoun's view that a 'Police Board' must be established without delay. In 1799 he was asked to draft more than one Bill, and became greatly excited, believing that at least some of the changes he had pleaded for were likely to take place quickly. He probably hoped the next year to succeed Sir William Addington as chief magistrate at Bow Street, having been widely tipped for this key appointment. Instead, it went to Richard Ford, a man with little of Colquhoun's energy or ability; then, without troubling to explain their reasons, the Cabinet dropped plans for action to improve the policing of London, and gave their attention once more to the war against Napoleon and the tracking down through Home Office agents of what they judged to be subversive political groups at home. Colquhoun's disappointment must have been acute. Already, however, he could point to one outstanding practical result of his *Treatise*. Westminster might have dithered, but commercial enterprise had not. Impressed by the mastery of detail and the urgent tone of his work, in 1798 the West India merchants, who had for many years been facing very large and ever-increasing losses from their ships on the river, took the initiative in setting up at Wapping New Stairs a Thames Marine Police headquarters, and contributed more than four-fifths of its cost.

The River Police, as they quickly became known, were badly needed. London had become the largest entrepôt or trading port in the world, with thousands of richly charged vessels jostling for space, and opportunities galore for pilfering. The basic problem was that as yet there were no proper docks. The quays had not been enlarged for more than a hundred years, being no greater in extent in 1795, according to the merchants of London, 'than they were in the year 1666'. Yet trade had expanded very greatly, so that by this date the annual tonnage of foreign shipping coming to the Port amounted to 620,000. Sea-going ships lay at anchor in the open river, sometimes for weeks at a time, because movement was so restricted. All about them were lighters and barges and other river craft; it was not uncommon for ships' crews to be discharged before cargo could be unloaded, which opened the way to large-scale robbery. Foreigners were regularly impressed by the sight of a forest of masts on the Thames, but it was just this overcrowding which exposed to a variety of types of theft many thousand pounds' worth of goods each week. Cargoes had to be unloaded for inspection by customs officers, not all of whom were honest, and whose warehouses, some of them unguarded barges, were peculiarly open to pilfering. So great was the congestion on the Thames that this process in itself often took days to complete. Vessels waiting to get rid of their cargo were known by those who frequented the quays as 'game' ships. The men who unloaded were called 'lumpers'; they wore loose clothing with large, concealed pockets, and it was an easy matter to make off with sugar, silks or other highly priced commodities. This went on all the time and, according to Colquhoun, enjoyed the kind of immunity from public disapproval traditionally given to smuggling – what was pilfering, amidst such wealth? Then there were other specialists, each with a pretext for being on the river, such as the ratcatchers who were regularly sent aboard cargo ships to get rid of destructive vermin in the hold. Time and again, said Colquhoun, they used the trick of carrying the same live rats from vessel to vessel, thus creating an opportunity to steal as they went.

Collusion between those on board and the waterside employees of various kinds who came in contact with them was commonplace. 'Mudlarks' and 'scufflehunters' were men, women and children who waded in the water or silt beneath moored ships and barges, catching packages thrown down to them from the craft which they helped to unload, either with official blessing or otherwise. For the most part, a mood of untroubled cheerfulness prevailed among the law-breaking lightermen, wharfingers and mudlarks, their assumption being that a mere fragment subtracted from the mighty trade of the Port was neither here nor there. That fragment cost half a million pounds a year, however, and in the past, when efforts were made to stop the constant trafficking in stolen goods by privately hired patrols or vigilantes, large fires had been started in the unprotected and dangerously close-packed warehouses beside the Pool of London. Behind the cheeky front of the casual workers who plied their illicit trade close to the Custom House was a tough determination to defeat those who set out to curb them. Often living in Southwark or Wapping, or in the old Alsatia district between Fleet Street and the river, these people were of the underworld, born and bred, and hostile to every sort of authority save their own subversive hierarchies.

Not until the building of large, enclosed docks – the West India Dock between Limehouse and the Isle of Dogs in 1802, the London Dock at Wapping in 1805, and the East India Dock at Blackwall Reach the following year – was theft on the river brought under really effective control. It was generally acknowledged, however, that the coming of the Thames Marine Police reduced very considerably the amount of stealing during the period when the docks were being planned and built. The office at Wapping employed more than sixty full-time officers – almost twice as many, in fact, as all of the Metropolitan Police Offices. Colquhoun was involved in every stage of its planning, suggesting, for example, the need for fire-engines, and he helped to draw up strict rules of conduct both for the River Police and for their associate team of specially trained honest 'lumpers'. The first resident magistrate in charge of the force was John Harriott, a swashbuckling ex-seafaring man with a thorough knowledge of the Thames and unshakable confidence in his own abilities. Harriott had a flair for publicity, and took every chance to let it be known that the Thames Marine staff were the first coherently organized police force in the country. While the West India merchants uncomplainingly footed the greater part of the bill for the new force, public funds were also involved. The Thames River Police Act of 1800, owing much to the sustained efforts of Colquhoun and Bentham, transformed the private venture into a public concern. This was a straw in the wind, and showed that the Government was aware at least of the need to protect the nation's prosperity in time of war, and especially to safeguard revenues from the customs dues. The key to getting things done, it appeared, was to win the interest of influential owners of property, who then put pressure on politicians.

One other action which brought about a reduction in crime was the revival in 1805 of the Bow Street Horse Patrol. This consisted of about sixty men whose duty it was to protect travellers on the principal roads within sixty miles of London. They were selected with care, and many had previously served in a cavalry regiment. On the main roads as far out as Epsom, Romford, Enfield and Windsor they created confidence with their clearly spoken greeting, 'Bow Street Patrol'. Their single most successful achievement was to rid Hounslow Heath of highwaymen. Like the other Bow Street officers they enjoyed a reputation for courage, and also for business acumen. Leon Radzinowicz has described them as 'a closely knit caste of speculators in the detection of crime, self-seeking and unscrupulous, but also daring and efficient when daring and efficiency coincided with their private interest'.

But while the river and the highways out of town were less densely infested by criminals than in the past, every other traditional setting for misdeeds continued to give trouble. And because there was as yet no means of combating crime by strategy rather than on an ad hoc basis, the recent improvements actually created new problems. Those youths who were denied the traditionally glamorous highwayman's role by the vigilance of the Bow Street Horse Patrol naturally looked about for other kinds of robbery involving people and goods in transit. A popular choice was stealing luggage, often by cutting the ropes which bound travelling chests to carriages. Or young men might adopt the common device of waiting in inn-yards, where they offered their services to carry trunks and baggage – and then stole them. In addition, the River Police and formidably secure new docks forced many members of the Thames-side criminal fraternity to look elsewhere for their income.

Interestingly, it was in the area near the river, rather than in robberies from travellers, that violence most often now tended to accompany crime. One reason was probably the tough quality of everyday life in that part of London which adjoined the main shipping area. Sailors in particular had a reputation for drunkenness and fighting. As they mixed with prostitutes, lightermen, coalheavers, lumpers and other groups who frequented riverside drinking-places, quarrels were frequent. But not only were those who dwelt in the narrow streets of Bermondsey and Wapping ready to use their fists on the slightest provocation, the blocking-off of customary opportunities for theft bred in some a deep sense of resentment against all authority; and this spirit sometimes issued in crimes of appalling violence. As long as such incidents were confined to bootings and knifings among lascars and other casually hired ships' crews, nobody took much notice. Such men were thought not fully to belong to the community. But when ordinary families were affected by violent crime, the response was altogether different.

In December 1811 two households, comprising seven people, were brutally clubbed to death within a period of twelve days, in different buildings close to the Ratcliffe Highway in the East End. The area was very close to the new London Docks, on the fringes of Wapping and Shadwell. In the first attack, a linen draper called Timothy Marr, his wife Celia, their infant child and an apprentice boy, were murdered in their home late on a Saturday night. News of this event caused panic far beyond the immediate district. The Ratcliffe Highway was well known as the main thoroughfare going east out of London, and the familiarity of the name combined with the appalling fate of a law-abiding citizen and his family sent a shudder of horror through the population at large. Then on Thursday 19 December an almost naked man escaped from an upstairs window of the King's Arms pub in New Gravel Lane, Wapping, exclaiming as he lowered himself by means of two sheets tied together, 'They are murdering the people in the house.' This was the bizarre prelude to the discovery, which aroused even more shocked fear among the public, that Williamson, the landlord, his wife, and their maidservant Bridget Harrington, had all been killed. Once again, the circumstances were peculiarly gruesome – and no murderer could be found. As Sheridan was to recall later in Parliament, all kinds of theories flew about as Londoners tried desperately to distance 'the murders in the Ratcliffe Highway' from themselves by looking for scapegoats:

people grew all of a sudden thoroughly persuaded that there was evidence upon the face of those murders to show that they were perpetrated by Portuguese, and by none but Portuguese. 'Oh, but who would do it but Portuguese?' was the general cry. Prejudice, however, did not long stand still upon the Portuguese. The next tribe of foreigners arraigned and convicted were the Irish – it was nothing but an Irish murder, and could have been done only by Irishmen!

John Harriott of the River Police, who was prominent in investigation of the crimes, spoke of 'a gang acting on a system', which did nothing to restore public confidence. One shopkeeper was said to have sold three hundred rattles, of the kind used by watchmen, within ten hours; doors were carefully barred; and according to Macaulay, who was in London at the time, there was terror on every face. The Home Secretary received numerous messages to the effect that there was 'a general Alarm not only throughout the City but throughout the Country'. The Government offered a reward of £500, the largest sum ever known, for information leading to the conviction of the murderer or murderers of the Marrs, and another large amount in the case of the Williamson killings. In Shadwell all the watchmen were sacked immediately and replaced by more active men; while messengers scurried everywhere, from the Thames, Bow Street and Shadwell Police Offices, and from Fleet Street.

In the end a man called John Williams, an inmate of another pub in the district called the Pear Tree, was arrested. He was a former shipmate of Timothy Marr's, who perhaps combined with a pathological nature a grudge against Marr dating back to a time when they both sailed in foreign waters in the *Dover Castle*. The evidence against him was merely circumstantial, and two writers who recently examined all the surviving records concluded that another man was also involved, a sinister figure called William Arblass, who once led a shipboard mutiny in which Williams took part. But Williams's guilt seemed to be confirmed when he hanged himself in Coldbath Fields Prison, 'cheating the gallows'.

The significance of the Ratcliffe Highway murders is not simply that they produced a temporary sense of panic, or led De Quincey to write a famous essay 'On Murder considered as One of the Fine Arts', or that they gripped the collective imagination of London as no murders were to do until the time of Jack the Ripper. It is, rather, that the citizens of London suddenly woke up to the fact that provision for their protection at the hands of the law was inadequate. Not even the destructive path of the Gordon Riots had stirred up such feelings of protest and such vigorous criticism of the old-fashioned apparatus of lantern, box and rattle. Parliament responded to the mood of the times by setting up an inquiry into the state of the nightly Watch. While its findings were disappointingly inconclusive, and the prejudice against the institution of police was to ensure the defeat of further measures of the sort during the next fifteen years, the end of an age was almost in sight.

TWO

THE LAST OF THE CHARLEYS

During the panic caused in the winter of 1811–12 by the murders in east London, the mere mention of the Ratcliffe Highway was enough to set people taking nervously about the frightening lack of a proper system of police in the capital to guarantee public safety. There was nothing to prevent something similar happening anywhere in the metropolis, and nearly everyone felt at risk. For the time being Londoners had been robbed of their sense of security, and news of distant victories in the Peninsular War was little compensation for the kind of gnawing fear which prevented people from sleeping at night. One of the problems of London, indeed, was that the Government was far more concerned with events abroad than with what went on at home . . . or so it appeared to those who read their newspapers.

The Press made the most of the situation by commenting at length upon what they judged to be the implications of the Ratcliffe Highway murders. Journalists had been quick to sense that the public was deeply interested, and they now gave considerable publicity to various proposals for amending the existing defective police system. The *Morning Chronicle* in particular took a leading part in campaigning for change, combining lurid accounts of actual and possible violent crimes to which London had long been exposed with practical suggestions for getting rid of the oldest and feeblest watchmen, especially from parishes near the river where the worst violence occurred. A completely new approach was urgently required to solve the growing problem of crime. Yet it would be a mistake, the *Chronicle* warned, to adopt a police organization along French lines. The police of Paris were nothing more than glorified state spies, 'most dexterously contrived for the purpose of tyranny'. On the other hand, if Parliament and the people wanted real change, they would have to act decisively, rather than simply carry on with what had been inherited from the past. Ruefully, the newspaper commented on the apparatus of law enforcement in Britain:

> We never think of taking down an old, shattered ruin of incumbrance, till we find it tumbling on our heads. This is the English beaten road of improvement. We always appear to improve less from choice than from necessity.

These words accurately describe the reluctance both of Britain's rulers and of the greater part of British society to abandon ways of dealing with crime which, for all their faults, had been handed down over generations; and they point to the painful struggle which lay ahead. Seeing the need for change was one thing, but actually doing anything new was another. An early indication of the prevailing mood came in this same year, 1812, with the publication of the report of the Parliamentary Select Committee which had been set up to inquire into the State of the Watch. While the report was sharply critical of policing methods, the Government failed to follow it up with appropriate legislation.

The Committee stressed that they had found many disquieting features, including an obvious lack of uniformity in arrangements made for the protection of different parishes. 'It would seem to be extraordinary', they remarked, 'that in such a Metropolis as London, there should be no Office in which information is collected, from which intelligence can be obtained as to the state of the Police.' This complaint perhaps reflected their frustration on trying to learn from a convenient central source about London's police, only to discover that there was none, despite the prestige of Bow Street and the authority of the Home Office. At any rate, they 'deeply felt' the necessity of introducing some system which would give unity and connection to the scattered parts of the metropolis, although they did not provide any detailed practical suggestions of how this might work. Until such a radical change took place, it was essential to relieve the Watch at least once during each night, if the watchmen were to be reasonably alert and efficient. The City, with its strict arrangements for changing the Watch, offered an example in this matter to the rest of London. The Committee on the Watch took the view that the River Police had proved themselves of great value. More money was now required, however, in order to protect Greenwich, and to provide police boats on the upper river above London Bridge, for the Thames-side thieves had moved into these areas in recent years. Similarly, receivers of stolen goods were elusive and hard to prosecute with success, and would remain so until police officers were issued with search warrants which could be used at night as well as during the day. Another troublesome group of criminals made use of Hackney coaches to move stolen goods, and had the habit of frequently changing number plates in order to escape detection. It would be somewhat easier to keep track of them if owners of Hackneys could be required by law to paint the numbers on the coach panels.

If the practice of changing number plates seems strangely familiar and up-to-date – another reminder that many underworld ruses are older than is often assumed – other topics in the report clearly belong to their age. The Committee had not long begun their task when they found themselves confronted by conflicting opinions over the question of rewards received by London's police. It was very common for victims of theft to offer sums of money to anyone assisting them in bringing the person or persons responsible to justice. In additon to these privately funded rewards, amounts ranging from £10 to £40 were fixed by statute as the appropriate financial incentives for those who successfully prosecuted for serious crimes. At the top end of this elaborate scale, a presiding magistrate was authorized to give a 'parliamentary reward' of £40 when a criminal was convicted of a capital charge: the popular expression was 'blood money'. Usually, the magistrate divided up the money, giving a certain proportion to the private individual who had prosecuted – for as yet, of course, Patrick Colquhoun's idea of a public prosecutor remained unrealized – and a part to each of the witnesses who had appeared in the prosecution. Very often, police officers figured as principal prosecution witnesses. They therefore stood to gain substantial sums from the reward system. On the other hand, their regular pay, in the form of the retaining fee they received from the Police Offices, was very low, in most cases less than enough to support a family. Everything was directed towards individual enterprise on the part of the thief-takers. It was openly recognized that police officers supplemented their pay by working for banks, theatres, business firms or private citizens, who employed them in particular cases. The assumption was that they were likely to be stimulated to track down and arrest wrong-doers by the prospect of winning a main share of blood money and other rewards.

What troubled the Parliamentary Select Committee of 1812 was the suggestion, heard from many sides, that police officers were unduly influenced by financial considerations. Sometimes, it appeared, they ran the risk of being discredited as witnesses because they had a strong personal interest in securing a conviction, irrespective of the facts of the case. No less seriously, they were said to 'nurse' certain criminals, allowing them to get off with minor crimes for which the rewards were slight until they 'weighed forty' or committed crimes for which blood money was offered. Either way, they were subject to corruption, and so corrupted justice. The Committee on the Watch recommended that the stipendiary magistrates should have 'further means of rewarding their different Officers for any extraordinary activity and exertions', thus recognizing that a supplement to regular pay was needed, but also as a corollary that police officers should cease to be eligible for the 'blood money' which seemed to lead to so many allegations of dishonesty and injustice.

Lord Liverpool's government chose to do nothing about this recommendation, at least for the time being. It would have been better had they acted straightaway, however, for four years later, when they had trouble enough on their hands with bread riots and political disturbances, they were suddenly faced with a major corruption scandal which threatened to destroy the reputation of Bow Street itself. The first hint the general public had that something was seriously wrong came on 18 July 1816, when *The Times* called for an urgent investigation into 'the horrible trade in blood demands'. There was only too much reason to fear, the newspaper reported, that there existed in London a regular system of conspiracy 'among certain police-officers and their associates to ensnare young men into the commission of crimes in order to betray them for the reward on conviction'. These were strong words, but they turned out to have a solid basis in fact. The Home Office had indeed already ordered an inquiry into the conduct of a number of officers suspected of conspiring 'for the sake of gain or reward'. Over the summer months more and more information came to light, and on 17 September *The Times* was 'happy to announce' that the government had decided to prosecute several men whose dubious activities had by now been thoroughly investigated. In the autumn six policemen were put in the dock. After a series of sensational trials, four of them were sentenced to death. The sentences were later commuted, but all of the lawbreakers were transported.

What was most alarming about the events of 1816 was that George Vaughan, the ring-leader of the corrupt police, had belonged to the crack Bow Street Foot Patrol, while his most prominent associate, Robert Mackay, had been a member of the City Patrol; so that from this time the two most respected units of police in London were seriously tainted in the eyes of the public. Essentially, what Vaughan had done was to revive and modify a crime which had first become notorious in London in the time of Jonathan Wild, the 'Thief-Taker General'. Using agents or 'decoy ducks', intermediaries who were known and trusted in the underworld, to help them, the police officers persuaded young professional thieves to carry out planned acts of burglary and house-breaking; then they switched sides, and with the assistance when necessary of other police, caught the thieves in the act, and so stood to gain large rewards. It was a risky business at the best of times, since it involved collusion with traditional enemies of the police, but Vaughan and Mackay had got away with it more than once before their eventual downfall. The fact that they had at different times used as agents William Drake, a forger who had done time in Newgate, and John Donnelly, a thief with a long criminal record, but in contrast chose as their victims inexperienced youngsters, was proof in the eyes of the sentencing magistrates that they had flagrantly abused the knowledge of the underworld which they had acquired in the course of their duties.

Vaughan's was the case most discussed because of his Bow Street connection, but three of the other officers, Brock, Pelham and Power, were guilty of a comparable crime, and had been responsible for having their dupes sentenced to death. One day in the Cheapside Market, Power and his agent Daniel Barry – in the Attorney-General's description 'a very bad man' – met up with two impressionable Irishmen called Reardon and Quinn. The conversation which followed obscurely suggested to Reardon and Quinn that there was money to be earned, but on unusual conditions:

'My master', said Barry, 'has plenty of employment for some smart fellows; but it is very *hard* work' – 'Oh!', answered the poor man . . . 'I want bread and do not mind how hard the work'. – 'Oh! but there is some *hazard* in it.' – 'Why,' continued the poor fellow, 'so has every kind of work; mounting a ladder five storeys high, with a heavy hod of mortar . . . is attended with great hazard; but an Irish labourer does not care much for danger.' – 'I know that,' said Barry, 'but this work is of a very peculiar kind, and I know that no man is bound to stay at a work he does not like . . . My master would not hire anyone, but such as will take a solemn oath that if he leaves the work, he never will speak about it.'

The upshot was that, together with a third Irish youth, Thomas Connell, Reardon and Quinn were sworn in. They were taken to a room which had been hired for the purpose by Pelham, and were given metal, file, scissors and other tools, and told to copy the design of a shilling which was put before them. One of them then realized that they were being employed to counterfeit money 'for which they might all hang'. They tried to leave, saying that they must go out for dinner, but Barry prevented this by claiming that a meal had already been ordered for them. He then went out, and not long afterwards Brock, Pelham and another police officer came in and arrested the boys. The police acted on the authority of a warrant issued to Brock, who had sworn before an alderman that 'he had just cause to know the coiners were at work'.

A peculiar feature of this case was that the three youths did not break their oath and denounce the conspirators in court, even though Barry was there in front of them and 'in a great fright', but instead allowed themselves to be convicted and sentenced to death. They may have feared reprisals more than the law, but a likelier explanation is, in the words of a nineteenth-century historian of London crime, that they were 'Irishmen and Catholics, and the rigid observance which they [Irish Catholics] pay to an oath is well known'. Had it not been for the vigilance of Sir Matthew Wood, the Lord Mayor and Chief Magistrate of the City, whose suspicion was aroused by a casual remark during the trial, no further investigation of the part played by police officers would have taken place. The convicted 'forgers' would have gone to the gallows, or if not, to Botany Bay, save for the timely intervention of a priest, who eventually persuaded them that they need not feel bound by an oath which had not been lawfully administered. This part of the story had a happy ending in that Reardon, Quinn and Connell were pardoned and discharged, and were enabled to return to Ireland and buy a small farm with money which came to them from a subscription appeal organized on their behalf by the Lord Mayor.

But the stock of the police of London had seldom been lower, for it had been conclusively shown that certain officers were ready to trade not only in justice but in the lives of innocent people and naive thieves alike. Moreover, the record of police units in controlling rioters was very poor, and it had been necessary for the military to be called in to the streets of Westminster in 1815 and on other occasions. It is hardly surprising that, with this background, the questions in the next few years were very searching. Time and again, magistrates and police officers found themselves asked to explain their procedures, and every hint of something amiss was followed up with great eagerness.

Interestingly, the move to set up a Select Committee in 1816 came from a leading Whig, Sir Samuel Romilly. Romilly was known principally as a very determined campaigner for a reduction in the number of crimes – still at this date over two hundred – which were punishable by death. He had scored his first notable success in 1808 when he managed to persuade a sceptical House that if the crime of picking pockets ceased to qualify for the death penalty, but instead was met by lesser punishments consistently applied, more convictions would be secured. Romilly's argument, and that of some of his fellow Whigs, was that private citizens were made reluctant to prosecute, and magistrates to convict, by the so-called 'bloody code' of English criminal law; it was a further indication of the need for change that, in practice, the death sentence was very often commuted to transportation or imprisonment. Thus his way of attacking crime followed a somewhat different course from that of, say, Patrick

Colquhoun. Until now Romilly and his followers had withheld support from the movement to rationalize London's police, on the ground that any systematic police organization was a threat to individual and corporate liberties. That he was now prepared to contemplate the possibility of a different kind of police for London was a clear indication of a change coming over public opinion. If noted Whigs, the champions of freedom, were softening in their attitude towards 'the police idea', there was at last a chance that the energies of police and criminal law reformers would become united.

The 1816 Committee did not bring forward specific proposals for reform, but instead concentrated on amassing a greater body of evidence about the state of everything relating to crime, the police and law enforcement than had ever before been made available to Parliament. The scope of their inquiries was much wider than that of the 1812 Committee. Every senior magistrate was interviewed, beginning with Sir Nathaniel Conant, who had charge of the Bow Street Office. The best-known Bow Street Runners, representative watchmen, parish officers and everyone with a known strong point of view or grievance, came before them. In addition, a number of the MPs who made up the Committee gave evidence themselves. Romilly, for instance, had an opportunity to show, with illustrative statistics, that more convictions for 'privately stealing from the person' had indeed taken place since this had ceased to be a capital offence.

Among the witnesses were men of colourful personality, who delivered their opinions with more than a hint of self-importance. John Harriott had now been in charge of the River Police for eighteen years, and he told the Committee that he did not wish to see his responsibilities as chief magistrate curtailed. If the work were 'apportioned to three separately, they would be jarring, and counteracting each other . . . I trust I may be allowed to say that I am the main key-stone of the plan'. He spoke reassuringly of 'a constant moving police on the river', which, in comparison with what it used to be, was now as smooth as a millpond. The fact that Harriott received few supplementary questions probably shows that the Committee broadly agreed with this description, even if they were bound to note his disinclination to share authority with others. Someone who was questioned at greater length was John Townsend, the most celebrated of all the Bow Street officers. There was no suggestion that he had been a party to corruption, but the Committee evidently placed a high value on the testimony of a man who had been a thief-taker at Bow Street for thirty-four years, and could make informed comparisons with the time of Sir John Fielding.

On the matter of rewards, Townsend was much more inclined to see changes made than were a number of his younger colleagues, who tended to be on the defensive. 'Officers', he mused, 'are dangerous creatures':

> they frequently have it in their power (no question about it) to turn that scale, when the beam is level, on the other side; I mean against the poor wretched man at the bar: why? this thing called nature says profit is in the scale; and, melancholy to relate, but I cannot help being perfectly satisfied, that frequently that has been the means of convicting many and many a man . . . Whenever A. is giving evidence against B. he should stand perfectly uninterested.

Townsend was very much the realist, who brought everything to the test of 'this thing called nature'. He himself had prospered to such a degree that he was above the conflict, for he regularly accompanied the Regent to Brighton, as well as working for the Bank of England and wealthy individual prosecutors, but he frankly admitted that, as the law stood, it placed police officers in a difficult situation: 'God knows, nature is at all times frail, and money is a tempting thing.' It was also true that a great number of offenders escaped merely because people were unwilling to go to the expense and trouble of prosecuting. He hinted strongly that something should be done to defray the legal costs of ordinary citizens bringing criminal actions for theft.

John Townsend agreed with other witnesses that whereas

theft was now running at an alarmingly high level in London, the capital was less violent than it had been in the previous century. Now, admittedly, there was jostling in the street from thieves of all sorts, but then 'they used to be ready to pop at a man as soon as he let down his glass; that was by banditties.'. But while he naturally welcomed this reduction in violence, he was not altogether in favour of the magistrates' growing leniency towards hardened criminals. There was a good deal to be said for putting the fear of death into the enemy. In 1783, he recalled, when Sergeant Adair was Recorder, forty men had been hanged at two executions. That was no example to the present age, yet it had an undoubted deterrent effect at the time. He quoted with some relish the remark of an old lag, 'Why, Sir, where there is one hung now, there were five when I was young' – and his own reply, 'Yes, you are right, and you were lucky you were spared.' Without question, the practice of hanging the bodies of executed criminals on a gibbet, to warn other would-be law-breakers, ought to be retained. Townsend illustrated this from a very recent case, that of two men who had been convicted and executed for murdering Revenue Officers. He himself had given the magistrate, Sir William Scott, the advice to display the corpses, and with good reason:

> There are a couple of men now hanging near the Thames, where all the sailors must come up; and one says to the other, 'Pray what are those two poor fellows there for?' – 'Why,' says another, 'I will go and ask.' They ask 'Why those two men are hung and gibbetted for murdering His Majesty's Revenue Officers.' And so the thing is kept alive.

Another witness whose long experience and family tradition allowed him to speak with especial authority on a number of key topics was William Fielding, the severely crippled son of Henry Fielding, and magistrate at the Queen Square Police Office, who exercised control over troublesome parishes such as St Martin-in-the-Fields. 'God knows,' he remarked at one point, 'I have seen a good deal of the police of the metropolis.' His main strictures were reserved for the herds of 'little vagabonds' who were forever pilfering in the streets. The bad old days of highwaymen had gone for good, but this was a new and serious menace. Significantly, however, the source of much crime in 1816 was the same as in his father's day.

In that treatise . . . *On the Increase of Robberies*, which has been rather a popular little thing, though not so great a favourite as his *Tom Jones*, his idea of the gin-shop was terrible. He then acted as a magistrate, and I believe, was then the only magistrate in London of any degree of consequence, and ought to know something of the subject.

Then it is your opinion that the gin-shops are increasing every day? – I should think so, and must increase, from the increased value of such property, for a man keeping a snug gin-shop has a much more profitable concern than if he kept a public-house, where he would only be selling his pints and quarts of beer, which is less profitable than selling glasses of gin.

The Committee must have been pleased to elicit this answer from the son of Henry Fielding, for it added weight to what was certainly one of their main findings, namely that London's licensing laws were so lax as to have allowed very many gin-shops and hole-in-corner drinking-places to spring up, causing a marked increase in crime. Reading between the lines, it is not hard to deduce that their animus against what they referred to as licensed 'houses of the worst possible character' was caused partly by such scandalous cases as those of George Vaughan, and of two former Hatton Garden officers who, they were told, had been guilty of taking 'hush money'. It was in low drinking-places, and particularly in 'flash-houses' frequented by thieves that police officers met their quarry, and there also, presumably, that the temptation to cross over to the wrong side of the law was at its strongest. Sir Nathaniel Conant of Bow Street faced persistent questioning about allegedly notorious public houses and gin-shops 'in the immediate district' of the Police Office, and also in the Covent Garden area. He was able to explain that public houses remained open very late near Covent Garden because of the market, the public theatres, and the fact that the watering-houses of Hackney coachmen were located there. On the other hand, he avoided going into much detail about drinking-places in and close to Bow Street, although he did point out that his men now had the use of a strong room in which to detain prisoners. Only two years previously, they had still been making use of a room in a Bow Street public house, the Brown Bear, which was known punningly in the underworld as the 'Russian Coffee-House'.

Collected evidence strongly suggested that in every part of London inadequate restrictions on the granting and renewing of licences had a great deal to do with crime, especially among the young. In such a situation much clearly depended upon the degree of professional integrity shown by individual magistrates who controlled the operation of the licensing laws. When a complaint was lodged against a particular licence-holder, whether for noise or immoral conduct on his premises, it was the magistrate's duty to investigate. If he found that the 'house' in question deserved its bad name, he had the power to take away the licence altogether. In practice, however, only crusading magistrates like Patrick Colquhoun were genuinely strict either about issuing licences, or about their renewal. The English preference for laissez-faire prevailed; and the saying among brewers who owned large numbers of public houses was that 'the walls keep no sin'. By this they meant that it was usually possible to persuade magistrates to replace publicans rather than to close places down. The profits to be made were very substantial.

The result of this was that in certain areas, and notably in those with particularly easy-going or dishonest licensing magistrates, every fifth or sixth door led into a drinking-place. One such area was the parish of Bethnal Green, which for many years had been in the grip of a local 'boss' called

Joseph Merceron. Originally a clerk to a lottery office-keeper, Merceron had learned much about money and power, and had since risen to possess both. Not only did he own eleven public houses and receive the rent from as many others, he served as treasurer of the parish, and chairman of the watch board, thus having command of its policing, and was in addition a Justice of the Peace. Every year he saw to it that licences were renewed among his placemen and friends, whatever the riotousness of their pubs.

In 1809, however, Merceron's hold on Bethnal Green had been challenged by a fearless new Church of England Rector, Joshua King. The condition of the police in Bethnal Green, King said, could only be described as 'deplorable'. Nor was it hard to understand why . . .

the treasurer of the parish, has amassed a large fortune, without any ostensible means; takes care to elect the most ignorant and the lowest characters, on whom he can depend, to fill all his parochial offices, and to audit his accounts.

'I have seen him instigate his creatures to riot and clamour', the Rector continued, 'even within the walls of the church.' Merceron had the habit of bringing a mob to vestry meetings, which made it practically impossible to oppose his decisions. No one had been allowed to examine the parish accounts for twenty-five years, and King claimed that a Parliamentary grant of £12,000 made in 1800 for the relief of the poor of the parish had been partly misappropriated. In 1812 he had indicted Merceron for fraudulently altering the Poor Rates, and for perjury over property belonging to a poor idiot and her orphan sisters.

The main burden of the Bethnal Green Rector's complaint lay here, in accusations of corruption which included much more than Merceron's alleged blatant manipulation of matters relating to the policing of the parish. The Select Committee heard, for instance, how the 'boss of Bethnal Green' was a close friend of Hanbury the brewer, who had large property interests in the area, and whom Merceron called 'a devilish good fellow'. But they were also treated incidentally to a vivid account of the life of the streets in that part of the East End, which shows how far from realization were the hopes of social reformers like Jeremy Bentham, Patrick Colquhoun or Samuel Romilly. In this parish, with its refractory population of weavers, and its widespread poverty, manners were still unruly; the wild spirit of eighteenth-century London was by no means dead.

Bitterly, the Rector spoke about the traditional Bethnal Green practice of chasing bullocks through the streets. The bullocks belonged to drovers going to Smithfield Market, and it so happened that they came into the parish on Sunday, in preparation for Market Monday. Because of this,

> every Sunday morning, during the time of Divine Service, several hundred persons assemble in a field adjoining the churchyard, where they fight dogs, hunt ducks, gamble, enter into subscriptions to fee drovers for a bullock: I have seen them drive the animal through the most populous parts of the parish, force sticks pointed with iron, up the body, put peas into the ears, and infuriate the beast, so as to endanger the lives of all persons passing along the street.

Only two months before, a bullock had actually been hunted in the churchyard during service. Merceron did nothing to prevent it: on previous occasions, indeed, he had spoken of his liking for bullock-hunting, thereby winning cheap popularity, and naturally therefore the parish officers also connived at the brutal chase. Once, the Police Office at Worship Street had intervened; but of course this was the kind of mob pastime which should in the first place be subject to local control. Market Mondays were even more riotous than Sundays, with as many as two thousand men and boys leaving their looms to join in the pursuit. It was not at all surprising that in the summer of 1815 a man was tossed and killed in Bethnal Green during a bullock chase, or that two men of Hackney parish were severely injured.

The story told by the Rector of Bethnal Green highlighted the conflict between the anarchic social life still going on in London and the reforming zeal of other citizens to whom such behaviour was genuinely shocking. Something else which a number of witnesses complained of was the practice of paying men in public houses on Saturday nights. Like the chasing of bullocks in the vicinity of Smithfield, this was a tradition inherited from the previous century. A stop would be put to it in most places by the mid-1820s, but while it lasted it caused every sort of havoc. Not only was it common for some men to drink away their whole earnings at a single protracted session each week, thus ensuring that the pawnbroker would be kept busy in the intervening period; there were many fights among the drinkers, and inevitably, too, between husbands and their distraught or gin-sodden wives. Again, matters were made worse by the fact that pubs were allowed to open very early on Sunday mornings. After imbibing for hours in the evening, those who wished to were able to move on to 'coffee-houses', which stayed open most of the night and in which spirits were often available. Then, if they were still capable of standing, they could make their way back again to their favourite pubs. One Sunday morning someone counted no fewer than 165 people visiting a typical pub for such revellers in Covent Garden, between the hours of 6.30 and 8.

The watchmen were kept particularly busy on Saturday nights, or at least those of them who worked conscientiously were. But as one person after another pointed out, vigilant watchmen were the exception rather than the rule. Many of them dozed away in their boxes, oblivious to the incidents on the streets calling for their attention, while others accepted small bribes from prostitutes in return for turning a blind eye to their activities. A very common trick was for a girl to waylay one of the intoxicated Saturday night drinkers; then she either stole from him herself, or created an opportunity for a male criminal to do so. Whether or not the theft took place, the watchmen did not want to know about it. John Lavender, a police officer with experience in the Bow Street and Queen Square offices, was asked:

Is it not a matter of common notoriety, that the watchman is generally a person, who supposing him to be awake, which he seldom is, is in the constant habit of receiving money from the women of the town who parade the streets in his district?

To this admittedly leading question, he replied:

That is too true, for I have seen it; I have absolutely seen the watchmen abused for not protecting the girls after they have given them money; and I have seen the watchmen abuse the girls, and beat them for not giving any money; I took a watchman off his duty in the Strand for doing that about a year and a half ago.

In the City, attempts to discipline the Watch were more systematic than in the rest of London, but even here the problem proved intractable. Matthew Wood, the Lord Mayor, dryly observed that

the beats or rounds of many watchmen are so short that they take only five minutes to walk them; which, being twice within the hour, he is either fifty minutes in his box, or what is more frequent, they meet two or three together, and are in conversation a considerable time; frequently they are employed in shutting up shops, or going on errands for the inhabitants, going into public houses with prostitutes; and although the streets are crowded with disorderly women, they will not interfere, or take the least notice of their conduct; also from the practice of their being fixed in stations or boxed for many years, there is no doubt but some of them receive bribes from persons who commit robberies in the streets as well as in houses; for it is a well known fact, that notorious characters attend Fleet Street and other public streets every night, and are in constant conversation with prostitutes, and must be well known to the watchmen.

The Lord Mayor earned a reputation for toughness, and provoked a number of satirical cartoons, by going on to the streets himself and supervising the efforts of the Watch to move prostitutes from their favoured nightly places of parade. His critics did not always realize, when they accused him of being a busybody, that his campaign had at least as much to do with crime as with morality.

From every quarter, then, the evidence came in of inadequacies in the policing of London, of corruption – serious and otherwise – among those charged with maintaining authority, and of persistent criminality and licentiousness in and around the rookeries. 'It is a weary life, and wears men out very fast', was the way in which John Vickery, an experienced Bow Street officer, summed up the difficult task of the few full-time police engaged in tackling the many different kinds of criminal to be found in London. Vickery had reason to know – two years before, he had got himself 'cut all to pieces' while attempting to arrest two men who had committed murder. He had not been expected to live, and had been laid up for six months. Understandably, he now objected strongly to the way in which magistrates and clerks, men with safe desk jobs, drew superannuation money, whereas he was ineligible for such payments. 'The officers', he complained, 'are considered nothing in the thing.' Vickery's concern was echoed by others. Yet this was only one type of problem among many facing those concerned with improving law enforcement. The real difficulty was to establish priorities and decide at which point to begin in the assault against crime. Two vicious circles seemed to be in operation: on the one hand, inadequate methods of policing bred inadequate police; while on the other young thieves who came out of the rookeries found their way to prison, and from there back to a life of crime. It was small wonder that those who knew the thief-takers and their quarry best were often cynical.

Cynicism was an easy response, but not the only one. A number of people, including Henry Grey Bennet, the chairman of the 1816 Select Committee on the Police, were inclined to make a start in combating crime with reform of the prisons. There was certainly scope for change. Prison, most observers agreed, did little to stem the flood of crime, and a good deal to make it worse. One basic trouble was that London's prisons were overcrowded and badly designed, another that the nation as yet lacked a consistent penal philosophy. In a number of prisons, felons who had committed very serious crimes mixed indiscriminately with unfortunate men and women incarcerated for small debts. Juveniles and hardened thieves were thrown together almost everywhere. Those brave individuals like Grey Bennet and Elizabeth Fry who had followed the example of the pioneering eighteenth-century student of prisons, John Howard, and risked contagion from gaol fever by actually visiting Newgate and London's other prisons, argued that they did more to destroy character than any other institution, with the two possible exceptions of the criminal flash-houses and another sort of prison, 'the hulks'.

England did not really believe in prisons. What the country wanted was to get rid of its criminal population. That is why in the seventeenth century the practice developed of sending to penal servitude overseas as many as possible of those wrongdoers who managed to escape the gallows. The most convenient dumping-grounds were the plantations in Virginia and other American colonies, and such islands as Jamaica and Barbados. But from 1775 the American War of Independence seriously interfered with the transportation of convicts, which, in its shipboard conditions, had come to resemble the slave trade. In due course Australia took the place of North America, but during the American war the experiment was tried of imprisoning convicts sentenced to transportation, for whom no transport ships were yet available, in the hulks of two old ships moored in the Thames. An Act of Parliament stated that convicts on the hulks were to 'be punished by being kept to hard labour in the raising of sand, soil and gravel, and cleansing the river Thames, or any other service for the benefit of the navigation of the said river'. What was hastily brought in as 'a temporary expedient' soon became a standard penal measure, and, from the prisoners' point of view, a particularly harsh and unpleasant one. In the late eighteenth and early nineteenth centuries there was almost always a shortage of ships ready to take men sentenced to transportation on the long journey to Botany Bay or to that dreaded place of no return, Norfolk Island. It became customary to send to the hulks many of those who would be 'going to sea' when transports arrived to take them; and, as the years went by, more and more criminals were despatched to the hulks anyway, usually for a period of several years. Converting ships which were no longer seaworthy into crude places of confinement cost far less than building new prisons, and during the war with France prisoners-of-war, as well as convicts, were soon also housed in hulks.

Conditions aboard the convict hulks were unspeakably horrible, with unwashed criminals packed together very closely on three decks, breathing permanently foetid air. At night, the hatches were simply screwed down, and the convicts were left to fight among themselves in wretched candlelight or claustrophobic darkness. Gambling was the main recreation, and, as one convict put it, 'crime was the constant subject of talk, and that after this they would never go to work again; must go thieving; intended to do it; wished to do it'. Newcomers were always relegated to the lowest deck. In time, if their stamina lasted – there were many deaths – they progressed to the middle deck, which inevitably had many sickly and diseased occupants. Then at last the upper deck was reached, and with it the possibility either of being transported or of eventual release. Yet even here violent attacks from fellow prisoners were commonplace, and the imitation, albeit incomplete, of the cruelty and squalor aboard the old slave ships continued to prey upon the nerves of the average convict. 'Hell on earth' was a common description of the life. Few of those with experience of the hulks were willing to quarrel with it, even although the actual location might be closer to mud and water. 'Whatever little remains of innocence or honesty a man might have is sure to be lost there', was one convict's summing-up. Whenever anyone died men gathered round like vultures, almost fighting 'to see if he had anything about the bed, so that they might take it, flannels or money'.

In 1816 there was a 'Convict Establishment' of 2,500 aboard five hulks, and this figure was to increase steadily until by 1828 no fewer than 4,446 prisoners were housed in ten ships. No proper provision was made for classifying and keeping apart prisoners of different types. From 1823 boys were held separately, first at Sheerness in the *Bellerophon*, a former man-of-war which had brought Napoleon to England after Waterloo, and then in the much smaller frigate *Euryalus* at Chatham; but overcrowding in the *Euryalus*, which produced merciless bullying – as well as scurvy and opthalmia – did away with whatever benefits there might have been in punishing young criminals apart from their elders. Instead of labouring ashore, boys were employed in making convict uniforms on board. During their exercise hour in the open air they walked round and round the upper deck in silence, like so many little old men. There was never enough food to go round, and the strong stole from the weak all the time. An ex-convict who served for a time as an orderly in the boys' hospital explained that he had known patients coming in there who had not tasted meat for three weeks: 'they have been obliged to give their portions to those Nobs [bullies] . . . and have fed themselves upon gruel and the parings of potatoes'. The hulks were loathed, but their overseer, J.H. Capper, was forced to admit in 1828 that, of boy-convicts, 'eight out of ten that have been liberated have returned to their old courses'. Among older criminals, the record was no better. The horrors of the hulks must have had some kind of deterrent effect; but they bred such hatred of authority and determination to take revenge on society, that everyone spoke of them as breeding-places of crime. In this, they resembled the generally much less rigidly controlled Newgate.

Newgate, situated close to the Old Bailey and maintained by the City Corporation, was the common gaol not only for the City itself, but also for the county of Middlesex. Steeped in criminal legend, it was known in the underworld 'by various names, as *the pitcher, the stone pitcher, the start,* and *the stone jug,* according to the humour of the speaker'. The *stone jug* had its own distinctive sub-culture. From time to time, elaborately staged 'prizefights' took place between prisoners, and this was only one way in which the outside world was aped and burlesqued. Mock-trials were held also, parodying the language of the courts and usually awarding harsh 'sentences' to unpopular criminals who had transgressed against the prisoners' unwritten code. The Recorder of London himself might have been proud of the legal knowledge displayed on these occasions, even if the proceedings had a way of ending up in anarchy. Riots and disturbance were commonplace. Whenever a group of convicts was due to be shipped overseas, they and their fellow-prisoners would go round the wards destroying bedding and smashing up furniture. This was one way of saying goodbye; enforced attendance at the 'Condemned Sermon' in chapel, when the clergyman specifically addressed those soon to be hanged, was another. Despite the ever-present threat of the gallows, however, Newgate was held by its most experienced inmates to be much less hard on a man than the hulks.

From the authorities' point of view, the most obvious drawback of the prison was that it was not nearly large enough to house separately the different types of offender who were sent to it. In addition to men awaiting trial at the Old Bailey Sessions, and others sentenced to death or transportation, women, boys and girls all found their way to Newgate. The buildings dated from 1770, and even then they had been crowded, a damp and ill-lit maze of yards, staircases, wards and passages, with no central vantage-point for control and inspection of the prisoners. 'That Newgate is too small', Henry Grey Bennet commented in 1818, 'cannot be too often repeated.' He went on: 'I think the prison, as it is, is one of the worst features of a bad police, and has been, and is, one of the leading causes of the increase of crime.' To Bennet, it seemed clear that as long as the common yards contained men and boys, first offenders and thieves with a long string of convictions, there could be little prospect of any improvement. There was, however, one ray of hope; he went out of his way to pay tribute to the changed conditions among female prisoners brought about by the work of the Quaker philanthropist, Elizabeth Fry:

I visited Newgate in the beginning of the month of May 1817, and went round, first, the female side of the prison: I had been there a few weeks before, and found it, as usual, in the most degraded and afflicting state; the women were then mixed all together, young and old; the young beginner with the old offender; the girl, for the first offence, with the hardened and drunken prostitute; the tried and the untried; the accused with the condemned; the transports with those under sentence of death; all were crowded together, in one promiscuous assemblage; noisy, idle, and profligate; clamorous at the gratings, soliciting money, and begging at the bars of the prison, with spoons attached to the ends of sticks. In little more than one fortnight the whole scene was changed, through the humane and philanthropic exertion of Mrs Fry, the wife of a banker in the city, assisted by others of the Society of Friends; and it is but justice to add, seconded by the Lord Mayor, Aldermen, and Sheriffs of London. In the first yard I visited were seventy-eight women, fines and transports together; the fines being persons under sentence of imprisonment for short terms; sixty-five of these were employed in needle-work which had been procured for them: there were also with these women, seventeen children. Of the seventy-eight, sixty-four were under sentence of transportation, and fourteen for short terms of imprisonment; twenty-two of them slept in one room, which was only twenty-four feet by eighteen. In one fortnight, the work done was three hundred and forty-two shirts, and sixty-four shifts, fifty-nine aprons, and two hundred and fifty pinbefores.

The initiative taken in this way by a practical-minded woman reformer who was ready to venture within the walls of Newgate into its foul-smelling courtyards, would indeed help to transform the lot of many prisoners from despair to productive drudgery or even something better. But the deadweight of neglect and cynicism within the prison system was so great, and the buildings in prisons other than Newgate so appallingly cramped, that it would have taken an army of Elizabeth Frys to counteract the tendency of all imprisonment in London to produce yet more crime.

Not far from Newgate was the Fleet, one of three prisons chiefly for debtors administered by the Royal Courts of Justice at Westminster; the other two, the King's Bench and the Marshalsea, were located to the south of the river. Debtors had privileges not granted to ordinary criminals, including the right to have their family stay with them, or to be visited. They could usually arrange also to be supplied with beer or spirits. These freedoms were abused, partly because of the presence in the prisons of law-breakers of another kind, and partly because the gaolers, who were in any case too few to be effective, had a profit-seeking attitude towards their charges. Thus in 1816 the Keeper of the Fleet actually described his prison to a group of MPs investigating the state of the prisons of the metropolis as 'the biggest bawdy-house in London'. The Fleet was probably the most chaotic of them all, because it received within its walls the largest number of variegated unfortunates. But in the other two also, something far short of order prevailed. At the King's Bench, in Southwark, where the annual profits to the gaolers from the sale of beer alone amounted to £800, a complicated set of rules of 'chummage' was in operation, whereby prisoners sub-let rooms to each other. This practice frequently led to quarrels among touchy debtors, and once again matters were made worse by the fact that the gaolers were unable or unwilling to handle several hundred prisoners with an degree of consistent authority. In the Marshalsea, issues of personal status led to constant friction, too, for here again petty debtors and their families found themselves lodged beside more serious offenders, including seamen under sentence of naval courts-martial for desertion, mutiny and other misdemeanours. The young Charles Dickens had to visit here, in consequence of his father's debts; and his lifelong sense of insecurity and injustice must have been partly caused by this humiliating experience.

A radical weakness of these and many other London prisons, 'houses of correction' and penal institutions of different kinds, was that they were not provided and run by the government, but instead bore all the signs of local rule and mismanagement. What made matters worse was that the government's own initiative in prison-building and administration was notably unsuccessful. At great expense, a huge 'penitentiary' was built between 1812 and 1821 at Millbank, on the site now occupied by the Tate Gallery. This was a drastically modified version of one of Jeremy Bentham's most cherished ideas. At one time, Bentham's brother Samuel had constructed a factory in Russia for Catherine the Great, and this provided the 'Father of Utilitarianism' with the model for what he called a panopticon, a penitentiary ranged around a central inspection tower in tiered layers of cells, all clearly visible to the keepers. Bentham's proposal, rejected by successive governments, was that he himself would run the panopticon as a moderately profitable concern. The profits would come from work done by prisoners persuaded by reason rather than by chains, and Bentham himself was to sit, as Edmund Burke put it, like a spider in the middle of a web. While Bentham's bold penal philosophy was foreign to Lord Sidmouth, the notably cautious Home Secretary in 1812, the penitentiary which was actually built beside the river resembled the panopticon in its design. It was run as a place which had as its main purpose the reformation of its inmates; but most people considered that all it actually achieved was a peculiarly rule-bound and soul-less form of detention. There was much criticism of what was deemed too generous a diet for prisoners, yet so erratic was the supervision of the Millbank institution that for a time near-starvation prevailed, along with 'a malignant and contagious disorder'.

The penitentiary idea was a sign of the times. If it was impossible to get rid of unwanted criminals – and the flourishing practice of transporting as many as possible overseas showed that this was still the chief objective – then they must cease to be criminal. Accordingly, increasing interest was taken in types of prison discipline which, it was believed, might inflict 'a just measure of pain' upon prisoners so as to bring about a fundamental change in their attitudes. One London prison which had pioneered a new technique, that of solitary confinement, was the House of Correction of Coldbath Fields. Significantly, Coldbath Fields was looked on as a thoroughly repressive institution by prisoners, who referred to it as the 'Bastille', the 'Stile' or the 'Steel'. The 'Bastille' did not fall into the hands of the prisoners, but there were repeated and violent demonstrations within its forbidding walls. Underworld opinion had it that the often brutal life of the older unreformed prisons was far preferable either to enforced separation, or to another new practice, the so-called 'silent system', which was aimed at reducing to an absolute minimum the amount of talk possible within prison. The theory behind the silent system was that hardened criminals would not have a chance to corrupt the young, and that all prisoners would profit by reflecting in silence upon their crimes. However, what tended to happen in practice was that a larger number of prisoners than usual broke down, in some cases becoming seriously deranged, while the majority fiercely upheld their individual and corporate identity by devising alternative sign-systems; for instance, they tapped in code on walls, window-bars, and, where these existed, waterpipes. It seems highly doubtful that strict rules of solitary confinement or silence made many criminals reform, but they certainly added to the degree of hatred and grievance which most prisoners soon bore towards all authority, and thus strengthened traditions of solidarity in the rookeries.

One symbol for prison inmates of all they loathed and despised in the new 'progressive' penal methods was the treadwheel. This huge revolving cylinder made from iron and wood, with steps like the slats of a paddle wheel, was invented in 1817 by Samuel Cubitt, one of the founders of a firm of building contractors. He had responded to an appeal from distraught magistrates in his native town of Ipswich for a new form of hard labour which would have a deterrent effect on law-breakers: there had been widespread riots in East Anglia in 1816, largely caused by hunger. Within a very few years, the treadwheel was in use in many English prisons. It was a common practice for people visiting a new prison such as Brixton – opened in 1821 – to watch the prisoners taking the forty-eight or fifty laborious steps a minute required to turn the wheel. Occasionally, the treadwheel was used productively, to grind corn or raise water, but far more often it merely beat the air, in many prisons for as much as ten hours a day, with prisoners stepping on and off it every twenty minutes. In the early years of its reign, which lasted until late in the century, the enthusiasm of some magistrates for the new 'corrective' measure knew no bounds, one JP going so far as to describe the treadwheel as 'the most tiresome, distressing, exemplary punishment that has ever been contrived by human ingenuity'. There was more than one fatality, with prisoners being mangled in the machinery; in some places, pregnant women and old men with hernias were forced to step on the wheel along with the rest. Yet it is unlikely that the 'shinbreaker' succeeded in achieving any penal end: instead it embittered old and young alike. The Whig reformer Sydney Smith saw its counter-productive potential for what it was, and wrote in irony:

We would banish all the looms of Preston jail and substitute nothing but the treadwheel or the capstan, or some species of labour where the labourer could not see

the results of his toil, where it was as monotonous,
irksome and dull as possible . . .

But his words were wasted on an age with a liking for
mechanical answers to society's problems.

It is commonly held that the 'bloody code' of eighteenth-
century English criminal law was perpetuated largely for its
symbolic worth as a means of showing the overwhelming
value placed on property by the nation's ruling classes. Even
when, with apparent inconsistency, the lives of poachers or
indeed robbers were spared, property-owning magistrates
were able to let it be seen that power ultimately lay with
them, as they invoked first the 'majesty' of law and justice,
and then – after a due interval for reflection on the part of the
guilty prisoner – 'mercy'. In a similar way, it might be argued
that the underlying rationale of certain of the harsher new
methods in early nineteenth-century prisons lay in the need of
an assertive but harassed society to instil in its rebellious
members an inhibiting sense of fear. In practice, in this
different context, 'mercy' was once again a feature of the new
code, this time in the form of remission for good conduct by
prisoners; but its application was now sparing and calculated.
Typically, the treadwheel, isolation, and silence for weeks on
end were there to be used on the refractory; rebelliousness, it
was thought, would soon be dealt with. The word 'corrective',
so often applied to punishment at this time, was frequently
only a hypocritical justification for the physical and mental
cruelty inflicted in prisons. The unspoken implication of
Coldbath Fields and Brixton was that the 'corrective'
resources of the gaolers would prove more than a match for
the criminal tendencies of the inmates. But the verdict of the
London underworld on the 'quods' or prisons of the Regency
period was that with minor exceptions – where individuals
like Elizabeth Fry had a genuinely philanthropic influence –
they increased the criminals' sense of being rejected as human
beings. Some prisons, it is true, were dreaded, as were the
hulks: but by members of a criminal class made more
determined than ever to cheat the law.

For these reasons among others, Peel's Prison Act of 1823, which attempted to classify prisoners according to their crimes and to standardize penal practice, was an essential first step on a long road to reform. In this, it can be compared to changes in criminal law which Peel, an altogether more enlightened Home Secretary than Sidmouth, managed gradually to introduce in the 1820s. The Criminal Law Act of 1826, for instance, greatly reduced the costs of prosecution for private individuals by introducing a regular system of expenses; although courts retained some power to pay rewards, this was no longer a dominant consideration when criminals were brought to trial. Thus the old reluctance to prosecute petty thieves began to disappear, and there was not now the temptation to indulge in reward-hunting. The next year, another act changed the status of receiving from misdemeanour to felony, even where the thief's identity was not known and regardless of his fate. This made the lives of receivers of stolen goods considerably harder by exposing them to a different range of sentences in the courts.

Important as these changes were, however, the long-term containment of the underworld depended, as Peel well knew, upon 'preventive' police. He had declared in 1822, 'I want to teach people that liberty does not consist in having your house robbed by organized gangs of thieves'. It must have been a bitter disappointment that when, as newly appointed Home Secretary in 1823, he set up a Parliamentary Committee on the Police, its final recommendations were bleakly negative, showing how strong was the continuing resistance to reform:

it is difficult to reconcile an effective system of police, with the perfect freedom of action and exemption from interference, which are the great privileges and blessings of society in this country; and Your Committee think that the forfeiture or curtailment of such advantages would be too great a sacrifice for improvements in police, or facilities in detection of crime, however desirable in themselves if abstractedly considered.

Peel had to bice his time for seven years; then, seizing the opportunity afforded by a fresh wave of public alarm over the amount of theft in London, he created a new and very carefully selected Committee, which reported unequivocally in favour of reorganizing the police of the metropolis. Skilfully, he bought off the opposition of the City of London by leaving its traditional control over its own police untouched for the time being, in the Bill which he proceeded to bring before Parliament. For the rest of London, however, the appointment of two commissioners, Charles Rowan and Richard Mayne, with authority to recruit a completely new and professional body of Police, brought to an end the days of the charleys, and of parochial autonomy.

Arguably Peel, with his long experience of handling difficult issues in Ireland, which bred coolness under pressure, was the only man in the land capable of achieving the kind of compromise which carried the day. And naturally enough, when the new legislation came into force he allowed the impression to be created that the entire impetus behind the movement for change had come from him. Patrick Colquhoun he referred to only once, in passing, rather patronizingly, as 'a Glasgow trader' who had been among the untrained stipendiary magistrates of 1793. That is the way of practical men of politics, of prime ministers in the making. In reality, however, Peel had not been alone, nor had his been a voice crying in the wilderness. What he succeeded in doing was to articulate at last within acceptable limits the political will and energy of the British people. He created out of a series of half-chances the means of doing something realistic, if inevitably limited and imperfect, to halt the headlong course of the criminals of London. He has his memorial in the Metropolitan Police and the still-familiar nickname 'bobby'.

THREE

NURSERIES OF CRIME

One of the most shocking aspects of the nineteenth-century underworld was that thieves appeared to be getting younger all the time. At least in the past, those who stole had usually been grown men and women. But now, it seemed, children were starting to pilfer as soon as they were old enough to walk, and by the time they were eight or nine some were already practised law-breakers, capable of making off successfully with money and goods from places where adult thieves dared not show themselves. This suggested that they were being trained by their elders in 'schools of vice' where crime was taught, quite deliberately, as a way of life.

The anxieties of prosperous householders, whose goods were naturally most at risk, were matched in a different way by those of the poorer people whose children, unlike those of the better off, might be exposed to the corrupting influence of criminal neighbours. It was sometimes not at all easy for the honest but poor parents of young children in Bethnal Green, the Borough, or Tothill Fields, living in cramped and depressing conditions, to ensure that their offspring stayed clear of the 'boys on the cross', or young criminals about town. Doubtless, many a word was spoken and many a thrashing handed out to drive the point home, but not always with the desired result.

It could be argued that the concern was alarmist and unnecessarily panicky. There *had* been some overall reduction in the level of serious violence in London's streets since the bloodbath of the Gordon Riots in 1780. But to contemporary observers crime nearly always appears to be increasing in scale and seriousness, and this is true especially of crime among the young. Each generation firmly believes that it faces a new and unprecedented crisis. However, with every allowance made for this, Regency London had due cause for its concern about young law-breakers. At this time, the children of the rookeries included in their number astonishingly callous and hardened criminals, veterans of the Old Bailey and of Newgate. Taught to steal from a very early age, both by precept and daily example, they were set on cheating authority and impressing their peers. Many would be transported to Australia while still in their teens; others would die on the gallows. Yet there always seemed to be new young thieves waiting to take the place of those who got caught. The life had a rough glamour about it, as indeed had the death. There was, in any case, little else for them to do; so they kept on stealing.

Their habit of masking despair under a cloak of bravado showed clearly in the way they talked about being transported or executed. 'Going to sea', meaning Botany Bay, was for many years an attractive, exciting prospect; or so they made out. They had heard stories about the horrors of penal servitude on Norfolk Island, as well as about boys dying in the disease-ridden convict ships which sailed to Australia. But against these things must be set the chance of finding a new life under the southern sky, a life far removed from the confining city which was all they had ever known. The ultimate penalty, still a public affair although one now taking place outside Newgate instead of at Tyburn as in the old days, was traditionally the chief way to get noticed in criminal circles. There was a special quality of reckless abandon about condemned youths. They spoke of 'dying game' or 'dying dunghill'. Their friends all followed them to the gallows. If they showed defiance to the last, and met their end wearing stolen finery, then their brief lives were crowned with a fitting glory. The climax was as it ought to be: a gesture of superiority and contempt for authority.

The number of boys and girls who stole for a living in Regency London was in the thousands rather than the hundreds. Henry Grey Bennet, Chairman of the 1816 Select Parliamentary Committee on the Police, informed his colleagues that in that year there were 'above 6,000 boys and girls, living solely on the town by thieving, or as the companions and associates of thieves'. He was at pains to point out that this was a conservative estimate . . .

I have seen calculations much exceeding this, but I am satisfied that no great dependence can be placed on them; and I mention the above number only to point out the evil, even on the least computation of its extent.

Grey Bennet himself visited Newgate and spoke at length with some of the younger inmates, and the evidence received by his Committee, including his own, shows in detail just how acute the problem of juvenile crime was felt to be – and also that there was little hope of conquering it in isolation from a whole group of related social evils. As well as the appalling overcrowding in the prisons, to which the young were too readily sent, and the absence of any proper system for separating first offenders – even when these were small children – from 'convicted transports' and other hardened criminals, there was a great deal of drunkenness in London, largely because of the lax control of licences and the habit of the poor of turning to gin as a solace for life's miseries. Schools and Sunday schools were lacking almost everywhere, and where they were not, were in need of funds and of staff. Children were being systematically corrupted by older thieves not only in prison but in flash-houses, which were at once brothels, drinking-places, and centres of criminal intelligence. The flash-houses ought to be put down; but instead their existence was connived at by the corrupt officers of a force wholly inadequate to the needs of the metropolis.

Witness after witness spoke of the 'late alarming increase' in the number of thefts committed by the young, and especially by boys. Thomas Vance, a magistrate from the Union Hall police office, whose district included Bermondsey, Brixton, Tooting and Vauxhall, claimed that many children were deserted by their parents, or badly neglected; poverty was partly to blame. Once out of parental supervision, there was a risk that the boys and girls – who needed to eat, after all – would become the tools of professional law-breakers. In his district, he pointed out:

> There are a number of designing thieves constantly on the look-out for children, who are naturally more inclined to be idle than to work, and who commence with petty thefts at the wharfs, and other places where property is exposed; these the confirmed thieves seize hold of, and make them the catspaw in doing those things which they otherwise would do themselves, and for which they would probably suffer detection and punishment, hoping that, in consideration of their youth, commiseration may be excited in the breasts of the Magistrates, and that they may be dismissed.

Similar information came from other parts of London. Sir Daniel Williams, a Whitechapel magistrate, who was questioned closely about licensing policy in Bethnal Green, remarked that children were frequently 'trained up' to steal by 'relatives and connexions'. James Bartlett, a watch-house keeper in St Paul's, Covent Garden, offered a fuller explanation of how children came under pressure from their elders:

> Their friends [i.e. relatives and friends] have generally sent them out begging, and if they do not bring home money as they ought to do, they flog them; that is the story we get from them.

Bartlett's words imply that he did not always believe every part of the story he heard from the urchins of Covent Garden, but the connection between begging and theft – and in particular, the practice of sending out to beg – was dwelt on by others also. Where criminals lived, it was common enough for the order to be explicitly given to steal if begging proved unsuccessful; and from this there was only a small step to rewarding children with payment, even payment in advance. As one witness put it, the older thieves would give them from time to time 'little sums, sixpence, or a shilling, or half-a-crown, to go and take an article'.

The views of Philip Holdsworth were of particular interest to the Committee because he held the key position of Marshal of London, and as such was directly responsible to the Lord Mayor for the policing of the City. As he saw it, the coming of peace had brought a very marked increase in the amount of stealing by the young. He did not develop this comment, but probably had in mind the sharp rise in unemployment in 1815–16, which was brought about in part by the return of soldiers from the war . . .

Do you consider the number of juvenile depredators as very much increased of late? – Yes, within the last twelve months, beyond any thing I ever remember.

What are the offences that are principally committed by the children? – Picking pockets; taking things off, on their hands and knees, from shops, such as haberdashers and linen-drapers; in the winter-time, with a knife at the corner of the glass starring it, and taking things out, which has occasioned the tradespeople having so many guard irons; but still there are shops not so guarded, and they can find opportunities of continually robbing: Boys upon all occasions, when there is any thing which excites a crowd, are very active, and many of them extremely clever; they are short and active, and are generally attended by men.

Holdsworth, too, was convinced that systematic instruction took place, much of it within particular 'gangs':

Do you consider these boys as acting together in gangs, and trained by thieves grown old in the practice? – No question; they are trained by thieves who are adepts; these boys are generally apprehended three and four together, but they go in larger gangs than that.

Are they of very tender age? – Many of them from six years old to ten.

The gangs he referred to were said by several people to have divided London into 'walks' for the purpose of picking pockets. They fought with each other over territorial boundaries, and sometimes regrouped or exchanged members, but there was scope enough for all. One reason for this, remarked Sir Nathaniel Conant, the Chief Magistrate at Bow Street, was simply that shopkeepers were too trusting. They did not protect their goods properly, but instead insisted on putting them on open display. Far too many tempting and valuable items were exposed each weekday at shop doors, within easy reach of prying young fingers. Nonetheless, it was admitted on all sides that, even when shopkeepers took due precautions against 'juvenile depredators', real danger of theft remained.

If the Marshal of London was an important witness, so also was the 'Ordinary' or Chaplain of Newgate Prison, the Reverend H.S. Cotton. His nominal main duty was to preach the traditional 'Condemned Sermon' in Newgate Chapel, addressed to those prisoners who were under sentence of death, and who sat grouped round a coffin. The idea was that even if the capitally convicted were beyond reclaim in this world, the occasion might serve as an awful warning to their fellow prisoners. But Cotton was possessed of a social conscience, as well as an unenviable benefice. He had responded to the challenge presented by the number of young criminals entering Newgate by starting a small prison school. There was much that he could tell the Select Committee, and accordingly he was questioned closely:

What are the average ages of boys you have now in your school? – About twelve years.

When was the school first established? – The 25th of August 1814.

How many have passed through since its establishment? –
One hundred and sixty.

Out of that number, how many have been convicted? –
One hundred and ten.

How many capitally convicted of the 110? – Eighteen.

Have many, and how many, been transported for life? –
Two.

How many have been transported for fourteen years? –
One.

How many for seven years? – Thirty-three.

In how many instances have the judgments been respited,
and the boys sent to their friends, or to institutions? –
Twenty-three.

What are those institutions? – The Philanthropic, the
Refuge for the Destitute, and the Marine Society.

What becomes of the remaining number ? – Thirty-three
fined or imprisoned in the house of correction, or
whipped, or so on.

Up to this point, perhaps, the Chaplain's evidence
contained few surprises for a group of MPs studying the
various questions associated with police reform. With more
than a hundred capital offences on the statute book, and
children of seven and over exposed to the full rigour of the
law, the harshness of the code of criminal justice was readily
recognized by thinking men. While the upsurge in juvenile
crime had already led to demands for still more severe
punishments, it was tacitly accepted in enlightened circles
that, wherever possible, children must be saved from the
gallows. In practice, magistrates handed out many more
sentences of transportation than of death to boys and girls;
these sentences were frequently themselves commuted to
terms of imprisonment; and if relatives or charitable
institutions such as the Refuge for the Destitute were
willing to take the law-breakers into their midst, late
pardons were quite often granted.

The Reverend Cotton must have given pause to the Select
Committe in subsequent answers, however, for he went on

to talk about the kind of habitual offender who came back time and time again to Newgate. The term 'recidivist' had not yet been invented, but the Newgate Chaplain had experience of trying to teach youthful recidivists:

Are there many of those boys who have repeatedly been in custody? – Four have been repeatedly in custody; upwards of seventy times between them.

Can you state their names? – Burnet, aged nine; Harper, aged twelve; Morn, eleven; and Sweeny, thirteen.

Burnet was capitally convicted, was he not? – He was.

If the committee mistake not, he was the boy who had been three years on the town, and who was without father and mother? – I think he has a mother.

The two boys Harper and Morn were those boys that travelled down to Portsmouth for the purpose of attending the fair at the head of a gang of boys like themselves? – Yes.

About what time was this? – In the summer-time, when Portsdown fair was held.

The Reverend Cotton here touched on two patterns of behaviour, one seasonal and the other having much to do with the fact that too many boys were sent out of prison penniless and with nowhere to go. It was the practice of a good number of London thieves who had spent the winter months in town to travel in the south of England during the summer. Most contented themselves with visiting the more attractive of the fairs which took place close to the capital each year; the Committee learned that no fewer than eighty such fairs, some of them lasting for several days, were held within ten miles of London between May and September. The bolder spirits, such as Harper and Morn, ventured further afield, seeking easy pickings and casual fun on the south coast and elsewhere. But there was another cycle, too, in which theft was followed by imprisonment, then in an apparently hopeless sequence by further and more serious theft, and so on. The Chaplain instanced a boy called

Wilson, who was acquitted of a crime while in Newgate 'and brought in again on the very same day'. He had since been sent to the Refuge, broken out of it, and been committed to the Bridewell in Tothill Fields, a kind of disciplinary institution for women and children.

All this was bad enough, but there was worse to come. The Ordinary of Newgate confirmed, as had already been suggested, that the boys in prison were as sexually precocious as they were prematurely expert in the ways of crime. Burnet, for instance, the nine-year-old who had been capitally convicted, had a 'mistress' of thirteen:

> Of the boys that you have in your school, did they not many of them, even of a very early age, profess to keep what are termed flash-girls, which they supported out of their thefts? – All of them. Burnet, who is only nine years of age, has also a person whom he terms his girl.
>
> Has it not often happened, that persons have presented themselves at Newgate, calling themselves sisters and relations of the boys, who had been prevented afterwards from coming, from its being found out that they were common prostitutes, and kept by the boys? – Repeatedly.

Further information on this point came from William Crawford, of Devonshire Square, a member of the Society of Friends who two years before had joined Peter Bedford, a fellow Quaker, of Spitalfields, in establishing a society 'for investigating the causes of the alarming increase of juvenile delinquency in the Metropolis'. Crawford had carried out extensive inquiries, centred principally on the prisons but involving also the families and acquaintances of young thieves; he could draw on detailed knowledge of eight hundred cases. The Select Committee already had before them a copy of his Report on Juvenile Delinquency, which gave details of typical young thieves . . .

> A.B. aged thirteen years. His parents are living; he was but for a short time at school; his father was frequently

intoxicated, and on these occasions the son generally left home, and associated with bad characters, who introduced him to houses of ill fame, where they gambled till they had lost or spent all their money. This boy had been five years in the commission of crime, and been imprisoned for three separate offences; sentence of death had been twice passed on him.

E.F. aged eight years. His mother only is living, and she is a very immoral character. This boy has been in the habit of stealing for upwards of two years. In Covent-garden Market there is a party of between thirty and forty boys, who sleep every night under the sheds and baskets. These pitiable objects when they arise in the morning have no other means of procuring subsistence but by the commission of crime; this child was one of the number; and it appears that he has been brought up to the several police offices upon eighteen separate charges. He has been twice confined in the House of Correction, and three times in Bridewell; he is very ignorant, but of a good capacity.

I.J. aged twelve years. Can neither read nor write; his father is a soldier, and his mother is deceased. This lad, with a younger brother, was sent to a workhouse, where it appears that he experienced harsh treatment, which induced him to effect his escape. When at liberty, he engaged himself to a chimney-sweeper, with whom he remained about a week. During this period he states that he suffered much from hunger and oppression. Early one morning he decamped with his master's watch; he was however soon apprehended and committed to prison.

Q.R. aged twelve years. He has had no education: has a mother who encourages the vices of her son, and subsists by his depredations. She turns him into the street every morning, and chastises him severely when he returns in the evening without some article of value.

This Report, which ranks historically as a pioneering attempt to understand young criminals rather than simply condemn them, listed a number of factors which were thought to lie behind the juvenile crime wave in London. Among them were parental neglect, due in part to poverty and the effects of the war, the want of schools and jobs, gambling in the streets, the severity of the criminal code, and the shortcomings of the police.

Crawford said he had no doubt at all that flash-houses were the source of a great deal of trouble, including the boys' habit of living with prostitutes. In some houses there was a promiscuous assemblage of men, women, boys and girls; while others were kept exclusively for the young. It was the rule rather than the exception for boys to cohabit with girls of their own age. There were several such houses in St Giles, and in one

> four hundred beds are made up every night; a boy who was in the habit of visiting this house confessed that he had slept there upwards of thirty times with girls of his own age, and he particularly named five: this boy was fourteen years of age, the girls were to be met with at the flash-house to which he resorted.

In every respect, the way of living of the young law-breakers was a close copy of older criminals' behaviour. For instance, when a boy went into prison – Crawford cited an example from Coldbath Fields – he expected his girl to try to keep on the lodgings which they had shared until he came out. If his sentence was a short one, she might well succeed in doing so.

William Crawford was a humanitarian of a remarkable sort. 'It is very easy', he told the Select Committee, 'to blame these poor children, and to ascribe their misconduct to an innate propensity to vice; but I much question whether any human being, circumstanced as many of them are, can reasonably be expected to act otherwise.' Grey Bennet, likewise a man bent on practical reform rather than one given to fulminating over the iniquity of youth, told of his own memorable encounter with Leary, a gang-leader described by the Chaplain of Newgate as 'an extraordinary boy'. Leary was clever and prepossessing; but he had grown up in one of the Irish ghettos, something had gone wrong, and he had taken to thieving. There was much to be learned from the tale of his exploits . . .

he was of about thirteen years of age, good-looking, sharp, and intelligent, and possessing a manner which seemed to indicate a character very different from what he really professed. When I saw him he was under sentence of death for stealing a watch, chain, and seals from Mr Princep's chambers in the Temple; he had been five years in the practice of delinquency, progressively from stealing an apple off a stall, to housebreaking and highway robbery. He belonged to the Moorfields Catholic School, and there became acquainted with one Ryan in that school, by whom he was first instructed in the various arts and practices of delinquency . . . he soon became captain of a gang, generally since known as Leary's gang, with five boys, and sometimes more, furnished with pistols, taking a horse and cart with them; and, if they had an opportunity in their road, they cut off the trunks from gentlemen's carriages . . . He has been concerned in various robberies in London and its vicinity, and has had property at one time amounting to £350; but when he had money, he either got robbed of it by elder thieves who knew he had so much about him, or he lost it by gambling at flash-houses, or spent it amongst loose characters of both sexes. After committing innumerable depredations, he was detected at Mr Derrimore's at Kentish Town, stealing some plate from that gentlemen's dining-room, when several other similar robberies coming against him in that neighbourhood, he was, in compassion to his youth, placed in the Philanthropic; but being now charged with Mr Princep's robbery, he was taken out therefrom, tried, convicted, and sentenced to death, but was afterwards respited and returned to the

Philanthropic. He is little and well-looking; has robbed to
the amount of £3,000 during his five years career.

This 'surprising boy' had since absconded from the
Philanthropic, committed further crimes, and been
sentenced to transportation for life. Characteristically, while
in Newgate he refused to accept the discipline of the school,
preferring to mix with older prisoners in the yard.

Grey Bennet was too honest to claim that he had any ready-
made answerto the problem posed by such extreme instances
of juvenile crime. There would be other Learys. In recounting
the criminal career of this one, it is possible that he was to
some extent simply voicing his own bewilderment. But he
wanted his fellow MPs to know the true facts. And about one
thing he was completely sure – something must be done to
put down the flash-houses. A number of witnesses from the
police offices had either denied that places answering this
description existed, or had argued that the police needed to be
able to visit them in order to pick up information about the
whereabouts of law-breakers who would otherwise escape
detection. The Chairman of the Select Committee on the
Police would have none of it. Flash-houses were a cause of far
more crime than they prevented, a cause, moreover, of the
corruption of youth:

I say then, that there are above two hundred regular flash-
houses in the metropolis, all known to the police officers,
which they frequent, many of them open all night; that
the landlords in numerous instances receive stolen goods,
and are what are technically called fences; that this fact is
known also to the officers, who, for obvious reasons,
connive at the existence of these houses; that many of the
houses are frequented by boys and girls of the ages of ten
to fourteen and fifteen, who are exclusively admitted, who
pass the night in gambling and debauchery, and who
there sell and divide the plunder of the day, or who sally
forth from these houses to rob in the streets.

He had reliable information that in some instances the officers levied a contribution from landlords in return for not reporting the nature of their houses to the magistrates; this practice was called 'going a boxing at Christmas to the public houses'. It was nonsense to pretend that flash-houses did not exist. What about the Black Horse in Tottenham Court Road, where the regulars had included such notorious thieves as Huffey White and Conkey Beau, and whose landlord, Blackman, 'has been considered a thief for fifteen years'? He could name other names even more embarrassing to the magistrates and police officers of Bow Street . . .

there is not a regular flash-house in London that is not known to the officers of the police, from the Rose, in Rose-street Long Acre, kept by Kelly [a well-known thief], which he kept long with impunity, to the Bear, opposite to Bow-Street office, the infamous character of which is notorious, and which unites the trades of brothel and public-house.

In one place alone, he suggested, was more thieving planned and more stolen property disposed of than in these 'hot-beds of profligacy and vice'. That was in Newgate, which must surely rank as the leading school of vice in London, whatever the general public might suppose.

Despite these strong words, Grey Bennet did not succeed in having the flash-houses closed, for he was up against the vested interests of brewers who were quite content to run pubs attracting the custom of the underworld, as well as of a lazy and partly corrupt police. But although he would have to wait until the 1820s for a substantial measure of reform – when Peel succeeded the cautious Sidmouth as Home Secretary – he had at least the satisfaction of placing before the House of Commons a formidable body of evidence, which has since been described accurately as a running commentary on crime in Regency London.

Grey Bennet had heard several witnesses speak about 'hush money' and underworld bribery, while others had warned him frankly that they did not want their names to become known in case of reprisals. Someone in this latter category had supplied him with a list of flash-houses known to the police, which he was not at liberty to divulge. As it happens, just such a list from this very year, 1816, is preserved in a notebook in the British Library. Who compiled the notebook can only be guessed at – the initials 'A.L.' appear, perhaps those of a police officer – but it is known that not long after this the notebook belonged to the Recorder of the City of London, Sir John Silvester. It contains detailed notes on receivers, and Silvester had told Grey Bennet's Committee that he believed there was a particular need to crack down on receivers . . . 'that is another mode of increasing crime, by the ease with which people part with stolen goods; if that could be prevented, and a greater difficulty thrown in the way of disposing of the property, the better it would be.'

The information on 'receivers of stolen property particularly from boys' in the Recorder's notebook throws fresh light on the twilit world of young thieves in the early nineteenth century, the world of *Oliver Twist*. Here we catch a glimpse of men and women capable of twisting the police officers of the day round their little fingers. Such a man was Lippy Allen, of Bell Lane, Spitalfields, who was ready to take action to protect his own son from the punishment about to be meted out to him by the law, but who would do nothing to save anyone else:

Fences from Men & Boys – deals in any thing – his Son from whom he fences was lately in Newgate School for Picking Pockets with another Boy, but he got acquitted through his Father stashing the Prosecution (as to him) with the Officer for 5 Guineas, but the other Boy was convicted & Transported for 7 years.

Among the women who held a complete and sinister control over young lives was Mrs Jennings of Red Lion Market, White Cross Street:

This is a most notorious Fence & keeps a house of Ill Fame. – She has secret Rooms by Doors out of Cupboards where she plants or secretes the property she buys till she has got it disposed of. Innumerable Girls & Boys of the Youngest class resort to this House as she makes up more Beds than any other House in that part of the metropolis; each room in her House (which is a large one) being divided into various divisions for Beds & the House is thronged every Night. She sanctions Robberies in her House which are continually committed by the Girls on Strangers whom they can inveigle into the House & whom the Girls will bilk into the bargain, as their Flash Boys never permit a connection under such circumstances.

Mrs Jennings had brought up her son to steal, just as Lippy Allen had; her boy was no common thief, either, but 'a notorious Cracksman or Housebreaker'. On one occasion, police officers took away from her house some housebreaking implements belonging to the son, but she herself had continued to prosper, in part through buying 'Silk Handkerchiefs, Gown Pieces & similar small Articles brought by the Boys & Girls'.

It is likely that many of the details about receivers listed in this notebook came in the first place from boys who had fenced with them, and who had since been caught. This would help to explain how it was known, for example, that Mrs Jennings had cupboards leading into secret rooms, in which she stored stolen goods. Quite often, the point of view seems to be that of one of the 'boys on the Cross' was telling part at least of what he knew in the hope of being treated leniently. Thus Mrs White of Barret's Court, Wigmore Street, a small-time operator in comparison with Mrs Jennings, but in her own way no less typical as a fence, is described as she must have been known professionally to her young clients:

Keeps an old Shoe Shop & buys chiefly Brushes, Pails, Coal-skuttles, &c., which little Boys sneak from Gentlemen's Houses, down the areas and at the doors.

Also pointing to an underworld source are the laconic words 'not known to the Officers', which follow many of the entries. Other entries would appear to combine facts newly gleaned from a young informer with what was already known to the police. The Recorder's complaint was that it was hard to bring receivers to justice. The list in his notebook was clearly aimed at shortening the criminal careers of habitual offenders.

Several different groups were at work. There were, for instance, women with barrows in the markets and streets, who simply hid away small objects supplied by thieves until it was safe to take them to a pawnshop or get rid of them in some other way. Sometimes, the objects were not so small, and ingenuity must have been required. An unidentified woman with a barrow at the corner of Gulston Street, Whitechapel, for example, received a whole range of stolen property from children, from petticoats and handkerchiefs to bacon, bread and cheese . . .

> Puts Handkerchiefs &c down her Bosom, and other things within her Barrow. She is known to all the little Cross Boys round the neighbourhood of whom she will buy anything if she can only get a penny by it, and urges them continually to get things of more value. The Officers have no knowledge whatever of this Woman and she excites no suspicion from her situation with her Barrow, but it appears this has become very lately a general practice with the lowest description of Fences (and who are chiefly those who buy from little Boys the most trifling Articles) to sit with Barrows at the corner of Streets & other Places, having within them secret places made for the Fenced Articles. This is very general, in particular through the Eastern parts of the City & Whitechapel.

Having a barrow gave a receiver the great advantage of mobility, and men could set up in much the same way, like a Mr Lawrence, of Fitzroy Place, who made use of a basket instead of a barrow, selling Banbury Cakes 'as a blind' . . .

his Basket (when he goes out) has private places where he Fences in the Street or at Fairs & Fights which he always attends, & his way is, to ask any one, who he thinks has any thing about him, such as a Pocket Book, Watch &c., to buy his Banburies, or sell him a Glass of Gin (which Lawrence always has secreted in his Basket), & while keeping the Party so engaged others who are connected with him play their part by Picking his Pocket etc.

Lawrence's was a classic method of fencing, but other types of receiver needed a horse and cart to carry away stolen goods. Here there was a sharp division between those who were dependent upon the assistance of someone else in the know and those who had their own transport at hand. Joshua Roberts, a pigeon-fancier of Pump Court, Duck Lane, Westminster, who fenced fowl, pigeons and rabbits, had to rely on a man coming occasionally to 'take things off'. Somebody with his own means of distribution, in contrast, was Edward Memmery, a coster-monger from Old Pye Street, who was both fence and cracksman. He, too, dealt chiefly in foodstuffs – butter, cheese, bacon and fowl – but he got rid of them himself by 'hawking about with a horse and cart in the outskirts of the town'. Coster-mongers, it seems, were particularly resourceful in this respect. His near neighbour, Robert Charles, who was supplied by 'innumerable boys', to whom he paid between one and two shillings for a duck or hen, made for outlying districts of London with his donkey, its baskets heavily laden. Sometimes it was easy enough to hire a horse and cart, but there were those who did not trust their fellow criminals in this way. Such was Brand, who kept an old rag shop in Tottenham Street, Tottenham Court Road. His special line was buying lead, which he conveyed in his bags packed with rags. Brand liked to work entirely on his own, having a mean streak . . . 'will not lend his Drag at a crack, but he goes himself & receives the Swag, & then plants it in his stable in Tottenham Mews, or lets it remain in the Drag till he further conveys it'.

Apart from food, the goods most commonly mentioned are small items of clothing, and especially handkerchiefs. These were stolen in astonishing numbers during the Regency. It was possible, in fact, for a resourceful woman with a well trained group of boys and girls supplying her, to specialize in fencing handkerchiefs alone. Mrs Diner, of Field Lane, Holborn, did so – and with impunity, for she knew how to outwit the police who came periodically to check up on her. Even while advertising prominently the goods in which she dealt, she had a hoard of purloined articles, and she always took care to get rid of the owner's marks from silk:

Keeps a Shop where numbers of Silk Handkerchiefs hang at the Window which she deals in & nothing else & has lived there 8 or 9 years in the same way buying them from Pick-pockets of every description, Men, Women, Boys & Girls, but chiefly Boys, whose practice it is. She has a Cockloft through a Trap Door at the top of her house where she had generally an immense quantity of Silk Handkerchiefs so bought by her. She is considered a Woman of Property. The Officers sometimes come here, but of no avail, as she take out the Initials or Marks, so that the Property cannot be identified.

There were fences who liked to concentrate on the 'things which Boys first going on the Town sneak for', a varied list including cheese, bacon, old brass and glass bottles. A man called Reed, with a rag and glass shop near Fitzroy Place, took such beginners and made them virtually apprentices to house-breakers. The initial stage in the process was to lend them instruments 'to get into new built Houses just finished & get off the new brass knobs to Doors, Shutters &c.' In this way, for an outlay of a few shillings, he received from three or four novices property worth £20. But breaking was merely a prelude to entering . . .

He instructs the Boys to get into these new buildings & go along the Leads or parapets to the Garrets of adjoining

Inhabited Houses to get into them & let in the Gang, or
rob the upper part of the House at the moment as may
appear best.

It is not hard to imagine, in view of the amount of
residential building which was going up in London at this
date, that Reed had made a great deal of money. His is one
of the names after which appear the words 'the Officers
have no knowledge of this man'.

Even when somebody had a known criminal past,
prosecution was difficult as there was no automatic right of
search and entry of premises suspected of harbouring stolen
goods. And in some cases the young thieves of London were
extremely loyal – either out of affection or fear – to their
fences. One impressive instance concerned a widow with a
little stall at the Holborn end of Fleet Market, who received
ribbons and trinkets from a large number of boys and girls,
and sold these again to the public as a blind. Her real
business was much more dangerous:

> This Woman fenced the Prince's Sash (so stated) valued at
> 25 Guineas & which was stolen from Mr Rowleys in St
> James's Street by two Boys (Frank Turner and Jack
> Robinson who were cast for Death, respited, & now gone
> off for Life) this Woman gave them only 12 Shillings for it.
> Every means were made with the above Boys to induce
> them at the time to give up their Fence for the above Sash,
> but nothing would tempt them. She Fences also from a
> number of Girls, some of whom are now Transported.

Perhaps not surprisingly, this particular receiver's bureau
was said to be 'full of stolen Property, principally Ribbons'.

Frank Turner and Jack Robinson kept their secret, quite
possibly, because they had been shown kindness by their
fence in the past. But many receivers were cowards by
nature, who thought nothing of using physical violence
towards juvenile thieves when they were dissatisfied, or,
more usually, of getting others to do the bullying on their

behalf. The thieves who stole watches and money from foolish outsiders visiting the bear-baiting at the Black Hell flash-house in Winfell Street, Whitechapel, were 'about 20 Boys & a great Number of Men of the most desperate description'. Boys doubtless had to yield the best prizes to the men; and heaven help them if they kept anything back. That was one kind of situation in which rough tactics were accepted as a matter of course.

Another might be found in St Giles, where 'Mother' Cummings ruled with a rod of iron, uniting in herself the functions of fence, bawdy-house keeper, and trainer of young criminals. She had rooms for men, women, boys and girls 'either to sleep there all the night or for what time they please, & from 1s. up to 5s. 6d'. She was jealous by nature, as could be seen in the way she kept tabs on her husband. Her complicated criminal business made it necessary for her to spend time in different houses (her own home was in Kentish Town, and she could seldom be found in 6 George Street, St Giles, after two in the afternoon), yet

she never if possible lets her Husband be out of her sight, or stay in Town without her, unless a Boy, named Billy is with him, & who is set as a constant watch upon him – this Boy she took out of some Workhouse (said to be Hampstead or Pancras) and he renders to Mrs Cummings an account of the Husbands transactions in her absence.

Billy was trusted; but it seems unlikely that she extended her goodwill towards all of those who brought articles to her because they had heard the prices were good, let alone towards the young prostitutes whom she employed. Their instructions were simple enough – bring a man to bed, then rob him:

it appears to be the common practice of this house that when a Girl has got in her prey, the more they are intoxicated the more secure, to ascertain the Property they have about them, when the Girl watches her opportunity to purloin it, leaves the Room immediately upon some frivolous excuse, & bolts the door on the outside or locks it (according to the fastenings to the different priced rooms) thereby confining the Man who either missing his Property or finding the Girl not to return, makes to the Door, when he commences a knocking, & a Woman who is always on the ready on the outside to unbolt it or unlock it, as soon as she thinks proper & by her conduct & language stalls off the Robbery by declaring they did not see the Girl go away, & that they know nothing of her, and such Property Mrs Cummings uniformly Fences, immediately, if she is at home, or the next morning as soon as she comes from her residence.

In Mother Cummings' eyes, men were fools, and the human race in general simply pawns, 'whenever her riches are brought on the tapis in St Giles's, the observation is, she may thank her Gangs of Thieves & Whores from whom she gets it all'. The young were simply to be exploited, and brought in line like everyone else.

FOUR

THE MEDICAL UNDERWORLD

Up the close and doun the stair,
But and ben wi' Burke and Hare.
Burke's the butcher, Hare's the thief,
Knox the boy that buys the beef.

(*Edinburgh street rhyme*)

'Look out, the bogey man will get you': the names of Burke and Hare are still enough to send a shiver down the spine in Edinburgh. The discovery in 1828 that two drunken Irishmen had, within the space of a few months, committed sixteen murders in the city, and had sold the bodies of all their victims to a leading anatomist for dissection, shocked the people of Scotland as no other series of crimes has ever done. Edinburgh itself, the 'Athens of the North', taking pride in its high degree of civilization and cultural distinction, was appalled. Until the passing of the Anatomy Act four years later – which for the first time guaranteed to British surgeons a legal and plentiful supply of dead bodies – the city was in a state of constant terror. Children were told to keep off the streets, and families stayed indoors from long before sunset. At no time in living memory had Edinburgh's locksmiths done such a roaring trade. Even tough labouring men took to coming home from work in groups rather than on their own, while prostitutes were no longer to be seen so openly in some of their old public haunts.

Long before Burke and Hare came on the scene, however – for a good thirty years before the passing of the Anatomy Act – few people could be sure, even though they might die a natural death, that their mortal remains would not be disturbed by bodysnatchers. In Edinburgh, and in London, Glasgow and Dublin, the other cities where anatomy was taught and studied, anxiety was very real. And the Burke and Hare murders deepened into panic the already widespread fear caused by the activities of 'sack-'em-up men' or resurrectionists. Something of the nature of that fear can be gathered from an extraordinary advertisement which appeared in *Wooler's British Gazette* in 1822:

Many hundred dead bodies will be dragged from their wooden coffins this winter, for the anatomical lectures (which have just commenced), the articulators, for those who deal in the dead, for the supply of the country practitioner and the Scotch schools. The question of the right to inter in iron is now decided . . . The violation of the sanctity of the grave is said to be needful, for the instruction of the medical pupil, but let each one about to inter a mother, husband, child, or friend, say shall I devote this object of my affection to such a purpose; if not, the only safe coffin is Bridgman's Patent wrought-iron one, charged the same price as a wooden one, and is a superior substitute for lead. Edward Lillie Bridgman, 34, Fish Street Hill, and Goswell Street Road, performs funerals in any part of the kingdom . . . Those undertakers who have IRON COFFINS must divide the profits of the funeral with EDWARD LILLIE BRIDGMAN. TEN GUINEAS reward will be paid on the conviction of any Parish Officer demanding an extra fee, whereby I shall lose the sale of a coffin.

Bridgman, an enterprising undertaker of the new industrial age, had won 'the right to inter in iron' only after a long struggle: churchwardens had not liked the idea of already overcrowded graveyards being cluttered up with imperishable newfangled coffins. But the public demand was there. This is shown both by Bridgman's subsequent advertisements, reporting the rapid sale of his patent coffins (which had interior bolts and cost £31. 10s. each), and by the number of iron slabs over early nineteenth-century graves, and 'mortsafes' or protective railings around them. While perhaps it seems a pity that there was no one at the time to expose the commercial hypocrisy associated with the Regency way of death, the scare-mongering claim that 'many hundred dead bodies will be dragged from their wooden coffins this winter . . .', had a basis in undeniable fact. Not only in the winter of 1822–3, but every year between October and May while the anatomical schools were in session, there was a demand for corpses. As a result, both the resurrection-men and Edward Lillie Bridgman flourished.

The basic problem was that by law only dead bodies of executed criminals could be used for dissection, which was an essential part of the rapidly growing study of anatomy, and medical students now greatly outnumbered capital convictions. The gap between the demand and the legal supply is hard to measure exactly, as statistical information for the period is often unreliable, but one writer estimated that

In all Great Britain, from 1805 to 1820, there were executed eleven hundred and fifty criminals, or about seventy-seven annually; and at the same time there were over one thousand medical students in London and nearly as many in Edinburgh.

In other words, there was sometimes only one body for a dozen students to work with, and sometimes none at all. London surgeons in the making counted themselves lucky on occasion if they received as much as a finger or toe on which to practise their skills in dissection, and all were more familiar with *papier-mâché* models than with actual human bodies. The lecturers responsible for teaching anatomy, for whom this situation was clearly most unsatisfactory, made sure that the resurrection-men were paid good money for additional bodies, and they did not always insist on asking where these 'things for the surgeon' came from.

It is important to remember here that anything which could properly be called British medical (or at least surgical) science was at this time very new – it was only in the eighteenth century that surgeons in England had succeeded in establishing themselves as a separate professional group from barbers. A law directing that up to four murderers' corpses a year should be given for dissection had been passed in the reign of Henry VIII, when a charter had first been granted to the Barbers and Surgeons of London (the law was changed to provide the bodies of all executed criminals for dissection in 1726). But the intention of the law had been as much to proclaim the wickedness of murder as to serve knowledge: public hangings were often followed by the public cutting up of criminals' corpses. It is easy to understand, therefore, the emotive and inextricable link between the idea of dissection, frightening enough in itself, and capital crime and a dreadful fate.

For the surgeons, of course, the matter was a much more practical one. Human bodies, in their eyes, were a source of information, and if they wished either to advance learning or to gain proficiency in carrying out operations they had no alternative but to obtain corpses for dissection. Their attitude was empirical and unemotional; they simply wanted to know as much as they could about the body and all its functions and abnormalities, in the same way that botanists, inspired by the work of the Swedish scientist Linnaeus, were seeking to understand and classify plants.

Just how sharply the outlook of pioneering anatomists differed from that of the rest of society is shown by an episode in the career of the 'father of modern surgery', the brilliant late eighteenth-century Scots surgeon John Hunter. In the early 1780s Hunter, like many of his fellow surgeons, took a keen interest in reports about the extraordinary size of a young Irishman, Charles Byrne. Byrne was well over seven feet six inches tall, and he completed a very successful tour of the British Isles billed as a giant. (One particularly impressive incident took place in Edinburgh when he lit his pipe at one of the street lamps of the city police.) But Byrne's lanky frame was too much for his heart to support, and in 1783, when still in his early twenties, he became fatally ill. John Hunter immediately decided that he must acquire the giant's skeleton, and told his servant Howison to watch Byrne 'while he [was] ailing'. This was because he was in process of building up an extensive collection of surgical 'specimens'; anything so unusual as an outsize skeleton was certain to add to its interest. (The collecting instinct and skill in medicine both ran in the family. His elder brother William's collection now forms the basis of the Hunterian Museum in Glasgow, while John Hunter's own can be viewed in the Royal College of Surgeons in London.) Hunter spoke freely to a number of people about his wish to display Byrne's bones in his collection, and waited impatiently for the tall man to die.

Then, as chance would have it, the dying Byrne heard of Hunter's intention, and quite understandably suffered a feeling of revulsion at the thought of the fate that was being planned for his body. Just as Hunter was determined to have Byrne in his collection at all costs, so it became an obsession with Byrne to elude the Scotsman's grasp. He gave orders that when he died his body was to be guarded day and night, and then placed in a lead coffin and buried at sea. However, upon Byrne's death, Hunter learned through his 'spy' Howison the name of the pub at which the men paid to look after the giant's body were in the habit of drinking, and offered one of the team £50 if he would allow the body to be stolen. Byrne's bodyguard was not to be persuaded so easily, for he could see that Hunter was more than ordinarily interested in closing the deal, and ruthlessly he put the price up and up. Hunter's Scots caution yielded to his overriding wish to obtain a prize item for his collection, and before the evening was out he had parted with £500. Hunter's great fear now was that a rival surgeon might give orders for Byrne's body to be stolen from him. So he saw to it that the corpse was smuggled to his house in Earl's Court under cover of darkness that same night. The copper boiler in his house had been stoked in preparation, for he had decided in the interests of speed to separate the giant's flesh from his bones by boiling rather than by the slower process of dissection. Byrne's skeleton in the Royal College of Surgeons is discoloured brown in consequence.

Believing that he had acted in the interests of science, Hunter could see nothing untoward in what he had done. But to some of his contemporaries who had no connection with surgery his action in pursuing Byrne's person, against the Irishman's express wishes, seemed both callous and gruesome. This notorious episode, as well as later incidents of a similar kind involving other surgeons, lies behind 'The Surgeon's Warning', a poem by Robert Southey which shows that the anatomist's proven lack of respect for the dead gave great offence:

> All kinds of carcasses I have cut up,
>   And now my turn will be;
> But brothers, I took care of you,
>   So pray take care of me.
>
> I have made candles of dead men's fat,
>   The Sextons have been my slaves,
> I have bottled babes unborn, and dried
>   Hearts and livers from rifled graves.
>
> And my Prentices now will surely come
>   And carve me bone from bone,
> And I who have rifled the dead man's grave
>   Shall never have rest in my own.
>
> Bury me in lead when I am dead,
>   My brethren, I entreat,
> And see the coffin weigh'd, I beg,
>   Lest the plumber should be a cheat.

And let it be solder'd closely down,
  Strong as strong can be, I implore;
And put it in a patent coffin,
  That I may rise no more.

If they carry me off in the patent coffin,
  Their labour will be in vain;
Let the Undertaker see it bought of the maker,
  Who lives by St Martin's Lane.
And bury me in my brother's church,
  For that will safer be;
And, I implore, lock the church door,
  And pray take care of the key.

And all night long let three stout men
  The vestry watch within;
To each man give a gallon of beer,
  And a keg of Hollands gin;

Powder and ball and blunderbuss,
  To save me if he can,
And eke five guineas if he shoot
  A Resurrection Man.

And let them watch me for three weeks,
  My wretched corpse to save;
For then I think that I may stink
  Enough to rest in my grave.

As 'The Surgeon's Warning' indicates, in the minds of the public, surgeons themselves were held to blame for the activities of the body-snatchers. However strongly Hunter and his successors might protest that they acted from sound motives in obtaining bodies, society at large was unconvinced. And in one sense at least, people were right to blame the surgeons. The latter, it is true, did not as a rule deal directly with resurrection-men, preferring to act through intermediaries such as hospital porters and surgical assistants. But the all-important orders which kept the practice going came from them: theirs was the need, and theirs the cash which rewarded the 'Sextons' (and others) who actually stole bodies from graves.

In London, the key figure from 1800 onwards was one of John Hunter's most gifted former students, Astley Cooper (1768–1841). Cooper, a man of driving energy, was astute enough to realize that, partly as a result of the number of injuries received by British soldiers in the Napoleonic Wars, surgical knowledge was at a premium. Besides having private patients, he held the two most important surgical posts in the large 'Borough Hospitals', being at once surgeon at Guy's and lecturer in anatomy at St Thomas's. At Guy's he had succeeded an uncle, and he in turn made sure that hospital appointments went to his own nephews. The fact that he did this several times was a sign of his personal authority, but advancement through nepotism was normal enough in his profession at this period. Similarly, Cooper's pluralism was exceptional among successful medical men only in degree and not in kind. He may well have been influenced by the example of his father, a prosperous clergyman with a number of benefices.

Cooper received his knighthood in 1821 for removing a tumour from the top of George IV's head. The King had insisted that the operation must be performed by Cooper, against the latter's wishes. 'I was very averse from doing it,' Cooper recalled later. 'I had always been successful, and I saw that the operation, if [a failure] would destroy all my happiness and blast my reputation.' His success on this occasion resulted in part from luck, as he well knew, but in part, too, from his breadth of experience. Throughout his career he worked a fourteen- or fifteen-hour day, and he liked to spend two or three hours in his dissecting room before breakfast each morning. It was said of him that he would dissect anything from a mouse to an elephant – he had in fact carved up an elephant from the Tower Menagerie in 1801, attracting a large crowd of interested spectators as he worked on its carcase outside his house at St Mary Axe in the City of London. That particular dissection, and others on smaller creatures which followed, served a branch of his subject which was becoming known among surgeons as 'comparative anatomy'.

Cooper's preference, however, was for human corpses, of which he needed a regular, and very often a daily, supply. He knew exactly how to obtain what he required, for while he avoided the kind of extravagance shown by Hunter in his pursuit of the Irish giant, he always paid well. Moreover, in Tom Butler, the porter in St Thomas's dissecting room, he had for a number of years a robust if bibulous middleman who was expert in the ways of the leading metropolitan bodysnatchers and whose career is interesting in its own right. When Butler had to leave his hospital job, Cooper did not lose touch with him, even though he had a shrewd idea that his old helper had begun to accompany the bodysnatchers on their nocturnal outings. Instead, he arranged for Butler to travel to Spain and visit Bransby Cooper, one of his medically inclined nephews, who was preparing himself for hospital work in London by spending some time at his uncle's request as an assistant surgeon with the Royal Artillery in the Peninsular War. Butler gave to the harassed army surgeon a letter which read:

> My dear Bransby, – Butler will tell you the purpose of his visit. I hope you are well and happy. Your affectionate uncle, Astley Cooper.

On being asked by Bransby Cooper what he wanted, Butler replied 'teeth', adding by way of explanation,

> Oh, sir, only let there be a battle and there'll be no want of teeth. I'll draw them as fast as the men are knocked down.

It was fashionable in the Regency to use human teeth instead of boxwood or other substitutes in making sets of false teeth, and there was an excellent market in London for recently drawn teeth. During the next few months, whenever Bransby Cooper went among the wounded on the battlefield, Butler followed him, pincers at the ready. On his return to England he sold the teeth that he had pulled from the dead and the dying for £300. He used the money, quite logically, to set up as a dentist in Liverpool; but then his liking for gin got him into debt, and he was sentenced to death for trying to pass a stolen five pound note. Butler appealed against the sentence, and while awaiting the outcome at Calton Jail in Edinburgh offered to 'articulate' the skeleton of the Jail Governor's favourite horse, which had just died. The practised skill with which he arranged bones caught the eye of a distinguished foreign visitor to Edinburgh. This visitor – one of the Austrian Archdukes – begged the Prince Regent to pardon Butler. The pardon was granted, but only on condition that Butler left the country. How he ended his days is not known, but it was rumoured in the 1820s that he went to Ireland and organized the supply of bodies from Irish graveyards to the surgeons of Edinburgh, a city to which he had a certain cause to be grateful.

Sir Astley Cooper was quite unrepentant about employing Butler and others like him. He wanted the law relating to the supply of bodies to surgeons to be changed, and took the view that in the meantime it was far better to obtain specimens for dissection than to allow students of anatomy to remain untaught. In 1828 he stated boldly to a House of Commons Select Committee inquiring into the matter:

> I would not remain in the room with a man who attempted to perform an operation in surgery, who was unacquainted with anatomy, unless he would be directed by others; he must mangle the living if he has not operated on the dead . . . A knowledge of anatomy consists not only in being acquainted with the names of things, but with their relative situation, and relative situation cannot be taught by casts or by models in *papier mâché*.
>
> The cause that you gentlemen are now supporting is not our cause, but yours; you must employ medical men, whether they be ignorant or informed; but if you have

none but ignorant medical men, it is you who suffer from it; and the fact is, that the want of subjects will soon lead to your becoming the unhappy victims of operations founded and performed in ignorance.

These words carried great weight, because by 1828 Sir Astley Cooper was President of the Royal College of Surgeons and Sergeant Surgeon to the King; among his other patients, as those who listened to his evidence were aware, were the Prime Minister and the Duke of Wellington. It may be that the MPs on the Select Committee were somewhat taken aback when their distinguished witness went on,

There is no person, let his situation in life be what it may, whom, if I were disposed to dissect, I could not obtain . . . The law only enhances the price, and does not prevent the exhumation.

But here, too, Sir Astley was speaking from experience. All his life he had shared John Hunter's interest in human beings with any physical abnormality. He thought nothing of asking for the bodies of such persons, and had a particular enthusiasm for the re-examination of former patients on whom he had performed experimental operations. This latter category was a large one, because he had carried out hundreds of operations at St Thomas's and elsewhere, and at this stage in the development of surgery more operations were to be described as 'experimental' than routine. Had the Select Committee asked to see his professional diaries, they would have found many entries which concerned payments made to resurrectionists specifically for making possible the post-mortem dissection of his more interesting former patients, as well as a larger group relating to the supply of the bodies of unidentified persons.

But while the great surgeon made no secret of his lifelong connection with the bodysnatchers, and spoke approvingly of the way in which the Home Secretary had discouraged magistrates from prosecuting surgeons, anatomical lecturers and bodysnatchers, he showed nothing but contempt for the night workers who made dissection possible. The resurrection-men, he claimed, were 'the lowest dregs of degradation; I do not know that I can describe them better . . .'

> there is no crime they would not commit, and, as to myself, if they should imagine that I would make a good subject, they really would not have the slightest scruple, if they could do the thing undiscovered, to make a subject of me.

It was only by exercising very firm control over his unsavoury associates, he implied, that he had been able to accomplish so much. No passage in Sir Astley's evidence was more emphatic than this complete moral dismissal of these men, to all of whom he was well known but whose existence he would never have acknowledged in the street. He no doubt recalled occasions such as that when he received a note saying,

> I have been informed that you are in the habit of purchasing bodys, and allowing the person a sum weekly; knowing a poor woman that is desirous of doing so, I have taken the liberty of calling to know the truth.

To this he had replied,

> The *truth* is that you deserve to be hanged for making such an unfeeling offer.

He had seen, as few others had been in a position to do, that the competition to sell bodies to the surgeons brought out the very worst in human nature.

Among the evidence received by the Select Committee in 1828 was a police statement to the effect that there were no more than a dozen full-time bodysnatchers in London although as many as two hundred men were believed to rob graves from time to time as a means of supplementing their (often criminal) earnings. Rival gangs who controlled the London trade were known to send surplus corpses for distribution in Edinburgh; and they guarded their rights jealously, for profits were very large. The Committee were told that a gang made up of six or seven of these men had earned well over £1,000 during the previous winter session of the anatomical schools from the sale of 312 bodies.

Confirmation of what had been said by surgeons and magistrates came from three resurrection-men. They gave their evidence anonymously, and it is easy to believe that care had to be taken to protect them when they were seen in public during the Select Committee hearings. 'A.B.' told the committee that the days of easy bodysnatching had long since gone. The trade was highly competitive, and increasingly dangerous. 'Every ground in London is watched', he claimed, 'by men put into them at dark, who stop till day-light with fire arms.' Under questioning, he admitted that rival gangs gave information against each other, and were responsible for vandalistic behaviour; but his main quarrel was with amateurs spoiling the game, rather than with fellow-professionals. 'They are nothing but petty common thieves,' was his contemptuous description. Asked about the greatest number of bodies he had ever 'lifted' in a single period, he spoke of taking twenty-four in four nights. But that had happened years before, when the business was less risky than now. The use of firearms to protect graves frightened him. In his recent experience, the lower orders in London would not mind shooting a man dead as a robber, if they caught him in a churchyard.

A similar story was told by 'C.D.', who complained that in 1820 'we had our men shot away from us, and it was very dangerous'. C.D. brought out that the connections of resurrectionists went beyond the capital. One source of supply was the Netherlands and Holland; and when lecturers in London had been unwilling to buy material at the going rate, it had been possible to sell corpses elsewhere in Britain. He also spoke about methods of obtaining bodies from workhouses by false pretences. A common ruse was to dress carefully, present oneself to the overseer of a workhouse as the relative of a pauper inmate known to have just died, and in this way claim a corpse 'for decent burial'. C.D.'s testimony, like that of A.B., was that of a master of his ghoulish craft.

While the answers of these men to their questioners in 1828 were revealing, they do not provide a detailed account of the nightly doings of resurrectionists. For that, we must turn to what is surely the most hair-raising of all early nineteenth-century diaries. By chance there is preserved in the Library of the Royal College of Surgeons a manuscript journal kept in 1811 by a member of the most successful bodysnatching gang in London. It shows among other things that – while the degree of public hostility was greater by 1828 – the essential features of the trade were all to be found seventeen years earlier. In this particular criminal underworld, as in others, continuity and not change were the rule. Hard drinking, mutual distrust, and violence were all endemic among resurrection-men.

The diarist, who does not name himself, was almost certainly C.D., who answered Select Committee questions about the number of bodies he had lifted by quoting from his 'book' for the years 1811 to 1813. He has been identified as Joseph Naples, of the 'Borough Gang' which had a virtual monopoly in supplying Guy's and St Thomas's. Naples was the son of a law-abiding shopkeeper, and had seen action in Nelson's navy aboard the *Excellent* at the Battle of Cape St Vincent. On being discharged, he had become a gravedigger at the St James's, Clerkenwell, burial-ground in Bowling Green Lane. In the eyes of the resurrectionists, gravediggers were marked men, to be bribed, bullied and put to work. Naples was recruited to the ranks of the bodysnatchers by a Scotsman called White, who did not actually take part in the exhumations, but who sold bodies to the hospitals. After Naples had assisted 'the Borough boys' on two or three occasions, White made him join the gang by the classic method of threatening to denounce him to the authorities.

The leader of the gang at this time was Ben Crouch, a leering, pock-marked character who owed his position mainly to the fact that he drank to excess less frequently than his mates. (James Bailey, who published an edition of Naples's diary in 1896 while Librarian of the Royal College of Surgeons, argued convincingly that Ben Crouch was A. B. of the 1828 Select Committee evidence.) Another member of the group was Tom Butler, especially valued for his long association with Astley Cooper. Someone who was handy with his fists was Bill Harnett, like Crouch and Butler an old hand at the game of 'placing' bodies with the hospital surgeons. Harnett's unruly nephew Jack copied Crouch, and not his inconspicuous uncle, in dressing in flashy clothes. He and Joseph Naples would appear to have had much the same standing in the gang. None of them liked Bill Holliss, who talked too much and cared only for his own skin, but Holliss owned a horse and cart, which had often carried their illicit merchandise about London. On the fringes of the Borough Gang were Tom Light, who had done time in the Portsmouth hulks for the theft of plate glass from gentlemen's carriage windows, and one or two others. Crouch had an unpleasant habit of turning over to the law individuals whom he suspected of lining their own pockets or of scheming to displace him. At one time or another everyone with whom he worked spent some time in jail, as he did himself.

Naples is a laconic, matter-of-fact diarist whose most frequent personal comment is 'got drunk', applied either to himself or to one of his colleagues. Despite this characteristic, however, or because of it, his record of work and of sales during the anatomy lecturers' season is imbued with a brutish underworld quality, the quality of Dickens's Bill Sykes in *Oliver Twist*, as the first few entries well show:

1811 November
Thursday 28th. At night went out and got 3, Jack & me Hospital Crib, Benjn, Danl & Bill to Harpers, Jack & me 1 big Gates, sold 1 Taunton Do St Thomas's.

Friday 29th. At night went out and got 3, Jack, Ben & me got 2, Bethnall Green, Bill & Danl. 1 Bartholow. Crib opened; whole at Bartw.

Saturday 30th. At night went out and got 3 Bunhill Row, sold to Mr Cline, St Thomas's Hospital.

Remarks, &c., December 1811

Sunday 1st. We all looked out, at Home all night.

Monday 2nd. Met at St Thomas's, Got paid for the 3 adults & settled; met and settled with Mordecei, made him up £2. 5s. 6d. and Receipt of all demands. At Home all night.

Tuesday 3rd. Went to look out and brought the Shovils from Bartholw. Met early in the evening at Mr Vickers, did not go out that night, Butler and me came home intoxsicated.

Wednesday 4th. At night went out and got 10 . . .

The general meaning here is quite clear, even if some of the detail is obscure. 'At night went out and got 3' shows that on each of the nights 28, 29 and 30 November the Borough boys managed to obtain three bodies. To increase their takings and avoid suspicion, they split up into twos and threes and travelled to different graveyards. 'Hospital Crib', which occurs frequently in the diary, is slang for one much visited burial-ground, adjacent perhaps to St Thomas's, and Harper is the name of a graveyard keeper who had been bribed to leave a private door open at night. '1 Bartholow. Crib opened' indicates that a body which had had a post-mortem performed on it was taken from the burial-ground attached to St Bartholomew's Hospital. Such a specimen would be sold for less than an intact corpse, if indeed the anatomy lecturers would buy it at all. The diary shows where the bodies were sold; for instance, three were disposed of on 30 November to Mr Cline, a surgeon at St Thomas's. It was essential for the bodysnatchers to know when funerals took place: hence on Sunday 1 December 'we all looked out'. Monday the 2nd was a day of financial dealings. First, Crouch's men were paid at St Thomas's for the material they had recently supplied. They they visited Michael Mordecai, a noted receiver who kept an old curiosity-shop in New Alley, and settled with him. With money in their pockets, Butler and Naples celebrated by getting drunk the next night.

This first extract is typical of the whole, and reveals the pattern of their lives. Nights of feverish activity were followed by bouts of indolence. The bodysnatchers' liking for strong drink brought them close to disaster on more than one occasion. The entry for Tuesday 10 December reads:

> Intoxsicated all day: at night went out & got 5 Bunhill Row. Jack all most buried.

For the most part, however, things seem to have gone smoothly, and it is plain that there was little difficulty in selling the bodies. Most were got rid of in London, with Edinburgh as an alternative outlet: 'packd 4 and sent them to Edinborough' is noted against 14 December. How far the gang drank to escape from the associations of their work – open graves, dissecting rooms, putrid human flesh – can only be guessed at. But they were hardened to what was, after all, a very lucrative occupation. No doubt at this time, as in 1828, Ben Crouch looked down on mere 'common thieves' with scorn. Naples records almost complacently on 20 December that he attended the theatre before going to his place of work:

> Went to St Thomas's, came home and went to the play, came home: at 3 a.m. got up and went to the Hospital Crib got 5 large.

'Large' in this context denotes an adult corpse, for which more was paid than for a 'small'. Naples is meticulous in listing these differences, which affected earnings crucially. A sub-classification occurs in the entry 'Ben went got 2 large & 1 large small'. Such was the level of mortality among children in early nineteenth-century Britain that there was no shortage of 'smalls' for the bodysnatchers. On Christmas Eve, each man's share was £8. 16s. 8d. from the common earnings. Naples spent Christmas Day and Boxing

Day at home with his family, but there was no question of his remaining idle for long. No fewer than six bodies were procured on Saturday 28 December. Three days later, one of the quarrels which swept through the gang from time to time took place in the Artichoke public house . . . 'Met at the Harty Choak, had a dispute about the horse.' As usual, Bill Holliss, on whom they depended for transport, was proving unreliable.

Astley Cooper is mentioned on 22 January 1812, when he seems to have argued with Naples and Bill Harnett about the price to be paid for a specimen to be used in his lecture course. When such disagreements occurred, it was Ben Crouch's way to threaten Cooper with withdrawal of supply. A month later the words 'sent 7 into the Country, distributed the rest about town' remind us that a number of doctors outside London occasionally asked for specimens, while there was a steady demand from private London surgeons as well as from the most prominent men at Guy's and St Thomas's.

Crouch's men were literally creatures of darkness. Naples copied into his diary notes on the lunar cycle, since it was too dangerous for the gang to go out when burial-grounds were lit up by moonlight. Towards the end of February 1812 a full moon made it impossible to go out, and much time was spent in drinking as a result:

Monday 24th. Bill Jack Tom and Ben with Nat Ure Getting drunk oblige to Come Home in a Coach which prevented us going out to Harps.

Tuesday 25th. At home all day, at Night met at Jack to go to Harps. the moon at the full, could not go.

Wednesday 26th. Went to look out. Could not go out Jack and Tom got drunk. Ben taken very ill.

Thursday 27th. Went to St Thomas's, sold the extremities. At night Tom & Bill got drunk at the Rockingham Arms, at Home all night.

Friday 28th. Met at Jacks Got 4 large 1 small and 1 Foetus, Harps. Took them to the London.

It is easy to imagine that tempers quickly became frayed when proceedings were held up in this way. So much money went on alochol that the gang were often in debt. One of the few value-judgments in Naples's diary occurs when he writes with some irritation on 18 March 1812: 'at home all night which was a very bad thing for us as we wanted some money to pay our debts to several persons who were importunate'.

Owing money to a Jew was bad enough, but the presence of a Jewish rival in the trade was intolerable to the Borough boys. Two long entries in Naples's diary in August describe how the gang followed 'the Jew's Drag till Dark and lost scent', and then, on learning that he had taken a male corpse to St Bartholomew's, 'had a row', presumably with the porters or surgeons there. The rival in question was probably Israel Chapman, a noted minor operator in the resurrection business. This August proved a particularly troublesome month for Naples, as an untoward incident took place the next night in a burial-ground at Islington. 'The dogs flew at us, afterwards went to Pancras found a watch planted, came home.' It may be that Israel Chapman had countered the gang's attempt to deny him trade by informing against them; such moves were by no means unknown. Quite possibly, the relatives of persons newly buried in the Islington and St Pancras graveyards had paid for the guard-dogs and watchmen. Naples was worried, and with reason: here was a portent for the future.

Something which he did not record in his diary, but which came out in response to Select Committee questions in 1828, was that by far the greater number of bodies snatched by the gang were those of poor people. Asked whether they had taken the rich or the poor, 'F.G.', an unidentified accomplice of Crouch and Naples, replied, 'Both classes; but we could not obtain the rich so easily, because they were buried so deep.' It was important to the Select Committee to establish firmly that it was the 'lower orders' who suffered most from bodysnatching depredations. A change in the law designed to regularize the supply to anatomists, which the Select Committee felt to be essential, could only be brought about if the poor, who deeply distrusted the anatomists, could be persuaded that reform of this kind was in their interest. The Committee heard witness after witness repeat that the first thing they must seek to do was to end the practice of having murderers' bodies dissected, since the association between the worst kind of guilt and dissection weighed heavily with everyone, and especially with the poor. As William Lawrence, a surgeon at St Bartholomew's, put it, the selection of criminals' bodies for purposes of medical research by official authority gave 'the most powerful sanctions, those of the legislature and judicature, to the horror and aversion which mankind are perhaps naturally disposed to entertain against what they deem a profanation of the dead'.

Having interviewed everyone from Joseph Naples and Ben Crouch to Sir Astley Cooper and Thomas Wakley, the crusading first editor of *The Lancet*, the Select Committee presented a strong case for reform. (Wakley was an able Devonian who married the daughter of a wealthy London merchant in 1820 only to be severely beaten up and have his fashionable house and medical practice in the West End burnt to the ground the same year, according to the Press in an act of retribution by underworld fanatics for the part he was alleged to have played as a masked assistant during the execution of the 'Cato Street conspirators', who had tried to assassinate the Cabinet.) They recommended, predictably, that the use of murderers' remains by anatomists should stop; and, more controversially, that a proper and adequate supply of bodies for dissection should be found in the unclaimed dead of the workhouses. In 1827, it was pointed out, more than 3,000 paupers in the London area had to be buried at the parish expense, and in a third of these cases no relatives were in attendance. In an attempt to justify a proposed change which would legalize the provision of bodies exclusively from the poorest class, the Committee noted how often poor families suffered at the hands of the resurrection-men, and commented on their workhouse scheme, 'where there are no relations to suffer distress, there can be no inequality of suffering'.

The Select Committee Report was an impressive document, but it took a series of brutal murders in Edinburgh, followed by another murder sensation in London, to bring home to the public that laws guaranteeing the provision of bodies for medical men had become absolutely essential.

Rumours of murders committed in order to obtain corpses were certainly not unknown, and among the most interesting evidence heard in 1828 was that of James Macartney, Professor of Anatomy and Surgery in Trinity College, Dublin. He admitted quite cheerfully that the resurrection-men of Dublin lived by exporting bodies. The arrival of the steamship made this possible. 'If bodies be cheap and plentiful in one part, a supply will be got from that part for those places where they cannot be so easily procured.' Nevertheless, these were troubled times. Within the past few months in Dublin, he went on,

A report was propagated which originally had been circulated in Scotland, that children were kidnapped for the purpose of dissection, and this became so currently believed by the populace, that it was necessary to protect one of the anatomical schools, for nearly a week, by means of the police. This strong feeling in the public mind arose chiefly from the supposition, that these children were to be sent over either to Scotland or England by the steam vessels. The difficulty has indeed been so very great within the last few months, that most of the schools in Dublin have been unable to finish their winter dissections at the usual period. The common people frequently of late have assaulted the resurrection-men, one of these men died in consequence of a severe beating, and another in consequence of being whipped with a sort of cat-o'-nine tails made with wire, and others were thrown into the water. In the first of these cases I paid the expenses of a prosecution for murder against the parties; they were not convicted, but the prosecution had a very good effect on the state of public feeling. I may add, that lately also, even medical men and medical students were assaulted by the people, and that at present the resurrection-men go to a great number of graveyards, some distance from Dublin, provided with firearms . . .

The belief that Irish children were being kidnapped and sold to be cut up in Scotland or England may or may not have had a basis in fact. Dublin is a city of rumours, and this one seems to carry an echo of one of Swift's most brilliant satires, published a hundred years earlier, 'A Modest Proposal for Preventing the Children of Poor People from Being a Burthen to Their Parents or the Country, and for Making Them Beneficial to the Publick'. Nevertheless, that the story should have been put about at this particular time is curious, for within a few months two desperate Irish bodysnatchers were to sell to an Edinburgh anatomist the bodies of no fewer than sixteen people, all of whom they had murdered.

Burke and Hare came together in Edinburgh by evil chance, and with their 'wives' – Burke was a bigamist, and Hare's marriage to the widow of his former landlord was grounded on habit and repute alone – lived in the shabbiest district of the Old Town. All four drank spirits habitually and to excess. In this they resembled some of Ben Crouch's associates; but neither Burke nor Hare had any professional knowledge of the body-snatching trade. It is conceivable that they were given the idea of luring innocent folk to their deaths by the scandalous story circulating in Ireland about children falling victim to the resurrection-men. But what actually got them started on their career in crime, in November 1827, was the death from natural causes at Hare's lodging-house of an old army pensioner named Donald. Hare suggested to Burke that they should together sell the corpse to 'the doctors', and Burke agreed. They made their way eastward through Edinburgh to the busy 'Surgeons' Square', close to the High School Yards; there a number of expert anatomists had their headquarters. They were pleasantly surprised by the amount of money they received at the anatomy school of Dr Robert Knox, and by the remark that he 'would be glad to see them again when they had another to dispose of'.

Such a one was easy to come by. After this chance beginning, the two men conspired to lead into the West Port lodging-house a succession of Edinburgh down-and-outs. Many were old women; one was a prostitute called Mary Paterson; another a retarded youth known as 'Daft Jamie'. In nearly every case, drink was produced to fuddle the victim's wits, and then he or she was smothered. Burke and Hare chose this method of murder – soon to be known as 'burking' – because the close examination of bodies by Dr Knox and his students was bound to reveal any marks of violence. At no time, apparently, were that anatomist's suspicions aroused by the new and surprisingly good source of supply he now had for his lecture course. Knox was a man with a career to make; there were some points in connection with his profession that he chose not to inquire into.

Burke and Hare's gruesome activities did not come to an end until November 1828, when the newly murdered body of the last of their victims was seen in the lodging-house by a lodger called Gray, who told the police. The trial which followed horrified the public, who had already been supplied with grim newspaper disclosures. On 28 January the largest crowd of spectators ever collected in the streets of Edinburgh – almost 25,000 – gathered in the Lawnmarket for Burke's execution. His body was partly dissected, then placed on public display in the university before being prepared for use in anatomy lectures. 'The corpse of the murderer Burke', wrote Sir Walter Scott on 31 January,

is now lying in state at the College, in the anatomical class, and all the world flock to see him. Who is he that says that we are not ill to please in our objects of curiosity? The strange means by which the wretch made money are scarce more disgusting than the eager curiosity with which the public have licked up all the carrion details of this business.

Hare, who had turned King's evidence and so escaped the retribution meted out to Burke, was allowed to leave Scotland.

Tradition has it that his identity having been discovered by some fellow-workmen, he was thrown into a lime pit, with the result that his eyes were destroyed. He is reputed to have become one of London's blind beggars, with a stance on the north side of Oxford Street, and to have outlived Burke by forty years.

The death of Burke and removal from Edinburgh of Hare did not satisfy the outraged citizens of the Scottish capital. Most people believed that Knox was guilty of a crime scarcely less dreadful than the murderers; for he had actively encouraged the two men, when he must have known they were totally disreputable incomers to the trade in corpses. On Thursday 12 February 1829 a mob assembled on the Calton Hill at nightfall. They carried a life-size effigy of a human figure, which had on its back a label inscribed 'Knox, the associate of the infamous Hare'. From the Calton Hill they processed to the quiet southern suburb of Newington, where Knox lived, strung up the dummy on a tree outside Knox's house, and then set it on fire. Considerable damage was done to the anatomist's property, but the police protected him from personal injury on this as on later occasions. Knox behaved coolly through everything, although his professional reputation was ruined and from this time on he was a broken man. Within a few years there was a falling-off in the number of his class, which until the scandal had been the most popular in Edinburgh. A move to Glasgow brought him no better luck, and he ended his days in obscurity and some poverty in Hackney. Certainly, the strength of the people's reaction serves to demonstrate the horror and fear which had been aroused by recent events.

In March 1829 Henry Warburton introduced into the House of Commons 'A Bill for preventing the unlawful disinterment of human bodies, and for regulating Schools of Anatomy'. This Bill incorporated the main recommendation of the Select Committee, but neglected to repeal the clause which ordered the bodies of murderers to be given up for dissection. It met with considerable opposition, despite the Burke and Hare panic in the north, and although it passed the House of Commons, it was rejected by the Lords. The decisive factor in bringing about a change of outlook in the Upper Chamber was the notoriety of another trial for 'burking', this time in London. On 5 November 1831, two men named Bishop and May called at the dissecting-room at King's College, London, asking the porter, whose name was Hall, if he 'wanted anything'. They explained that they had the body of a boy of fourteen, for which they asked twelve guineas – the price later came down to nine. In the afternoon they came back with another man called Williams, and Shields, a porter, who carried the body in a hamper. The appearance of the body made Hall suspicious, he told the Demonstrator of Anatomy, Mr Partridge, and Partridge managed to delay the men until the police were summoned. A coroner's inquest brought in a verdict of 'wilful murder against some person or persons unknown'. At their trial at the Old Bailey, Bishop, Williams and May were found guilty of murdering Carlo Ferrari, an Italian boy from Bethnal Green who had made his living by showing white mice. His empty mouse-cage was found in the rooms of Bishop and May.

The fate of the poor street-urchin aroused a wave of sympathy for Carlo Ferrari, just as 'Daft Jamie' had been pitied in Edinburgh. There was intense interest in the trial and its aftermath. May escaped the gallows, being instead transported for life, but Bishop and Williams were both executed. The *Weekly Dispatch* sold more than 50,000 copies of the issue which contained the confessions of the murderers. But the significant outcome of the Bishop and Williams case occurred in December 1831 when Henry Warburton introduced a much improved Bill into the House of Commons. It passed safely through both Houses, and became law on 1 August 1832. Section 16 of the Anatomy Act did away once and for all with the dissection of the bodies of murderers, while a steady supply of the unclaimed bodies of the inmates of workhouses was guaranteed to the anatomists. No doubt a shiver went through many London workhouses; but the days of the resurrection business were at an end.

Thomas Rowlandson's Touch for Touch. *(Courtesy of Museum of London)*

A satire on the infidelity of George IV as seen by James Gillray.
(Courtesy of Mary Evans Picture Library)

Lord Byron in an engraving by G. Sanders. (Courtesy of Mary Evans Picture Library)

The pillory at Charing Cross by Pugin and Rowlandson.
(Courtesy of Museum of London)

LAST DYING SPEECH.

Rowlandson's Last Dying Speech.
(Courtesy of Museum of London)

The Old Bailey in session as seen by Ackermann. (Courtesy of Museum of London)

A production at Sadler's Wells Theatre, 1809. (Courtesy of Museum of London)

The Strand in Uproar, *by Boitard. (Courtesy of Museum of London)*

Drunken youth under arrest by a charley. (Courtesy of Museum of London)

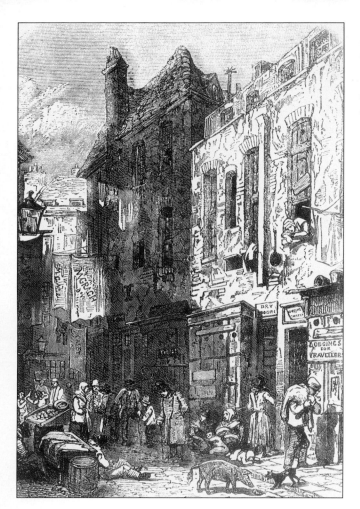

The rookery, St Giles, from Clinch's Bloomsbury, c. 1800. (Courtesy of Museum of London)

Interior of a Police Office. (Courtesy of Museum of London)

Patrick Colquhoun
(1745–1820), 1818.
(Courtesy of Mary Evans
Picture Library)

A scene from Hogarth's Industry and Idleness, 1747. (Courtesy of Mary Evans
Picture Library)

Tom & Bob Catching a Charley Napping, *1822. (Courtesy of Museum of London)*

John Townsend, the most famous of the Bow Street Runners, 1804. (Courtesy of Mary Evans Picture Library)

The TOWNS-END.

Mr. Townsend, Police-Officer, Bow-Street.

Prostitutes at Covent Garden outside Tom King's coffee-house, from Hogarth's Times of Day. *(Courtesy of Mary Evans Picture Library)*

A drinking house from Egan's Life in London. *(Courtesy of Museum of London)*

The *Discovery* at Deptford, *by Samuel Prout, 1825.*
(Courtesy of Mary Evans Picture Library)

The 'Condemned Sermon' at Newgate prison chapel by Pugin and Rowlandson.
(Courtesy of Museum of London)

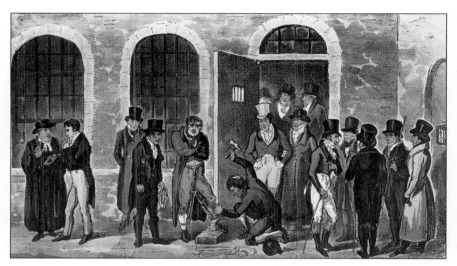

Tom & Jerry at Newgate, from Egan's Life in London.
(Courtesy of Museum of London)

The gateway to the Fleet prison, by G. Shepherd, 1810. (Courtesy of Museum of London)

The courtyard of the Fleet prison, by Pugin and Rowlandson.
(Courtesy of Museum of London)

The water engine at Coldbath Fields prison, 1808.
(Courtesy of Museum of London)

The treadmill at Brixton prison. (Courtesy of Museum of London)

The pass room at Bridewell, by Pugin and Rowlandson, 1808. (Courtesy of Museum of London)

A young pickpocket at work, c. 1830. (Courtesy of Mary Evans Picture Library)

Resurrectionists *(John Holmes and Peter Williams) by Phiz, 1777. (Courtesy of Mary Evans Picture Library)*

Sir Astley Paston Cooper in middle age. (Courtesy of Mary Evans Picture Library.)

William Burke, 1828. (Courtesy of Mary Evans Picture Library)

William Hare, 1828. (Courtesy of Mary Evans Picture Library)

The execution of William Burke, Edinburgh, 1828. (Courtesy of Mary Evans Picture Library)

Tom, Jerry and Logic tasting wine from the barrel, from Life in London. *(Courtesy of Museum of London)*

Tom and Bob from Real Life in London.
(Courtesy of Museum of London)

Tom Getting the best of a Charley, *from* Life in London, *1820.*
(Courtesy of Museum of London)

Tom & Jerry in Trouble after a Spree, *from* Life in London.
(Courtesy of Museum of London)

The Cruikshanks' depiction of an evening at All-Max.
(Courtesy of Museum of London)

Gambling on a fight between a dog and a monkey.
(Courtesy of Museum of London)

Loan contractors as seen by Rowlandson. (Courtesy of Museum of London)

Beau Brummell (1778–1840).
(Courtesy of Mary Evans Picture
Library)

A 'Modern Hell' or Fashionable Gaming House.
(Courtesy of Museum of London)

John Hatfield (1759–1803)
The Famous Seducer,
engraving of c. 1805.

Frederick Augustus, Duke
of York (1763–1827), from
Jesse's Life of Brummell.
(Courtesy of Mary Evans
Picture Library)

Mary Anne Clarke, c. 1805. (Courtesy of Mary Evans Picture Library)

Note the list on the headboard! (Courtesy of Mary Evans Picture Library)

An illustration from Harriette
Wilson's Memoirs, 1825. (Courtesy
of Mary Evans Picture Library)

The Duke of Wellington refused admittance
to H. Wilson.

Harriette Wilson, 1825.
(Courtesy of Mary Evans
Picture Library)

Mr Grimaldi as Clown.
*(Courtesy of Mary Evans
Picture Library)*

*Becky Sharp in a scene
from* Vanity Fair, *drawn
by W.M. Thackeray.
(Courtesy of Mary
Evans Picture Library)*

FIVE

TOM AND JERRY

Tom and Jerry have changed over the years. The cat and mouse who play out their endless feud before cinema and TV audiences world-wide may seem to be stereotyped beyond all change. But they are not the first Tom and Jerry, who were created by cartoonists long before the coming of motion pictures and of Hanna Barbera and Warner Brothers. Robert and George Cruikshank, as gifted visual satirists as any in Regency London, were the inventors of Corinthian Tom and his 'country cousin', Jerry Hawthorn – humans, not cat and mouse. Or more exactly – there was much argument about it afterwards – they shared the invention with their friend Pierce Egan, an Irish sporting journalist: he wrote the words, they drew the pictures. To amuse their fellow Londoners in 1821, the brothers Cruikshank designed and etched 'scenes from real life' showing the adventures about town of Tom and Jerry. Their hand-coloured illustrations appeared in printshops and bookshops each month, accompanied by Egan's racy commentary, which included copious use of slang and occasional comic songs as well as the story.

Corinthian Tom and Jerry Hawthorn set out to 'see life' in the capital, and get into every kind of company and all sorts of scrapes. They hobnob with the wealthy and fashionable at the Royal Academy and in the clubs of St James's, and drink blue ruin – cheap gin – in the East End. Egan and the Cruikshanks portray them as fun-loving and easy-going, equally ready to wink at pretty girls in the Burlington Arcade or to use their fists in a brawl.

Something about the pair, and their madcap companion Bob Logic, the Oxonian, caught on, and Corinthian Tom and Jerry Hawthorn became cult figures. Serial publication rapidly led to a book made up of the original pictures and text with additional material . . . *Life in London Or, The Day and Night Scenes of Jerry Hawthorn, Esq., and His Elegant Friend Corinthian Tom, Accompanied by Bob Logic, the Oxonian, in Their Rambles and Sprees through the Metropolis.* Jerry, who is named first in the subtitle, is the innocent stranger being introduced for the first time to the temptations of London life. The frontispiece shows him carousing along with Tom and Logic, while Tom sings a verse from Burns in keeping with the carefree outlook of the trio:

> Here are we met, THREE merry boys,
> Three merry boys I trow are we,
> And mony a night we've merry been,
> And mony mae we hope to be!

By placing the merry-makers half-way up (or down) an architectural column representing various classes of society, the illustrators bring out that Tom, Jerry and Logic have easy access to every group in London, from the rich and high-born to the 'tag rag and bob-tail' far beneath them. The rich visual symbolism of this column is explained in a lengthy note by Egan, who makes it clear that the 'ups and downs' and 'ins and outs' of life in London have all come within the experience of the heroes. Tom and Jerry are open-minded students of human nature, not stand-offish snobs or dandies.

Life in London was an instant success. Within a few months a rival team of artists, including the brilliant Rowlandson, and a journalist called Jonathan Badcock who felt that he had an old score to settle with Pierce Egan, brought out in two volumes *Real Life in London*, which claimed to give a more truthful and detailed account of contemporary London than the original, though in fact it made use throughout of the same basic formula as the first work, and cheekily varied the names only a little (*Real Life in London: Or, The Rambles and Adventures of Bob Tallyho, Esq., and His Cousin, the Hon. Tom Dashall, through the Metropolis . . .*) It was the first of many imitations, all of which were to enjoy some part of Tom and Jerry's popularity. Soon, 'copycat' titles included *Life in Paris* and *Real Life in Ireland*, 'By a Real Paddy'. Nor was the craze limited to prints and books. Visitors to London were urged to buy Tom and Jerry snuff-boxes, handkerchiefs, fans and ornamental screens. And Egan's 'flash' language – talk of *coves* and *charleys*, *traps* and *flats* – was soon on everyone's lips. This was largely because the theatres took up the theme, with such enthusiasm and inventiveness as to give a completely fresh impetus to the original idea. *Life in London*, in fact, became the theatrical hit of the decade. Egan's casual picaresque plot was exploited and added to by a number of professional stage writers. Before the end of 1823, half a dozen versions, with new comic songs and additional characters, were staged in various London and provincial theatres. Feeling piqued as well as flattered, Egan decided that he must adapt the work himself, and did so, but with less success than W.T. Moncrieff, whose *Tom and Jerry* ran at the Adelphi Theatre for ninety-three successive nights.

The craze was to burn itself out, as crazes usually do. Its very intense phase lasted for no more than three years, and the fame of Tom and Jerry for perhaps ten – Egan and the Cruikshanks published *The Finish to the Adventures of Tom and Jerry*, a deft sequel to *Life in London*, in 1828. But there were to be many revivals of the Tom and Jerry plays during the next half-century, both in Britain and abroad. One of these, an American stage version of *Life in London*, inspired someone in the United States to name a drink – made up of rum and hot water, sweetened and spiced – after the two heroes. (The drinks mentioned most frequently in *Life in London* are actually 'heavy wet' (porter) and gin). It seems that in fact the twentieth-century Tom and Jerry, cat and mouse, have received their names from the drink, and not from their early nineteenth-century forebears. Yet by one of the mysterious continuities within change of popular art, the bold conspiratorial spirit of the first Tom and Jerry, intent always on their own rambles and sprees, seems to have found its way inside the skins of the modern cartoon 'enemies'.

The popularity of *Life in London* in the 1820s lay in part in the London theme, in part in the characters of Tom and Jerry themselves. The Cruikshank–Egan Tom and Jerry are still engaging as comic characters, even if their initial appeal has inevitably faded with time and changing tastes. Tom, the more sophisticated of the two, mixes on equal terms with the proudest people in London, and likes to be thought of as decidedly raffish; he is, after all, a Corinthian or 'swell'. Jerry lacks some of Tom's social poise, but has about him the frank, likeable manner of a countryman come to town. Both are brave, fond of female company – especially when the company is young and attractive like that of Kate and Sue, their favourite companions – and ready for every kind of activity which promises to be entertaining. They are drawn with exuberant energy and skill by the Cruikshanks. George Cruikshank, best known today as the illustrator of Dickens, was making his name at this time, and was as yet no enemy to conviviality: later in life, he signed the pledge and became somewhat sanctimonious. The *Life in London* illustrations, executed in full partnership with his brother (who in 1828 laid claim to having been the 'sole inventor' of the series), are among his finest work, observant, fresh, and amusing. 'Jerry in training for a "Swell"', for instance, one of the earliest pictures of all, seems to catch the exact nuance of Tom's knowingness as, lounging in his *Chaffing Crib*, he supervises Mr Primefit, his 'knight of the thimble' or tailor, measuring Jerry for a *swell suit*. Nearly all of the thirty-six illustrations are of the same high quality.

Whereas the illustrations can stand on their own, Egan's text now appears very mannered when divorced from its accompaniment. He is inordinately fond of exclamation marks and of LARGE CAPITALS!!! But although his copy must have given many problems to his publishers, Sherwood, Neely and Jones, it is nonsense to state, as W.B. Boulton does in *Amusements of Old London* (1901), that 'in his prose English style surely sank to depths which it has never reached before or since'. This is to ignore the key point that illustrations and text were published together in serial form. Egan's role was to provide for each 'episode' words which would at once explain and in a sense match the eye-catching, detailed drawings. There is a carry-over of visual stimulus from picture to page:

TOM and JERRY, previous to the arrival of the *apparel-furnisher*, had been discussing the advantages resulting from *dress* and *ADDRESS*: and the CORINTHIAN had also been pointing out to his Coz. not to *skim* too lightly over so important a subject, but to peruse with the most marked attention that *grand* living BOOK of BOOKS – MAN!!!

Jokes, exclamations, changes of typeface, good-humoured digressions and billowing footnotes all fall into place naturally within such a scheme. Egan writes with the restlessness and watchful eye of a boxing reporter, the best of his generation. If it is sometimes annoying that he never seems to stay still for a moment, a triumph of his art is to suggest that the same is true of his subject, and he tells the story itself with relish . . .

JERRY, dashing along in his hunting career, was so intent upon the scene before him, that he had nearly passed his 'fair *Nun*', who was in company with another female, without observing her, when his eye suddenly caught sight of her lovely shape, as she was about to quit the Masquerade. HAWTHORN, in an instant, was all raptures; and, with more boldness than prudence, he immediately made up to her, and in a low tone of voice, almost whisper, said, 'My fair *Nun*, I have made out your riddle. I beg your pardon, I ought to have addressed you as my dear Lady WAN——' 'Hush, for heaven's sake, hush!' replied the lady, dropping the arm of her companion, and retreating a few steps, 'the Baronet is near at hand; and if you expose me here, I shall be ruined for ever!'

'Only let me, fair *Nun*, claim your promise
   Then *hunt* me out, I will you greet
Kindly welcome, when next we meet,
   and I'll be as silent as a *poacher*', cried JERRY.

As a writer Egan put on a performance in *Life in London* rather like that of a music-hall impresario, with puns and flourishes and alliteration. This helps to explain the ease with which his work was adapted to the stage by men expert in the conventions of early nineteenth-century *burletta* and musical drama.

But neither the genius of the Cruikshanks, nor the quirky originality of Pierce Egan's style, can account in full for the impact of *Life in London* in the 1820s. The idea of exploring high and low life in the capital – always an intriguing one – held special appeal in this period. One reason was that the nation was going through a curious post-war phase, at once jingoistic, questioning and frivolous; another that the public who bought prints and books and went to the theatre were genuinely ignorant of London's social diversity, and especially of the conditions in which the poorest lived. It is true, of course, that by simply walking into Whitechapel or Southwark, a middle-class visitor could see for himself abject poverty – and also the purlieus of crime. But it took courage to venture into such areas, where pockets were picked even more readily than in the Strand. Many preferred to stay within what they conceived to be the bounds of polite society, and to gain their knowledge of uncharted London in their own libraries or in the theatres, with *Life in London* as a guide. That way, they could learn and observe while at the same time enjoying an escape into fiction. For *Life in London* offered not only what Pierce Egan insisted was 'a complete CYCLOPAEDIA' of the *real world*, but also entry into a holiday realm of catchy tunes and characters set free from jobs and from every kind of serious responsibility:

LONDON TOWN's a dashing place
For ev'ry thing that's going,

> There's *fun* and *gig* in ev'ry face,
> So natty and so *knowing*.
> Where NOVELTY is all the rage,
> From high to low degree,
> Such pretty *lounges* to engage,
> Only come and see!

A great deal in *Life in London* turns upon the idea of contrast, which must have been among its chief attractions in 1821. If in one episode, for example, Tom and Jerry pursued Lady Wanton and other idle rich women at a masquerade, readers could be sure that before long the pair would turn up instead among the 'unsophisticated sons and daughters of Nature' in a cadgers' kitchen near Covent Garden or Smithfield Market. Cleverly, Egan used the organizing principle of the work as an excuse for writing repeatedly about the least respectable groups in London, prostitutes and thieves, and for playing upon the fascination of the middle classes for what lay beyond their ken:

The EXTREMES, in every point of view, are daily to be met with in the Metropolis; from the most rigid, persevering, never-tiring industry, down to laziness, which in its consequences, frequently operates far worse than idleness. The greatest love of and contempt for money are equally conspicuous; and in no place are pleasure and business so much united as in London. The highest veneration for and practice of religion distinguishes the Metropolis, contrasted with the most horrid commission of crimes: and the *experience* of the oldest inhabitant scarcely renders him safe against the specious plans and artifices continually laid to entrap the most vigilant. The next-door neighbour of a man in London is generally as great a stranger to him as if he lived at the distance of York. And it is in the Metropolis that *prostitution* is so profitable a business, and conducted so openly, that hundreds of persons keep houses of ill-fame, for the reception of girls not more than *twelve* and *thirteen* years of age, without a blush upon their cheeks, and mix with society heedless of stigma or reproach; yet honour, integrity, and independence of soul that nothing can remove from its basis, are to be found in every street in London. Hundreds of persons are always going to bed in the morning, besotted with dissipation and gaming, while thousands of his Majesty's liege subjects are quitting their pillows to pursue their useful occupations. The most bare-faced villains, swindlers, and thieves walk about the streets in the day-time, committing their various depredations, with as much confidence as men of unblemished reputation and honesty. In short, the most vicious and abandoned wretches, who are lost to every friendly tie that binds man to man, are to be found in swarms in the Metropolis; and so depraved are they in principle, as to be considered, from their uncalled-for outrages upon the inhabitants, a *waste of wickedness*, operating as a complete terror, in spite of the *activity* of the police. Yet, notwithstanding this dark and melancholy part of the picture, there are some of the worthiest, most tender-hearted, liberal minds, and charitable dispositions, which ornament London, and render it the delight and happiness of society.

This passage belongs to a *genre* which dates from long before the Regency, the *Stranger's Guide*, or *Guide to the Evils and Frauds of the Metropolis*. Such publications were common in Shakespeare's time. They multiplied after the Restoration, and Ned Ward in *The London Spy* produced a classic account of the seamier side of Queen Anne's London. (Interestingly, one of the imitations of *Life in London*, by 'Bernard Blackmantle', was entitled *The English Spy*.) But the fact that Pierce Egan wrote within a tradition of social reporting and moralizing which included authors such as Ned Ward and Defoe, did not in any way lessen the force or novelty of his words on their first appearance. The London underworld is always waiting to be discovered, even though it is very old. Every generation believes that it has exposed the 'waste of wickedness' for the first time, and his was no different.

What was new about *Life in London* was the freedom with

which it used both fiction and up-to-the-moment facts, and combined them unpredictably. The Cruikshanks drew from life, thinking nothing of going into mean pubs and coffee houses to study possible subjects; and the same was certainly true of Egan, an habitué of sporting and glee clubs in more than one quarter of town. Rumour had it, quite plausibly, that the three main characters in the series were the creators themselves in disguise: the small, bespectacled figure of Bob Logic being Egan, the bluff newcomer, Jerry Hawthorn none other than Robert Cruikshank, and Corinthian Tom of the aquiline features and brisk decisive air his gifted brother George. Typically, the artists and writer turned this unofficial public identification with the characters in the series to advantage. When Pierce Egan was late on one occasion in supplying copy for the printers he filled up the space by explaining to subscribers in a note entitled 'The Author in Distress' that he had stayed out rather late on a spree with Bob Logic, one result of which had been that his 'reader' or pocket-book was stolen by some 'troublesome customers'. Luckily, he had been given it back since this festive outing, but the accident had prevented him from keeping his engagement with his public on 'The First of the Month'. The illustration was aptly captioned 'Peep o' Day Boys. A Street Row the Author losing his "Reader", Tom & Jerry "showing fight", and Logic floored'.

Now it is quite possible that Pierce Egan was indeed mugged on his way home from drinking *daffy* with his friends: there is no way of being completely sure one way or the other, despite the suspicious pun on 'reader'. But the most celebrated incident of all in *Life in London* was undoubtedly made up – even though it had an authentic origin in the life of the streets, both as a common occurrence and an old joke. This was the business of 'Tom Getting the Best of a Charley'. According to the plot, Tom and Jerry had had no reason to love watchmen ever since one of that aged fraternity reported them to a magistrate at Bow Street when they had run into a spot of bother one night on their way from Covent Garden to the West End. Tom was not a man to bear a grudge, but when some weeks later he was returning from a convivial evening in Tothill Fields he could not resist the chance to tip over a charley's box . . .

> TOM had the CHARLEY in his box down in an instant.
> HAWTHORN laughed immoderately at the dexterity of TOM, and with the utmost glee said to the CORINTHIAN, 'My dear Coz. the CHARLEY had the "best of us" last time, at Bow-Street, but we have got the best of him now, and therefore let us keep it!'

London watchmen, with their rattles and ineffective lamps, had for decades been considered fair game for satirists. Solemn citizens objected that through such scenes *Life in London* was not only condoning but actively encouraging lawlessness and immorality; but the great majority laughed and thought otherwise. The Cruikshanks' cartoon of Tom tipping over the charley was much admired and reproduced. Copies appeared in *Real Life in London* and elsewhere. This incident figured prominently in a bestselling twopenny broadside version of 'the Sprees of Tom and Jerry attempted in cuts and verse', printed close to the heart of the underworld by 'Jemmy' Catnach in Monmouth Court, Seven Dials, where in truth charleys and other figures of authority received scant respect. The Seven Dials rule of life was *look after your own*. Recognizing that John Pitts and other rival ballad printers might 'steal' Tom and Jerry from him, Catnach on his title page warned 'those persons who are in the habit of pirating my copyright that if they dare to print any part of this Sheet, they shall be proceeded against according to Law'. Who was to guess that he had himself pirated his woodcuts, each of which shows the reverse image of a Cruikshank illustration?

Part of the appeal of 'Tom Getting the Best of a Charley', both in Seven Dials and in Bond Street, lay in the fact that Tom was not a vagrant or a thief but a gentleman. The eighteenth century had forgiven sporting young bloods about town nearly everything, in art if not always in reality, and the eighteenth-century tradition of robust knockabout encounters in the street was still alive. By joining in the popular sport of 'baiting a charley', Tom shows that he is prepared to mix it, to ignore the restrictions imposed by caste, and this, too, is a key to his popularity. There was something deeply reassuring to an early nineteenth-century public in his combination of good birth with a strong dislike of social exclusiveness. *Life in London* is to be understood in the light of a recent historian's comment that 'the separation between the upper classes and the rest of the population was probably at its height in 1800'. Although social division was an accepted part of life, it was a source of disquiet, as was the continuing extraordinarily rapid increase of population in London. The comedy of Tom and Jerry worked, as comedy so often does, by playing upon very real fears and anxieties – including the fear of the breakdown of law and order.

Life in London helped to create a myth, cherished by its readers, that theirs was a capital in which with a bit of luck, determination, and the right friends a 'true gentleman' – whether defined by birth, appearance or character – could move in and out of different social groups more or less at will. Not only did he enjoy to the full what is now called upward social mobility, even to the point of dining with countesses and earls, he might also, if he chose, experience the opposite pleasure of 'slumming' among beggars and thieves. A myth it undoubtedly was, though one with a scandalous basis in reality at this time: class barriers and various taboos made instant coming and going in everyday life impossible, although there was no shortage in the Regency either of social climbers or of noblemen who sought out street-girls. But the idea of being free, at least for a time, to move up or down the social ladder at pleasure, was extremely attractive to Pierce Egan's readers. Hence the outstanding popularity of two contrasting episodes in the series, showing Tom and Jerry 'in the East' and 'in the West', at ALL-MAX and Almack's.

The first describes a visit to the kind of back-street gin-shop ('Max' is one of many names for gin used in *Life in London*) where the charleys did not go if they could avoid it, a place of meeting for both sexes, different races, and down and outs:

> Lascars, blacks, jack tars, coal-heavers, dustmen, women of colour, old and young, and a sprinking of the remnants of once fine girls, &c., were all *jigging* together, provided the *teazer of the catgut* was not *bilked* out of his *duce*. *Gloves* might have been laughed at, as dirty hands produced no *squeamishness* on the heroines in the dance, and the scene changed as often as the pantomime from the continual introduction of new characters. *Heavy wet* was the cooling beverage, but frequently overtaken by *flashes of lightning*. The *covey* was no *scholard*, as he asserted, and, therefore, he held the pot in one hand and took the *blunt* with the other, to prevent the trouble of *chalking*, or making mistakes.

At this point, Egan explains in a footnote that by an odd coincidence the name of the proprietor of ALL-MAX is Mace, 'which is a slang term for *imposition* or *robbery*'. Almost certainly the name is made up to let him slip in yet another pun, and there is a fictional element in the whole scene. But the pub has been identified as the Coach and Horses in Nightingale Street, East Smithfield; and there is no reason to doubt that this is in essential respects an accurate account of one of the notorious early nineteenth-century 'Cock and Hen Clubs' where, according to witnesses interviewed by the 1816 Parliamentary Select Committee on the Police, 'lewd and riotous' behaviour was commonplace. Egan's angle of vision, however, is not that of a police reformer intent on doing away with flash-houses, nor of a member of the Society for the Suppression of Vice. His moralizing is in a vein of his own. As a man of the people, he writes cheerfully, even sentimentally of the scene:

> the parties *paired off* according to fancy; the eye was pleased in the choice, and nothing thought of about birth and distinction. All was *happiness*, – everybody free and easy, and freedom of expression allowed to the very echo.

Bob Logic, who before the night is out 'pairs off' with African Sall, is evidently the author's mouthpiece in announcing,

'It is, I am quite satisfied in my mind, the LOWER ORDERS of society who really ENJOY themselves. They eat with a good appetitie, *hunger* being the sauce; they *drink* with a zest, in being *thirsty* from their exertions, and not *nice* in their beverage; and as to *dress*, it is not an object of serious consideration with them. Their minds are daily occupied with work, which they quit with the intention of enjoying themselves, and ENJOYMENT is the result; not like the rich, who are out night after night to *kill* TIME, and, what is worse, dissatisfied with almost every thing that crosses their path from the dulness of *repetition*.'

At this stage, while they have had many opportunities of observing and mingling with 'the higher ranks of society', they have not yet visited Almack's. The chance soon arises, and Egan is careful to point the contrast between the East End pub and the assembly rooms in King's Street, St James's, which in real life were the setting of the most exclusive fashionable gatherings in Regency London. No strong drink was allowed in Almack's, which was ruled over by a group of imperious, aristocratic ladies. Anyone arriving late, or wearing the wrong clothes, was liable to be turned away – even if the clock was only a few minutes past the hour and the latecomer was the Duke of Wellington. Almack's was the high citadel of social power:

If once to ALMACK's you belong,
Like MONARCHS, you can *do no wrong*;
But Banished thence on Wednesday night,
By Jove, you can do nothing right.

Tom and Jerry, who have on this occasion left Logic at home because he likes fun and African Sall more than etiquette, are acutely aware that they do not 'belong' at Almack's in the full sense. Tom knows his way about, or thinks he does, but for once even he feels nervous:

'I must once more remind you, my dear Coz.' said TOM, 'that we must be on our Ps and Qs; and if you should find me *tripping*, as I by no means consider myself infallible, you will gently bring me back to my recollection by merely saying "LETHE"; and, in turn, if necessary, I will perform the same kind office towards you.' 'I shall bear it in mind,' says HAWTHORN.

Each is as good as his word. They spend a correct evening among 'high and mighty Commanders – mobs of Earls and Lords – Generals – Admirals – Right Honourable Ladies like flowers in a garden' and 'lots of rich but *plain* Mistresses'. The tone throughout is of pointed social satire, and it is strongly implied that, despite the presence of Lady Wanton and moments when he has to be pulled up short by Tom, Jerry sees much less to interest him than at ALL-MAX.

Tom and Jerry, indeed, clearly find low life more congenial than the elegant but vapid diversions of the rich and well connected. The point is confirmed by what Egan describes as 'the grand climax' of the series, when they disguise themselves as beggars and 'masquerade it' at the Noah's Ark – a gathering for life's survivors – in the *back slums* in the Holy Land. The 'Holy Land' was the traditional nickname of a rookery largely inhabited by the Catholic Irish poor, close to Buckeridge Street in St Giles, not far from Bloomsbury. It was a meeting place for London's beggars and mock-beggars, the 'freshwater sailors', able-bodied cripples, and other charlatans of the streets. Tom tells his friend what to expect . . .

the *Beggar* who has been writhing to and fro all the day in the public streets in terrific agony, to excite your charity and torture your feelings, here meets his fellows to laugh at the *flats*, count over his gains, and sit down to a rich supper. The wretch who has also pretended to be *blind*, and could not move an inch without being led by his dog, can here *see* and enjoy all the good things of this life, without even *winking*. The poor married woman with twins, who you are led to imagine, from her piteous tale, has been left in distress, in consequence of her husband having been sent to sea, you will find is a single woman, and has only *hired* the children from poor people, who lend them out for the purpose, joins the party, at the *Noah's Ark*, to laugh at the fools who may have relieved her pretended wants in the course of the day.

The impostors they are going to see practise countless cynical tricks upon the public each day, he claims, despite the 'exertions and exposé of the Parish Officers, the Police, and the Mendicity Society'. Tom's stern warning is exactly in the style of a chapbook Guide to the Frauds of London. But once the friends actually enter the Noah's Ark, where the party is in full swing, the note of disapproval becomes less insistent. Among this motley crew of rapacious tricksters and mountebanks, the Cruikshanks and Egan provide a glimpse of anarchic social merriment – here are people set free from the restraints of conventional society. At the centre of the picture, Egan explains, is Peg the ballad-singer (Jemmy Catnach in neighbouring Seven Dials needed many ballad-singers to sell his wares) . . .

Peg, the ballad-singer, all in tatters, and covered with various-coloured rags, yet her pretty face did not escape the roving eye of TOM, upon her winking and leering her ogles at him, and chaunting the ballad, 'Poverty's no sin', in hopes to procure a new *fancy-man*. Massa Piebald, as they termed him, on account of his *black* mug and white *mop*, was chaffing the little *cove*, that, as he had no *pins* to stand upon, he must have a *perch*; and, as he was no *starter*, he proposed him for their chairman. The *no-pinn'd* hero, on being elevated, gave, as a toast, 'success to FLAT-*catching*', which produced roars of laughter and shouts of approbation. The fellow sitting near the stove, whose face seems on the grin, from the pleasure he feels on *scratching* himself, offers to lay a quart of *heavy* that he has not *cut his nails* for the last twelve months, he has had such active employment for them. Quarrelsome old *Suke*, who has been *hobbling* all the day on her *crutches* through the streets, now descends the ladder quickly to join the party, and is *blowing-up* her *ould man* for not taking hold of her crutches 'as he knows she doesn't vant 'em now'. Behind the stove, the row has become so great, from the copious draughts of liquor and jollity of the *Cadgers*, that the gin measure and glasses are thrown at each other; and their crutches and wooden legs are brought in contact to finish the *turn-up*, till they are again wanted to *cadge* with the next day. The black one-legged fiddler is *strumming* away to enliven the party; and the *peck* and *booze* is lying about in such lots, that it would supply numerous poor families, if they had had the *office* given to them where to apply for it.

This 'rich view of human Nature' includes one or two individuals who can be conjecturally identified from other sources, as well as types of beggar familiar in early nineteenth-century London. In 1817 J.T. Smith, Keeper of Prints in the British Museum, published *Vagabondiana, or Anecdotes of Mendicant Wanderers through the Streets of London, with Portraits of the Most Remarkable*. His aim, he explained, was to record curious customs of the beggars, including the 'idle and sturdy', before it was too late – already, new laws threatened to drive many off the streets. The sort of thing Smith describes ranges from the way of life of Grannee Manoo, who begs old shoes to sell to the 'Translators' (cellar-dwelling cobblers in Monmouth Street), or stall-holders in Food and Raiment Alley, Rosemary Lane, to the funeral of Jack Stuart, sometime model for the sculptor Flaxman and notorious freshwater sailor:

After lingering for nearly three months, Jack died on the 15th of August, 1815, aged 35; his funeral was attended by his wife, and faithful dog, Tippo, as chief mourners, accompanied by three blind beggars in black cloaks; namely, John Fountain, George Dyball, and John Jervis. Two blind fiddlers, William Worthington and Joseph Symmonds, preceded the coffin, playing the 104th Psalm. The whimsical procession moved on, amidst crowds of spectators, from Jack's house, in Charlton Gardens, Somers Town, to the Churchyard of St Pancras, Middlesex. The mourners afterwards returned to the place from whence the funeral had proceeded, where they remained the whole of the night, dancing, drinking, swearing, and fighting, and occasionally chaunting Tabernacle hymns; for it must be understood, that most of the beggars are staunch Methodists.

Vagabondiana offers information about men and women who gain their livelihood by means which, in the author's opinion, the prosperous cannot even conceive of: among them are dog-tooth sellers ('to bookbinders, carvers, and gilders, as burnishing tools'), bone-pickers and grubbers. Smith relates how a bone-picker was followed for several hours through many streets, alleys and courts, in the parish of St Martin's-in-the-Fields. At Moor's yard, a place for the execution of criminals in former times, he was accused of stealing door-mats, and dogs were set on him. Then 'in Hartshorn-lane, in the Strand . . . he was seen to take up a brick, and throw it at two curs fighting for a bone, which he picked up and put into his bag. These bones are bought by the burners at Haggerstone, Shoreditch, and Battlebridge, at two shillings per bushel.'

Smith's definition of a beggar seems to include anyone who makes his living by picking up what does not originally belong to him. 'Grubbers' and Thames-side coal-gatherers both fall into this category. The first group, who are sometimes employed to clear gully-holes and common sewers,

> grub out the dirt from between the stones with a crooked bit of iron, in search of nails that fall from horse-shoes, which are allowed to be the best iron that can be made use of for gun-barrels; and though the streets are constantly looked over at the dawn of day by a set of men in search of sticks, handkerchiefs, shawls &c that may have been dropt during the night, yet these grubbers now and then find rings that have been drawn off with the

gloves, or small money that has been washed by the showers between the stones.

Such smelly toil, Smith concedes, is bad enough – he does not take into account that the coming of peace meant a dwindling of demand for iron, and therefore more work in the sewers – 'and yet Ned Flowers followed this calling for forty years'. Far worse, in his view, because extremely unhealthy, is the lot of 'a more wretched class of being than grubbers', who never know the comfort of dry clothes:

> they are like the leech, perpetually in water. The occupation of these draggle-tail wretches commences on the banks of the Thames at low water. They go up to their knees in mud to pick up the coals that fall from the barges when at the wharfs. Their flesh and dripping rags are like the coals they carry in small bags across their shoulders, and which they dispose of, at a reduced price, to the meanest order of chandler-shop retailers.

In comparison with these pitiable creatures, the beggars lucky enough to have a regular stance in a busy street and a successful 'line' – whether honest or assumed – are a class apart. And he makes the point that two sets of beggars are especially privileged: 'black people, as well as those destitute of sight, seldom fail to excite compassion'. Smith cites many examples of 'cunning and witty black men' like Charles McGie, a Jamaican with an excellent pitch at the Obelisk, at the foot of Ludgate Hill, who regularly attends Rowland Hill's meeting-house on Sundays and who 'is supposed to be worth money', and Toby, of Church-lane, St Giles, a 'cripple' who always seems to become tired close to the pubs selling the best gin. While Smith notes that many blacks have 'short names such as Jumbo, Toby, &c.', it seems reasonable to assume that this particular gin-loving Toby appears in the Cruikshank plate of the Noah's Ark. Another drinker common to *Life in London* and *Vagabondiana* styles him as the 'King of the Beggars' – he had thirty years' experience – and mentions his regular pitch, when sober, outside the door of Coutts' Bank. When they visit the 'Holy Land', Tom and Jerry hear the 'little cove' nominated as chairman of the festivity.

The stage versions of *Life in London* made capital out of the audience's familiarity with the appearance and behaviour of a number of London beggars and dustmen, and with the Cruikshank-Egan manner of treating them. In W.T. Moncrieff's *Tom and Jerry*, the fiddler Billy Waters, Little Jemmy the sledge-beggar, and Dusty Bob the dustman are given an importance in the comic development which they do not have in the original. They were all recognizably based on actual figures who could be seen each week in the streets. No doubt the most resourceful of the beggars exploited this fame by coming into view outside the theatres. But according to one story, the dramatized adventures of Tom and Jerry broke the heart of the real Billy Waters, a one-legged musical black, 'who died in St Giles's work-house, on Friday, March 21, 1823, whispering with his ebbing breath, a mild anathema, which sounded very much like: "Cuss him, dam Tom – mee – Tom – mee Jerry!"'

Already accepted by the public as an expert on everything to do with 'the Fancy' or boxing fraternity, Pierce Egan established himself through *Life in London* as no less of an authority on thieves' cant and London slang in general. He at once took the chance to bring out a fresh edition of the first really good book on English slang, the eighteenth-century antiquarian Francis Grose's *Classical Dictionary of the Vulgar Tongue*. Recent opinions on Egan as a student of slang have varied, but Egan's contemporaries undoubtedly admired his knowingness. He *appeared* to be a 'master of cant', as well as of all the other kinds of language exemplified in his tales of Tom and Jerry. There was evidently no limit to his resources of vocabulary, nor to his liking for repetition. Some readers of the series, indeed, objected at an early stage to the sheer number of slang words which it contained. Egan's reply to their criticism shows the ready ease with which he could move from using one set of terms to another . . .

I am anxious to render myself perfectly intelligible to all parties. Half the world are *up* to [the slang]; and it is my intention to make the other half *down* to it. LIFE IN LONDON demands this sort of demonstration. A kind of *cant* phraseology is current from one end of the Metropolis to the other: indeed, even in the time of Lord Chesterfield, he complained of it. In some females of the highest rank, it is as strongly marked, as in *dingy* draggled-tail SALL, who is compelled to dispose of a few sprats to turn an honest penny: and while the latter, in smacking her lips, talks of her *prime jackey*, an *out-and-out* concern, a *bit of good truth*, &c, the former, in her dislikes, tossing her head, observes, it was *shocking, quite a bore, beastly*, stuff, &c. The duchess, at an Opera, informs the Countess of a 'row' which occurred on the last evening with as much *sang-froid*, as CARROTTY POLL mentions to a *Costardmonger* the *lark* she was engaged in, at a gin-spinner's, and in being turned out of the *panny*, got her *ogles* taken *measure* of for a *suit of mourning*.

On this occasion, as it happens, he is guilty of an unconscious confusion, and an interesting one. By his reference to 'a kind of *cant* phraseology . . . current from one end of the Metropolis to the other', Egan prepares us for the use of thieves' slang. Now the *argot* of the criminal underworld is certainly used with flair and precision elsewhere in *Life in London*. But what this passage actually goes on to illustrate is not cant as such but instead something wider and more inclusive – demotic London speech, the English of the streets and back-streets and in particular of the East End. Carrotty Poll, who is turned out of the pub with two black eyes, talks in a way which for the moment Egan wishes to place at the opposite end of the social scale from the conversational manner of the Duchess at the Opera. Poll's snatch of London slang represents what later writers will describe as 'Cockney'. The significant thing is that Egan takes Cockney to be so intimately bound up with cant language that the two can be carelessly confused; words originating with criminals, in his view, are a main element in the daily usage of a large number of Londoners.

This tells us a good deal both about Pierce Egan and about early nineteenth-century London. It has of course long been recognized that, from a date some two hundred years before this, cant words were progressively absorbed into London speech. Modern authorities on the subject, anxious to prove that Cockneys are no longer tainted by the criminal origins of some of their words, like to point out that the spread outwards from rookery to law-abiding population of colourful, expressive terms is a natural process in the history of the language. From this point of view, when Egan writes of *swell kids, mollsters* and *boozing kens,* he is simply to be described, like Ned Ward before him, as participating in that process. But such a bland judgement ignores two other points – Egan's claim that cant was still being used in Regency London as a kind of secret code by those with something to hide, and the fact that his first readers welcomed *Life in London* as an exposé. They took delight in his skill in 'blowing the gaff' on the criminal underworld.

By 'explaining' in the course of its dialogue a number of slang words, Moncrieff's 'Extravaganza Burletta' *Tom and Jerry* serves to show where the boundary between familiar terms and unfamiliar for London theatre audiences ran – although, as in Victorian music-hall, part of the joke lies in spelling out what is quite elementary. Introducing Jerry to Bob Logic, for instance, Tom says:

He is now come to see life, and rub off a little of the rust. In effecting this desirable consummation you can materially assist; under so skilful a professor of the flash as you, Bob –
Jerry. Flash! I'm at fault again, Tom.
Tom. Explain, Bob.
Logic. Flash, my young friend, or slang as others call it, is the classical language of the Holy Land; in other words, St Giles's Greek.
Jerry. St Giles's Greek; that is a language, doctor, with

which I am totally unacquainted, although I was brought up at a Grammar School.

Logic. You are not particular in that respect; many great scholars, and better linguists than you, are quite ignorant of it, it being studied more in the Hammer Schools than the Grammar Schools. Flash, my young friend, or slang, as others call it, is a species of cant in which the knowing ones conceal their roguery from the flats; and it is one of the advantages of seeing Life in London, that you may learn to talk to a rogue in his own language, and fight him with his own weapons.

This allows Logic to do no more than run over his ABC, but a little later he is able to teach Jerry some especially useful phrases . . .

Logic. It's the blunt that does it – blunt makes the man, Jerry.

Jerry. Blunt! I'm at fault again.

Tom. Explain, Bob –

Logic. Blunt, my dear boy, is – in short what is it not? It's every thing now o' days – to be able to flash the screens – sport the rhino – show the needful – post the pony – nap the rent – stump the pewter – tip the brads – and down with the dust, is to be once good, great, handsome, accomplished, and everything that's desirable – money, money, is your universal God, – only get into Tip Street, Jerry.

For Logic as a seasoned man about town, as for Lord Byron in *Don Juan*, 'cash rules'.

Moncrieff's *Tom and Jerry* makes clever use in a number of exchanges and choruses of underworld diction, and incidentally anticipates Dickens by fifteen years in burlesquing Cockney speech mannerisms: *v*'s are regularly substituted for *w*'s, and vice-versa, *h*'s added and dropped, and so forth. But the authenticity of the thieves' language which is bandied about so freely by Egan and by Moncrieff is to be tested by comparison not with the brilliantly idiosyncratic usage of Dickens, but with word-lists set down in sober earnest during the Regency period itself by two men whose professional business lay respectively in law-enforcement and law-breaking: representatives of the species *trapp* and *prigg*.

In the manuscript collections of the British Library are two small notebooks which at one time belonged to Sir John Silvester, who was Recorder of London from 1803 until 1822 and as such an Old Bailey judge of considerable authority and influence. The value of these notebooks lies most obviously in the wealth of detailed information they supply about receivers who were active in early nineteenth-century London, but it is also of great interest that the later of the two, dated 1816, included a criminal vocabulary. It seems possible that the 'A.L.' whose initials precede this 'list of cant words with their meaning', as well as the notes on fences under surveillance, was one of the police Runners with whom Silvester had dealings. Here, at any rate, is a source close to the seat of criminal justice in the City. Cant was spoken daily by prisoners at the Old Bailey, and in the course of his work on the Bench, the Recorder must have learned to 'translate' all of these underworld terms:

Noseing: Telling everything you know. *Napping a Bob*: Getting a shilling. *A Crack*: Housebreaking. *A Sneak*: Going privately into a Shop. *A Sneaksman*: Do. *A Scamp*: A Highwayman. *A Spice*: A Footpad. *A Jump*: Getting into a One pr of Stairs Window. *The Hoist*: a Shoplifter. *The Rush*: Knocking at the Door & rushing in. *The Truck*: Pinching of half Gn. or Palming do. *The Burst or Spank*: Forcing a Door open with violence and art. *A Knucler*: Pickpocket. *A buzman*: a little Pickpocket. *Napping a Peter*: cutting Portmanteau or Trunk. *Dragsman*: robbing of Waggons. *Starring a Glaze*: Cutting Window & taking things out. *Napping a Snow*: Sneaking Wet Linen. *Doing out & out*: Murder. *Crapping*: Hanging. *Teased*: Whipping. *Standing in the Stoop*: Pillory. *Lagged*: Transported. *Start*: Newgate. *Done in the Start*: Imprisoned in it. *Tumbler*:

a Cart. *Showing the Tumbler:* Whipped at Cart tail. *Patter:* to try. *Pattered:* to be tried. *Making Whites:* Coining Shillings. *Making Browns:* Coining halfpence. *Smashers:* Utterers of bad Money. *Upright Sneak:* Stealing Pewter Pots & Pans. *Quod Cull:* Keeper. *Trapps:* Thieftakers. *Horneys:* Constables. *Old Scouts:* Watchmen. *Beaks:* Judges & Justices. *A Tick:* A Watch. *A Tawnee:* a Ring. *A Cast:* a Hat. *A Smitch:* a Shirt. *A great Tog:* a Great Coat. *Hickseys:* a pr of Breeches. *Hock or Dock:* Shoes. *Wedge:* Silver. *Ridge:* Gold. *Lower:* Money. *Sack a Clie:* Pocket. *Mounters or Buffers:* False Witnesses. *Fence:* a Receiver. *Turning Snitch:* Turning Evidence. *Napping a Reader:* Stealing a Pocket Book. *Napping of Skreens:* Stealing of Bank Notes. *A Clout:* a Handkerchief. *Sharps:* Gamblers. *Flatts:* those who lose their money to Gamblers. *Oliver Widles:* Moonlight night. *The Gaff:* The Play-house. *Darkey:* a Dark night. *A Queer Pin:* a sore Leg. *A Queer Morley:* a sore Head. *A Pop:* Pistol. *A Lash:* a Cutlass. *Dabbs:* Picklock keys. *A Rooke:* an Iron Crow. *A Cheive:* a Knife. *A Pratler or Bounder:* a Coach or Chariot. *Old Prigg:* an old Thief. *A Flashman or a Needle:* a Sharper. *A Topper:* a blow on the Head. *Fray:* cant word. *Grubbige:* Hungry. *Sucky or Suck as a Buffer:* a Drunkard. *Milling a Fellow*: Beating a Fellow. *A Swell*: a Gentleman. *A Lagger*: a Sailor.

At least half of the words and phrases in this *trapp*'s (or *beak*'s) key to the cant of Regency thieves can be found in *Life in London*. It is true, of course, that Silvester's list includes a number of terms – some of them, like *fence*, still in common use – which must have been familiar to people outside the criminal courts, even if thieves and thief-takers had more frequent occasion to use them than anyone else. Also, one or two expressions, such as *milling a fellow*, have a slang origin rather than one in cant. Nevertheless, the list offers a reliable guide to the special vocabulary of crime in early nineteenth-century London as it was actually heard and noted down, and the accuracy with which this vocabulary is reproduced by Pierce Egan and by the best of his imitators is remarkable.

A very different 'control' against which the underworld talk in *Life in London* can be judged is *A New and Comprehensive Vocabulary of the Flash Language* compiled and written in 1812 by James Hardy Vaux, a petty thief and confidence trickster who, in the course of a notably unsuccessful criminal career, was twice transported to Australia. During his second spell in the southern continent, Vaux began work on his 'flash' dictionary, which was published in London in 1819 along with his *Memoirs* (recently described as one of the earliest works of Australian literature). Vaux's list of words is much longer than Silvester's, and his definitions are more detailed, so that on occasion he can be used to clarify a compressed entry in the Recorder's notebook. For instance, he glosses *jump* as 'a game or species of robbery effected by getting into a house through any of the lower windows', and adds, 'to *jump* a place, is to rob it upon a *jump*. A man convicted for this offence, is said to be *done* for a *jump*'. (Interestingly enough, Vaux had once escaped from being 'done', apparently through the obtuseness of the Recorder. In 1808 Silvester had acquitted Vaux when he was tried at the Old Bailey for stealing a silver snuff-box; Vaux's *Memoirs* convey his low estimate of the Recorder's powers of intelligence.) The *Vocabulary of the Flash Language* is perkily eloquent where the British Library notebook maintains silence, as for instance in defining *kiddy*: 'a thief of the lower order, who, when he is breeched, by a course of successful depredation, dresses in the extreme of vulgar gentility, and affects a knowingness in his air and conversation, which renders him in reality an object of ridicule; such a one is pronounced by his associates of the same class, a *flash-kiddy* or a *rolling-kiddy*'. Egan once more passes the test as an author thoroughly versed in terms which occur in Vaux's *Vocabulary*. This time, however, the point must be put more tentatively, as it is of course possible that he actually made use of the old lag's notebook in the course of writing *Life in London*.

An 'anti-language', such as that of criminals, serves its original purpose only in so far as it keeps secrets or maintains group morale and identity. *Life in London* did not destroy the confidence of the kiddies on the town who liked to talk flash; indeed, some argued that 'Tom and Jerry and all that nonsense' merely glamorized the shabby dealings of law-breakers. On the other hand, the code in which the criminals liked to communicate with each other was no longer secret. James Hardy Vaux had nosed or grassed. But most people would have given the credit to Tom, Jerry and Bob Logic.

SIX

A TRADITION OF GAMBLING

The history of gambling is long and dishonourable, but some of the citizens of Regency Britain deserve a place among the boldest risk-takers of all. The Regency was a time when Englishmen (not to mention Irish, Scots and Welsh) were ready to bet on almost anything, even if they lost their lives as a result. The *Morning Chronicle* of 26 March 1811 reported an incident which was in keeping with the mood of the times.

> A blacksmith at Stroud ate on Tuesday, for a trifling wager, a pint of periwinkles with the shells, in the space of ten minutes. Being desired to repeat this disgusting feat he readily did it, but he is now so dangerously ill that he is not expected to recover.

Physical bravado was the blacksmith's undoing. He seems to have been unluckier than most, but he was by no means alone in his outlook. A year later the *Annual Register* gave details of another wager.

> *15th April 1812.* On Wednesday evening an extraordinary investigation took place at Bow Street. Croker, the officer, was passing along the Hampstead road, when he observed, at a short distance before him, two men on a wall, and, directly after, saw the tallest of them, a stout man, about six feet high, hanging by his neck, from a lamp post attached to the wall, being that instant tied up

and turned off by the short man. This unexpected and extraordinary sight astonished the officer; he made up to the spot with all speed; and, just after he arrived there, the tall man, who had been hanged, fell to the ground, the handkerchief, with which he had been suspended, having given way . . . both were brought to the office, when the account they gave was that they worked on canals. They had been together on Wednesday afternoon, tossed up for money, and afterwards for their clothes; the tall man, who was hanged, won the other's jacket, trousers, and shoes; they then tossed up which should hang the other, and the short one won the toss. They got upon the wall, the one to submit, and the other to hang him on the lamp iron. . . . The tall one, who had been hanged, said, if he had won the toss, he would have hanged the other. He said he then felt the effects of his hanging in his neck, and his eyes were so much swelled that he saw double. The magistrates expressed their horror and disgust . . .

Between the lines of this account, we can detect the underlying desperation of the men involved. On the canals of England, and certainly for canal navvies, life was still nasty, brutish and short – it could be of small account if it was shortened a little further. The 'horror and disgust' expressed by the magistrates was no doubt their personal reaction, but they also wanted to issue a warning against the dangers of such wagers. When it was confined to the upper classes, outrageous gambling was bad enough – but it must not be allowed to take such a form as this among artisans and the poor. The 'contagion of bad example' was a cause of real concern to those in authority.

In 1829, when John Wade wrote his *Treatise on the Police and Crimes of the Metropolis*, gambling was still mainly thought of as an upper-class vice, even though it was undoubtedly practised also by street urchins tossing up buttons, by boastful blacksmiths and by navvies. Wade like to work with clear categories, and he described the prevalence of different bad habits in this way:

The crimes and vices now most rife in London are gaming among the higher and more opulent classes – theft, swindling, and fraud, among the middle classes – drinking among the lower classes, chiefly labourers.

Few of his contemporaries would have challenged the truth of at least the first part of this analysis. Whatever the vices of the middle and lower classes – and Wade's middle-class readers are not likely to have welcomed his comment on 'theft, swindling, and fraud' – it was readily accepted that gaming was the characteristic vice of the wealthy and high-born. As such, it was the frequent subject of shocked or simply amused comment by people who did not have entry to that particular social world, but who read in the public prints of estates changing hands over card-tables in St James's, of notorious practices in London's gambling 'hells', and of the growing power and fortune of William Crockford. By this date, Crockford was already a household name – and so too were the disrespectful nicknames 'Old Crocky' and 'The Fishmonger'; he was perhaps the richest self-made man in London. Readers of newspapers and magazines who had never laid a bet in their lives knew the whereabouts of his plushly appointed club, said to be even more splendid within than the Palace of Versailles. In the same street in the West End of town many non-gambling Londoners would also have been able to point out to an inquiring stranger the much longer-established White's, with its recently added bow window in which Beau Brummell had sat and held court, and the neighbouring Brooks's. If high play and high birth went together, there was no embargo on general knowledge or on London gossip.

The upper classes, who had the means, had been indulging in games of chance for centuries. What took place in the Regency was a kind of Indian summer and brilliant late flowering of an old and – in the literal sense – noble tradition. Even in Shakespeare's time, gaming had been looked on as a pastime of the landed gentry, although they already had imitators among the would-be sophisticates and

Italianate 'cits' of London. Inevitably, the Puritans of Cromwell's time had cracked down hard on the activities of *homo ludens*; they banished card-games altogether, but the result of this was that after the Restoration gambling flourished as never before. It was as if a good part of the aristocracy had been starved during the years of the Commonwealth of something necessary to their very existence, and they proceeded to make up for lost time. In its frenetic pleasure-seeking spirit, the Restoration was like an ancitipation of the early nineteenth-century mood. *'Gaming'*, wrote Cotton in the *Compleat Gamester* (1674),

> it is an enchanting *witchery*, gotten between *Idleness* and *Avarice*: an itching disease, that makes some scratch the head, whilst others, as if bitten by a *Tarantula*, are laughing themselves to death; or, lastly, it is a paralytical distemper, which, seizing the arm, the man cannot chuse but shake his elbow.

Gamesters, according to Cotton, were incapable of giving serious thought to anything except their obsession. They were the slaves of dice, always in extremes – whether of hope or of despair – always in a storm. Samuel Pepys, who had seen 'deep and prodigious gaming' on many occasions at Court, confirmed this impression. Ladies as well as dukes of the realm played very deep, squandering away 'vast heaps of gold' as if they were baubles.

A little later, the reforming essayists of Queen Anne's age issued anxious warnings about the dangers of a love of the tables. The indignant Swift was known to shake his fist in anger at the windows of White's Chocolate House in St James's Street, home from home of many a rakehell young nobleman, while Addison poured scorn on gambling in *The Spectator*. Sir Richard Steele, who had about him rather more of the cavalier taste for risky pleasures than either of these writers, obligingly backed up their strictures in his literary journalism with lessons drawn from his own lightly disguised experience. He also wrote, a little absurdly, about the particular risks run by women of vogue and fashion who developed a taste for gambling:

> Now, there is nothing that wears out a fine Face like the Vigils of the Card Table, and those cutting Passions which naturally attend them. Hollow Eyes, haggard Looks, and pale Complexions, are the natural Indications of a Female Gamester. Her Morning Sleeps are not able to repair her Midnight Watchings. I have known a Woman carried off half dead from *Bassette*, and have, many a time grieved to see a Person of Quality gliding by me, in her Chair, at two a Clock in the Morning, and looking like a Spectre amidst a flare of Flambeaux. In short, I never knew a thorough paced Female Gamester hold her Beauty two Winters together. But there is still another Case in which the Body is more endangered than in the former. All Play Debts must be paid in Specie, or by an Equivalent. The Man who plays beyond his income, pawns his Estate; the Woman must find out something else to Mortgage when her Pin Money is gone. The Husband has his lands to dispose of, the Wife, her Person. (*The Guardian*, 29 July 1713)

Words like these may have sent a shiver down the spine of regular readers of *The Guardian*, but it seems unlikely that there were many hardened 'female gamesters' among them.

It was the belief of Queen Anne's ministers, and of those who followed them in the Georgian era, that gambling must be reckoned among the most seductive and dangerous pursuits in London for those with money to burn, or simply with time on their hands. Successive parliaments passed laws to curtail the 'rage for gaming', but with little lasting effect. Laws, it seems, did not deter men who looked on it as their born right to do as they wished with their own or their fathers' money. It can be argued, in fact, that legislation against gambling in the eighteenth century merely succeeded in making matters worse by forcing those who wished to indulge in high play to do so behind closed doors. The effect of making gaming illegal in coffee houses and public houses was rather like that of prohibition two hundred years later in the United States. At least as much dicing went on as before, but it took place now in specialized private clubs, places of secrecy which lacked the wholesome moderating influence from everyday living that might have come through open acknowledgement and integration within society. These places where gaming regularly took place came to be known as 'hells', implying that men who ventured within them were lost souls. The name stuck, and with it the social stigma.

The politicians and magistrates who sought to banish gambling had powerful reasons for acting as they did, even though their best efforts failed. The throwing of dice undermined the stability of property, and property was very highly valued by eighteenth-century society. One can detect a double standard here. The social conservatism of the English combined with what might be called the Restoration tradition to persuade many people that there was little wrong with noblemen gaming among themselves. If a landowner chose to 'make a sport' of his property and to lose it, say, at the game of hazard, to another son of broad acres, that was his prerogative. But if, on the other hand, he was foolish enough to throw away what he had inherited to low-born adventurers or, worse, to Jewish money-lenders, the loss was invariably considered serious. The nation's rulers judged it a threat to their own kind when an estate or any significant part of one passed into the 'wrong hands'.

There was also an ethical consideration. Gambling, which Dr Johnson defined as playing extravagantly for money, set an example of the worst kind. It was a practice which destroyed morals as well as property, and as such it was better out of sight. After all, while land was given only to the few, a love of play was something shared by people of very different social backgrounds. Young men in commerce and trade were judged to be especially at risk. Dire tales were told of industrious apprentices who allowed themselves to be led to ruin through keeping bad company. Hogarth drew these and other evils for all to see. White's, still a centre of high play although now a private club instead of a chocolate house open to all comers, was included in his most famous series of satirical cartoons, 'The Rake's Progress'. Both Hogarth and Fielding took the robust eighteenth-century view that gambling should as far as possible be confined to the social class which might be said to have been bred to it. Fielding worked hard as a magistrate in the mid-century to contain what he saw as a source of misery for Londoners comparable with strong drink itself.

The opening years of the reign of George III brought something of a reaction against the excesses of the preceding period. The new king was not at all inclined to dabble in what he thought of as the decadent ways of English noblemen with too little to do; he scorned that kind of time-wasting. However, before his eldest son came of age, the stern and censorious George III had been made sharply and uncomfortably aware that such English folly was not something his family could escape. The Prince of Wales was a gambler by instinct. His notably flamboyant and expensive habits included a taste for horse-racing and for the betting which accompanied it. In the 1780s, he was a generous royal patron of the turf, living by the principle that it was not enough to own good horses – one must be seen to back them. In addition, he numbered among his intimate friends some of the most dedicated gamblers in London.

The most famous and gifted of these men was the Whig politician Charles James Fox, a son of Lord Holland. Fox was an astonishing combination of serious-minded politician and frivolous man-about-town. He was a member of White's, and also of a new and equally popular gaming club in Pall Mall, Almack's, which in 1778 moved to St James's Street under the new name of Brooks's, that of its wine-merchant proprietor. One of Fox's friends, Frederick Byng, said of him rather unkindly in later life,

Charles loved only three things, women, play, and politics. Yet at no period did he ever form a creditable connection with a woman; he lost his whole fortune at the gaming-table; and, with the exception of about eleven months, he has remained always in opposition.

Perhaps the truth was simply that while he was young it suited Fox to be in opposition, and later on there was little he could do to change that state of affairs. His routine, or lack of it, was established as early as the time of the American War of Independence, of which, as a lifelong rebel, he firmly approved. He liked to be free to move from Parliament, where he outshone all his rivals as an orator, both to his clubs and to the great houses of London hostesses, and also, when the mood took him, to Newmarket and the race-courses of the Home Counties. His stamina was enormous: he gambled for the sheer excitement of play, and enjoyed his various activities so much that he could go for long periods without sleep. Horace Walpole described one characteristic episode in this way:

He had sat up playing Hazard at Almack's from Tuesday evening, 4th February, till five in the afternoon of Wednesday 5th. An hour before he had recovered £12,000 that he had lost, and by dinner, which was at five o'clock, he had ended losing £11,000. On Thursday he spoke, went to dinner at past eleven at night; from thence to White's, where he drank till seven the next morning; thence to Almack's, where he won £6,000; and between three and four in the afternoon he set out for Newmarket. His brother Stephen lost £11,000 two nights after, and Charles £10,000 more on the 13th; so that in three nights the two brothers, the eldest not twenty-five, lost £32,000.

Stories such as this improved with the telling. It was pointed out at Westminster that the speech which Fox fitted in on 6 February between the end of his marathon session at Almack's and the beginning of his night at White's was a long one, on the notably serious and intricate subject of the Thirty-Nine Articles. Some muttered darkly that before he finished Fox would have more than thirty-nine articles in pawn.

The Prince of Wales found all this admirable, and saw nothing reprehensible, either, about the fact that Lord Holland had been obliged to pay his eldest son's debts to the tune of £140,000; Lord Holland, after all, could afford such a sum. The brilliance of Fox's conversation was recommendation enough to the Prince, who was already in rebellion against the earnest and frugal lifestyle of his father the King. He tried consciously to model his own conduct on that of Fox, cultivating his powers of wit and mimicry partly as a tribute to the example of his friend's celebrated eloquence and quickness in repartee. Very soon his hedonistic extravagance was the talk of the nation. Gambling was never more than one element in the pattern, along with women, pictures, clothes and places in which to live; but it was one to which the King and Parliament took particular exception because of the influence of royal example. Before long, half of the moralists in the land were attacking gambling once again as vicious, depraved and likely to corrupt. Anti-gambling societies sprang up, sermons were preached before the Prince, and politicians who disapproved of the way in which Fox lived found ways of marking the difference between it and their own lifestyles. The evangelical MP William Wilberforce, for instance, let it be known in 1790 that he had declined an invitation to be Steward of York Races. As it happened, both gambling and the devil-may-care *milordism* of the English aristocracy were entering a phase of hectic new life; but they did not do so unopposed.

Two of the factors which made gambling flourish with renewed intensity in the first two decades of the new century were the insecurity born of the nation's prolonged involvement in war, and an exceptionally lax system of credit. There had been many wars in the eighteenth century, but none on the scale of the struggle against Napoleon. To many of those who lived through it, the war waged to stop French imperial ambitions seemed all but interminable. It was like a shadow hanging over the British people, and among other things it produced a level of boredom and dissatisfaction almost without precedent. This particularly affected those at home with frustrated military aspirations, like the Prince Regent, and many of the actual combatants. Between periods of fighting, officers and men alike found time hanging on their hands. Months and even years would go by in which they had very little to do, and the obscure and uncertain course of the war did nothing to help; any sense of meaning was reduced to the immediate horizon.

It was practically inevitable, then, that some of Britain's fighting men should develop the habit of taking part in games of chance for money. Quite heavy gambling sometimes went on while they were actually in the field. As a result of this practice, the less cautious might run up sizeable debts before returning home. But the largest debts were nearly always incurred away from the gunfire, in London. Naval officers often had 'bounty' to spend – reward money for their part in capturing an enemy ship or otherwise adding to naval wealth. Many army officers came from landed families, and they too received good money for completing a tour of duty. Among the high-born, a taste for gambling was traditional, while others responded to the appeal of novelty. Frequently, George III's officers would celebrate the return to Britain with a spree in town, including play at the gaming tables. Then, unsettled by the contrast between campaigning and their present inactivity, a certain number would fall victim to the gambling habit, unable to live from week to week without the stimulus they derived from putting themselves at risk. Half-pay officers, in a condition of life which was by definition betwixt and between, were especially vulnerable, for they were likely to be both bored and under-financed. The problem was that they were often unable to come to terms either with themselves or with economic reality. With the curb of military discipline removed, officers and half-pay officers who deluded themselves that they had the means tended to gravitate towards club society and to play to the limit along with peers of the realm.

This was in a sense understandable. Their status could command respect in London, and it bolstered their self-esteem to be treated on more or less equal terms with noblemen and with clever men-about-town in the mould – however remotely – of Charles James Fox. The time passed more agreeably that way. What is more, if one had the right connections credit was fairly easy to obtain. It depended essentially upon social standing, and a period of service in a 'good' regiment was certainly a recommendation in the eyes of the tight little cliques which ran the leading clubs. Gamblers who managed to avoid notoriety were able to obtain credit because bills of exchange and paper currency had acquired a dominant new role in all financial transactions, both public and private. Deferred payment of debts was something quite normal and, as a rule, unquestioned.

One reason for this was that provincial banks as well as the Bank of England had by now been given the right to print their own banknotes. In the Regency there were several hundred such banks in competition with each other. Most were ready to advance money to county families with any semblance of discretion in their behaviour – in the period 1810–15 alone the private banks of the provinces issued notes to the value of £20,000,000. William Cobbett, who longed for a return to the good old days of gold and silver trading, sneered at the country bankers as 'country rag merchants'. But the junior nobility, officers, and gentlemen with a liking for dice and horseflesh were quite willing to pocket as many 'country rags' as they could lay hands on and scribble promissory notes for still more. The bolder spirits reckoned that when this resource failed – and a certain number of country bankers did fail – they could turn to moneylenders, most of whom were Jewish. Meanwhile, play continued.

At White's, there had existed since 1743 a betting book in which members recorded some of their private wagers. They did this as a safeguard against convenient lapses of memory, and also, it would seem, for the entertainment of the club at large: wit and originality were the keynotes. Many of the bets were purely personal – who would outlive whom –

> Ld Lincoln bets Ld Winchilsea One Hundred Guineas to
> Fifty Guineas that the 'Dutchess' Dowager of Marlborough
> does not survive the Dutchess Dowager of Cleveland,

that such and such a member would marry within two
years, that he would succeed in fathering a son before a
daughter, and so forth. But during the early Regency,
when Beau Brummell and his fellow dandies were cutting
a dash at White's, there came to the fore in the betting
book intense and even obsessive speculation about the
likely outcome of the war. In particular, members were
concerned about the fate of Buonaparte. Brummell seems
to have specialized in bets on this topic. He made two on
a single day during the Russian campaign:

> Mr Brummell bets Mr Irby one hundred guineas to ten
> that Buonaparte returns to Paris (Decr. 12th, 1812)

and

> Mr Brummell bets Mr Methuen 200 gs to 20 gs that
> Buonaparte returns alive to Paris, Decr. 12th, 1812.

Methuen had the news of the day on his side, but the
soundness of his judgement is in doubt. On another
occasion he placed a rather fuddled bet with a Colonel
Stanhope that if

> a certain worthy Baronet understood between them, does
> not of necessity part with his gold ice-pails before this day
> twelve-month, the ice-pails being found at a pawnbroker,
> will not entitle Col. Stanhope to receive his ten guineas.

Three years later, the final stages of the fighting produced a
flurry of bets, mostly for smaller amounts. One page of the
book at White's reads as follows:

> Capt. Capel bets Mr Brummell 5 gs that Napoleon is not

at the head of the French government in Paris within ten days from this day.

March 15th, 1815   George Brummell.

Col. Ponsonby bets Mr Raikes one hundred guineas to fifty, that Buonaparte enters Paris as a Conqueror on or before 1st May, 1815.   Pd.

Sir G. Talbot bets Mr W. Howard fifty guineas to five that Buonaparte is not at Vienna in three months.

March 17th, 1815.   W. Howard
                                                   G. Talbot
                                                   Pd G. Talbot.

Lord Cassillis bets Mr Greville 10 gs that Brussels belongs to Buonaparte in two months.   C. Greville
                                                   Cassillis pd.

Major Churchill bets Mr Greville 10 gs that Buonaparte did not enter Paris before daylight on Wednesday morning the 13th inst.   C.H. Churchill
                                                   C. Greville

Mr Bouverie bets Mr Raikes 20 gs that Buonaparte did not enter Paris before ¼ past 6 o'clock on the 17th inst.
                                        Chas. H. Bouverie pd.

Mr Bouverie bets Mr Greville 10 gs on ye same.
                                                   C. Greville
                                        Chas H. Bouverie, pd.

It was, of course, entirely natural for Englishmen to take a keen interest in the fortunes of the French Emperor, whose military record had given him a reputation for invincibility. For all that, there is in the betting book (still at White's) a clue to a major preoccupation of those who used their credit to place wagers in London clubs at this time. In making their bets, Brummell and his fellow-gamblers were seeking to establish a personal connection with the theatre of war and vicarious control over it. The dandies and their adherents were substitute soldiers, with their own rules and code of conduct. In the betting book, at least, George Brummell had not yet relinquished his commission.

The dandies were snobs and poseurs to a man, and it must have been especially galling for anyone outside their exclusive set to lose money to one of their number. But Brummell himself had a capacity for occasional acts of largesse at the tables which surprised those who thought of him as consistently hard-hearted and calculating. One night at Watier's, where the excellent cuisine and tradition of bold play were both to his liking, he came to the rescue of the dramatist Sheridan's consumptive elder son Tom, who had plunged too deeply into a game of maccao and was glumly facing his last ten counters, having lost several hundred pounds. Quietly suggesting to Sheridan that he should take his place, Brummell added £200 to Sheridan's £10, and, with the game running his way, soon won £1,500. He generously gave half of this to Sheridan, saying, 'Now go home Tom and give your wife and brats a supper, and never play again.'

Incidents of this kind confirm addiction-prone gamblers in their ways by making them believe that fortune will continue to smile on them. Brummell was already addicted. He managed to disguise for several years the fact that he survived in London society solely on the strength of his connections with royalty and with a string of noblemen who admired his wit and the cut of his coat. When the Prince Regent tired of him and he was foolish enough to make out that he, Brummell, had 'cut' the Prince, his credit could no longer hold. Captain Gronow, a keen observer of the social scene who disliked Brummell, wrote that

In the zenith of his popularity he might be seen at the bay window of White's Club, surrounded by the lions of the day, laying down the law, and occasionally indulging in those witty remarks for which he was famous. His house in Chapel Street corresponded with his personal 'get up' . . . His canes, his snuff-boxes, his Sèvres china, were exquisite; his horses and carriage were conspicuous for their excellence.

But now, Brummell's days of authority at White's were numbered. No longer would the Dukes of Rutland, Dorset and Argyle wait on his every word, no longer could he expect the plaudits of Lords Sefton, Alvanley and Plymouth. The final bet recorded under his name, in March 1815, 'that the Bourbons are on the throne of France on May 1st next', is marked 'not paid, 20th January, 1816'.

A few months later, Brummell's massive gambling debts caught up with him, and he was obliged to take refuge from his creditors in Calais. 'He has done quite right to be off', remarked his friend and successor on the throne of dandyism in the club, Lord Alvanley, 'it was Solomon's [a leading moneylender's] judgment'. As was customary in the period, an auction was held of the property of 'a gentleman of fashion lately gone to the Continent'. Some came to watch, with no intention of buying, as is the way in every age. This marked the point of no return for Brummell, although he continued for many years to nurse false hopes of being restored to his old haunts and his former glory. In 1819 his star had sunk so low that a scion of the minor nobility at White's – the very type of Englishman who had once treated him with such respect – wrote in the betting book,

> Ld Yarmouth gives Lord Glengall five guineas to receive one hundred guineas if Mr G. Brummell returns to London before Buonaparte returns to Paris.

With the ending of the war, France was now accessible for the first time since 1802. One of the ironies about what became the rush to Europe in the years which followed was that in a good many cases financial embarrassment was the main motive for leaving home. Life in a provincial town in France, Italy or the Low Countries was inexpensive, and sometimes it was possible to make a completely fresh start. A discredited gambler, however, faced particular diffi-culties arising from the combination of debt and notoriety – there were so many Englishmen abroad that his identity was soon known to local shopkeepers. The curious would sometimes break their journey at Calais hoping for word or glimpse of Brummell; he was like a bear tethered to a post, a mere tourist sight.

But Calais was not the only place in Europe with a claim upon the traveller's attention of this kind. Steadily over the years the number of 'broken dandies' on foreign soil increased. Dieppe, Bruges, Venice and, inevitably, Paris, all came to harbour fugitives from English gambling debts, members once of fashionable London clubs and now part of what might be thought of as the dandies' diaspora. Whether or not they followed Brummell into alcoholic disillusionment, most of these lovers of cards and dice found themselves at some point in their Continental exile unable to resist the lure of the green baize table. A few contrived to pay the rent that way, and even occasionally to clear part of the debt against their names at home, but none readily regained the status which they had once held in London society.

Someone who took a keen interest in the reported migrations and doings of the unsuccessful gambling dandies was Lord Byron, himself a voluntary exile from England since April 1816, although on account of a broken marriage rather than of bad debts. The dandies, he once explained, had been kind to him in his minority, when he lived a fast and careless life about town, and he liked to remain loyal to his friends. One gambling-prone friend from his undergraduate days at Cambridge in particular held his wry affection. This was Scrope Berdmore Davies, clergyman's son, wit, dandy and Fellow of King's College, Cambridge. Early in 1820, Davies 'rather plunged' at Newmarket, which was too close to Cambridge for his own good, and lost more than £20,000. Recognizing that he was ruined, he hurriedly packed and left the university town in which, tiresomely, the proctors had been in the habit of mistaking him for an unruly undergraduate. Shortly before quitting the country, he deposited a locked trunk with his banker, Morland, Ransom and Company, in Pall Mall. On 3 March 1820 Byron speculated on his fate in a letter sent from Italy to John Cam Hobhouse in England:

So Scrope is gone – down-*diddled* . . . To you and me the loss of Scrope is irreparable; we could have better spared not only a 'better man', but the 'best man'. Gone to Bruges where he will get himself tipsy with Dutch beer and shoot himself the first foggy morning. Brummell at Calais; Scrope at Bruges, Buonaparte at St Helena, you in your new apartments and I at Ravenna, only think! so many great men! There has been nothing like it since Themistocles at Magnesia, and Marius at Carthage.

Hobhouse probably enjoyed the poet's jest about Davies shooting himself on the first foggy morning. Davies had long been notorious for his threats to commit suicide, usually made during or immediately after a run of particularly bad luck at the tables. His friends knew him to be of a volatile temperament, but suspected him of sometimes seeking to bring pity into the hearts of those to whom he owed money. The ploy, if that is what it was, had quite often worked – but Davies now faced a new kind of challenge altogether.

As far as the evidence shows, he seems to have adapted to life in exile with a fair measure of success; he was, after all, a practised survivor. In the mid-1830s, when Byron had been dead for ten years, Scrope Davies was living quietly in Ostend. The old liking for individuality had not disappeared. His home was a converted hayloft approached by a ladder, and an English traveller who visited him wrote that

Scrope Davies had filled two rooms, fashioned in the loft, with relics from all the distinguished men he had known, and was visited by many eminent people as they passed through Ostend to pay their respects to King Leopold at Brussels.

Later, he moved to Paris, where he was said by Captain Gronow, now also in exile, to bear 'with perfect resignation' the loss of the wealth he had once possessed. According to Gronow, Scrope Davies 'daily sat himself down on a bench in the garden of the Tuileries' to gossip with his acquaintances, and for the rest occupied himself by writing notes about the famous men he had known in Regency London. He paid two or three brief and unobtrusive visits to London in his later years, and died in Paris, scarcely noticed, in 1852.

For a century and a quarter Scrope Davies remained all but completely forgotten. His name was known to students of Byron as that of a wild companion of the poet's youth and whetstone of his wit, but his Memoirs had been destroyed or lost, and allusions to his brilliance and folly in Byron's letters were virtually all that survived to show the kind of man he had been. Then, in 1976, the Directors of the main branch of Barclays Bank in the West End of London, at 1 Pall Mall East, decided to open a number of locked trunks which they had inherited from a private nineteenth-century bank on the same site. (Barclays Bank was formed when twenty private banks were amalgamated, and 1 Pall Mall East is named Kinnaird House after Byron's banking friend Douglas Kinnaird, once the senior partner of Morland, Ransom and Company.) The main object of their interest was a studded leather chest bearing the name Scrope Davies – the very one which he had hurriedly packed and lodged at his bank when he was forced to flee the country after his final indiscretion at Newmarket in 1820. When the trunk was opened, it was found to contain the characteristic personal papers of a Regency gambler, including betting slips, promissory notes, and unpaid bills on spikes; a series of passionate love-letters to Davies written by a noted society beauty, Lady Frances Wedderburn-Webster, whose name was at different times linked with those of both Byron and the Duke of Wellington; and literary manuscripts of great value, including the lost original of Canto 3 of *Childe Harold's*

Pilgrimage (a gift to Davies from the poet), several letters from Byron, and previously unknown poems by Shelley.

The contents of the trunk were described in *The Times* of 20 December 1976 as 'the literary find of the century'. But the significance of what had come to light went beyond literature to include social history. Mr Martin Davies, a collateral descendant of Scrope Davies, called the discovery 'a time capsule, perfectly preserved . . . a microcosm of the later Regency period'. There were, for example, invitations from Lord and Lady Holland and the Duke of Wellington; a recipe for gooseberry wine; lists of Latin and English aphorisms, evidently prepared for 'spontaneous' delivery by Davies at dinner parties; a bill from his bootmaker, George Hoby, for a pair of tennis shoes and a pair of red slippers; bills of exchange making plain Davies's financial embarrassments, with a summons on a debt of £7,000 among them; a bill from his shirtmaker, C.H. Hemans, for twelve long cloth shirts (12 gns) and six Indian muslin handkerchiefs; and a statement of account for Elphick and Son, late Thomas, breeches maker to the Emperor of Russia. There were also drawings of Napoleon by Scrope Davies's midshipman brother who accompanied the former Emperor to St Helena on HMS *Northumberland* in 1815.

Before he went abroad, everyone who had known him had a story to tell about Scrope Davies. There was, for instance, the incident of the 'dormeuse'. On this occasion Scrope had won a great deal of money from a young man who had been gambling on the eve of his marriage and who faced both disgrace and financial ruin as a result. On a generous impulse, Scrope had given back all of his winnings with the single exception of a little carriage in fashion at the time, called a dormeuse from its being fitted up with a bed. 'When I travel in this,' he remarked, 'I shall sleep the better for having acted rightly.'

This quixotic action brings Brummell to mind, but among gamblers of the period Scrope Davies had been quite exceptional in his intellectual gifts. He alone of the dandies had the kind of quickness of mind and sardonic phrase prized by such reckless tippling gamblers of an older generation as the dramatist and orator Sheridan. A King's Scholar at Eton, Davies had in later years been able to converse with Byron on near equal terms on subjects both serious and ribald; hence the latter's comment to Hobhouse in 1818 that 'such a man's destiny ought not to be in a dice-box, or a horse's hoof, or a gambler's hand'. When it came to gambling, however, the 'profane jester' Davies did not know where to draw the line, and he was always ready to engage in a duel when he felt his honour to be impugned. (He took care, though, to practise regularly with his duelling pistols.) In a letter to Tom Moore in 1813, Byron described how he had been placed in the unwelcome position of having to help resolve one of Davies's quarrels. Scrope had fallen out with Lord Foley, a committee member at Brooks's and another gambler notorious for his rashness and folly. Byron seems to have believed that if the duel had taken place, Foley would have been killed by his friend:

I was call'd in the other day to mediate between two gentlemen bent upon carnage, and – after a long struggle between the natural desire of destroying one's fellow creatures, and the dislike of seeing men play the fool for nothing – I got one to make an apology and the other to take it, and left them to live happy ever after. One was a peer, and the other a friend untitled, and both fond of high play; and one, I can swear for, though very mild, 'not fearful', is so dead a shot, that, though the other is the thinnest of men, he would have split him like a cane.

Although expressly forbidden by law, duelling went on from year to year throughout the Regency, and disagreements between men who indulged in heavy gambling were perhaps the most common cause of such meetings. The quarrel might begin in the tense atmosphere of a late-night session in a gambling hell, with nerves strained beyond the limit by a one-sided game, the hint – real or imagined – of crooked play, and an indiscreetly voiced suspicion that dice had been wrongly thrown or cards marked in advance. (It was not unknown for the unscrupulous to cut their losses by resorting to false accusations, but dishonest practices of other kinds also existed, and these were commonplace when hardened gamblers sat at the same table as novices or 'pigeons'.) If the word 'liar' were used, a challenge to 'satisfy the honour of a gentleman' would almost inevitably follow. To be labelled a coward was even worse than to be accused of cheating. With seconds appointed, the duellists would agree to meet at some quiet place far from the attention of Bow Street Runners in order to settle the matter. The lonely parkland at Chalk Farm to the north-west of London was one traditional duelling ground, but any level place remote from the public eye would serve the turn. More often than not, the first shots would be badly aimed, either deliberately or through inexperience, and at this point the seconds might persuade their principals that honour had been satisfied; but from time to time it was a matter of 'pistols for two, and breakfast for one'. When a fatal duel was known to have taken place, an inquest and trial would be held as a matter of course. In such circumstances, the surviving duellist sometimes judged it wise to escape for a few weeks or longer to the Continent. It did his chances in court little good when the cause of the duel was reported as an altercation over cards or dice.

The 'code of honour' of challenge, acceptance and duel, which found so natural a sphere of action in the lives of gamblers, was strongly affected at this period by military example. According to Gronow, British officers in Paris between 1815 and 1820 were forever being challenged by Frenchmen, in dozens of little affairs which were perhaps intended to make up for the great affair of Waterloo. A foreign influence therefore came into play. That apart, however, duels between serving officers of the British army were looked on as normal occurrences, and society at large appears to have approved of them. To a certain extent, the same applies to the quarrels which took place among titled and propertied members of London clubs. Regimental camp and gentleman's club were judged to be socially interchangeable, and it was a natural consequence that procedures adopted in one tended to be carried over into the other. This held good for gambling. While any man was free to defend his honour with his fists, it was widely accepted that persons of social standing would choose to have recourse to a form of redress belonging specifically to officers and gentlemen.

To those who sought their amusement in the West End of town, the status of gentleman was vitally important; apart from anything else, credit depended upon it. Somewhat ironically, however, many of the places where gambling flourished were run by men whose roots were not in the middle or upper classes at all. Brooks's and White's had committees of management made up of club members; but if one walked a few hundred yards from the door of either to any one of half a dozen well-known hells, a class barrier was crossed. Every effort was made in such places to give to the interior a degree of comfort and plushness which might tempt the well-to-do; this provided a change from the rather austere décor of the more exclusive clubs. Moreover, it was still possible in a gambling hell, as in the clubs, to engage in a private game against a friend or acquaintance, someone of known background. Frequently, though, visitors to these establishments took part in organized games against 'the house', meaning the proprietors; and the proprietors ranged from former prize-fighters to the ambitious and crafty sons of costermongers and fishmongers. In an atmosphere of bonhomie calculated to deceive the unwary, the unobtrusive redistribution of personal wealth went on all the time. Newspapers reported some of the more spectacular individual losses, but such incidents as

April 3, 1811. A young gentleman of family and fortune lost £7,000 on Sunday Morning, at a gambling house in the neighbourhood of Pall Mall

were merely the tip of an iceberg. The most successful of the gaming-house proprietors were financial entrepreneurs of a new kind; they saw to it that the odds over any medium or long run of play were consistently in their favour.

An impression of a number of West End gaming-houses is contained in a pamphlet of 1817, *The Pigeons*. The anonymous author explains that most owners setting up in a business with a bad reputation chose to call their premises 'club' in order to create an outward impression of respectability. He points out that

> by a house of fashionable resort being called a club-house, the proprietors are enabled to exclude *wolves in sheep's clothing*, i.e. spies and informers; for, by taking a mere trifle for a subscription, you get a knowledge of the subscriber, whether a *good man and true*, or not; and, being entered in a book – before he can *turn over a new leaf*, he may be *turned* to good account.

This leads to another and more damaging criticism:

> Where the houses are not really, or apparently, club-houses, large sums are often paid to police officers, as well as to more imposing reformers, who contrive to introduce themselves. Bob Holloway pretty well knew this, as he was, literally, in the pay of them all. Hush money varies according to the magnitude of the concern, from £250 to £1,000 per annum.

Several passages in *The Pigeons* suggest that in certain establishments the author may have been treated with less respect than he believed to be his due. An unsuccessful gambler's resentment perhaps colours his description of the owners of different categories of gaming-house, which include:

SUNDAY HOUSES

Our moral readers may start at the designation of this department; yet common sense will tell them that, as the Sunday Houses are but few, their profits must be the greater. Don't tell me about religion, morality, decorum, etc. Those who hear *gentlemen* express themselves in these sinks of corruption, will at once discover that they are men of the world, who can adapt their conversation to their hearers. First under this head is

77 JERMYN STREET
GEORGE SMITH, GEORGE POPE AND CO.

The scenes which nightly occur at this house, beggar all description. It is a hazard table, where the chances are little in favour of the uninitiated player. The first proprietor is low in stature as in breeding, a corpulent, self-sufficient, strutting, coxcombical, irreligious prig. Mr P. is a respectable, decent, modest personage enough in his way. He is humble, and is forced to succumb to the other, who is the monied partner. Many tradesmen, broken, breaking, or in the *right way*, honour this house with their presence. This house, not being large enough for its trade, the proprietors have opened another in St James's Street.

OLDFIELD, BENNET AND CO.,
27 BURY STREET

Mr Oldfield is not a well-proportioned man. He has red hair, and soon betrays his dunghill origin. He is a pragmatical, bloated, officious, flippant coxcomb, with the *tout-ensemble* of a waiter.

At the Sunday houses, Mr Kelly, proprietor of the public rooms at Cheltenham, which are not sufficient for him, is a steady hand, and, being a stout stentor of an Hibernian, keeps all his comrades in great awe. He, like Lord Y—, frequently plays by deputy; but that is only for small sums. However, like the bear in the boat of Gay –

> '– He thought there might be a picking
> Even in the barest bones of a chicken.'

Bennet of Jermyn Street is tall and robust, with black hair and eyes, and a rather blue beard; and, as for Crockford, 'Do you know me? Excellent well! You're a fishmonger.'

In 1817 Crockford's greatest triumphs still lay in the future, but already the jokes about him were beginning to circulate as he came to be recognized for what he was, the most formidable of all those men of humble birth who had moved west within London – he had begun his working life in a bulk shop near Temple Bar, amid the smell of fish – to exploit the upper-class taste for gambling. Rowlandson, who was a gambler of erratic fortune as well as a brilliant cartoonist, portrayed the squat and unprepossessing Crockford as 'The Shark'. The nickname, if obvious, was also truthful. Since the start of the century Crockford had been quietly studying the habits of betting men with the purpose of one determined to turn their weaknesses to account. His manner towards those who gambled against him was deferential to the point of servility, and his speech was that of the East End. But along with unctuous behaviour and dropped aitches went the cool judgement of a mathematician. From dingy and minor hells near Billingsgate he had risen, by means of successful private wagers and judicious betting at Newmarket, until he was able to go into partnership in a gaming-house in Piccadilly. Gossip had it that he was set on his way by a single win of £100,000 after a twenty-four hour session against a group of dandies with money to burn. (The *Dictionary of National Biography* repeats this story, identifying the players in question as Lords Thanet and Granville, the notoriously foolhardy Ball Hughes, a friend of Scrope Davies known in the clubs as 'Golden Ball', and 'two wealthy witlings whose names are not recorded'.) He prospered increasingly as the years went by, and was shrewd enough to buy the loyalty of his staff by sharing part of his profits. At the close of the 1824 season, for example, he divided £1,000 among the waiters in his club, and the head servant received £500 as a new year's day present. Two qualities gave 'Crocky' the advantage over all rivals – implacable determination, and speed in calculating the odds while giving every appearance of being stupid.

His ambition was to open a club which would cream off the richest takings in town and at the same time conform in every way to a high standard of elegance and cuisine. In 1827 he moved into the very heartland of aristocratic gambling by buying 50–53 St James's Street and commissioning a fashionable architect, Benjamin Wyatt, himself a gambler as it happened, to design a building which would be worthy of his grand scheme. In the months that followed, the noise of demolition and construction work was so great that Crockford's new club was spoken of as 'The Pandemonium' – when it was not referred to as 'Fishmonger's Hall'. Traffic in St James's Street was completely disrupted, greatly to the neighbours' annoyance, and one result of the endless digging and laying of drains was that on 9 November 1827 the building of the eminently respectable Guards' Club, which adjoined Crockford's property to the north, fell in with a great crash. Tom Moore recorded this incident in verse:

> What can these workmen be about?
> Do, Crockford, let the secret out,
>   Why thus your houses fall.
> Quoth he: 'Since folks are not in town,
> I find it better to pull down,
>   Than have no pull at all.'
>
> See, passenger, at Crockford's high behest,
> Red-coats by black-legs ousted from their nest;
> The arts of peace o'er matching reckless war,
> And gallant Rouge undone by wily Noir!

When the outraged guardsmen demanded financial satisfaction for the loss of their club and dignity, Crockford had no alternative but to contribute handsomely towards the costs of rebuilding. As always, however, he calculated in advancing his money. He knew that it was desirable to win the goodwill of the existing clientèle in St James's Street if his new venture was to thrive, and boldly looked forward to seeing some of the regulars from the Guards' Club – after good relations were restored – as members of his own club.

Crockford took a great deal of trouble over two other matters. The first was the choice of a chef who would confer upon his house the reputation of serving the best food in London. He was aware that Watier, formerly chef to the Regent, had very successfully launched the club which bore his name by offering Continental dishes which made a welcome change from the endless round of joints and beefsteaks served at White's and Brooks's; and Watier's had quickly established itself as a centre of high play. Crockford decided to employ a French chef of the same quality as Watier, and to give him every opportunity to excel. His choice fell upon Louis Eustache Ude, a brilliant, temperamental figure whose pride in his art was such that he would argue heatedly with anyone who dared to criticize either sauce or entrée. Crockford paid him between £1,200 and £2,000 a year, an unheard-of salary for a chef. Ude proved to be worth every penny, for London was gastronomically a dull city. It was rumoured that some members enjoyed provoking the chef to storm into the dining-room: certainly, Ude had publicity value.

No less important was the appointment of what Crockford called his 'Management Committee of Noblemen and Gentlemen'. *The Times* hinted on 29 November 1827 that subscriptions to the new club were being taken out by men from the city who should have known better – 'the counting house and the hazard table do not well accord' – and Crockford was at pains to demonstrate that the most respected names in the land were associated with the new premises in St James's Street. Not only did he manage to recruit leaders in the sporting world such as the Earls of Chesterfield and Lichfield, he succeeded in due course in enlisting the support of the Duke of Wellington himself, a lifelong non-gambler ever since indiscreet gaming in Dublin when he was a young officer had all but cost him his commission. Wellington made it clear that what attracted him to Crockford's were its excellent food and general amenities as a club. This was entirely to the liking of the owner, who was eager to promote the belief that he was in business primarily to meet the innocent social requirements of those who paid the thirty-guinea annual subscription – the highest, incidentally, of any club in London.

His genius, nevertheless, was for gambling management, and soon after Wyatt's imposing three-story club building opened its doors in January 1828, very large sums of money began to change hands at Crockford's. It is true that Crockford's expenses were large; staff costs apart, he spent about £2,000 a year on dice alone, providing three new pairs made from the finest ivory at a guinea a pair at the opening of play each evening. But from the beginning the takings were never in doubt, and one contemporary estimated that Crockford's gross income in the first two seasons must have been more than a quarter of a million pounds. The game which made him this new fortune was hazard, in which – although the players were lulled into believing the odds would operate in their favour – in terms of probability the house had an 'edge' over all comers of at least 15 per cent. All that was necessary to ensure very large profits was that players should remain at the table for longish sessions. This was the real point of serving tempting food and wine, and Crockford made it a rule that for those who took part in gaming everything was on the house. If a noble lord took a sudden fancy to peaches or grapes out of season, his whim would normally be gratified, even if Ude had to send his minions out from the 'Ascot of gambling' on hurried journeys across London to the markets.

The room in which Crockford was usually to be found was less immediately impressive than the magnificent staircase, state drawing-room and dining-room in the club. It was described in this way in a magazine article of the period:

The *Sanctum Sanctorum*, or *Play Room*, is comparatively small, but handsomely furnished. In the centre of the apartment stands the *all attractive Hazard Table*, innocent and unpretending enough in its form and appearance, but fatally mischievous and destructive in its conjunctive influence with box and dice. On this table, it may, with truth, be asserted that the greater portion, if not the whole of Crockford's immense wealth was achieved; and for this piece of plain, unassuming mahogany, he had, doubtless, a more profound veneration than for the most costly piece of furniture that ever graced a palace. . . . At another part of the room is fixed a writing table, or desk, where the Pluto of the place was wont to preside, to mete out loans on draft or other security, and to answer all demands by successful players. Chairs of easy make, dice boxes, bowls for holding counters representing sums from £1 to £200, with small hand rakes used by players to draw their counters from any inconvenient distance on the table, may be said to complete the furniture, machinery, and implements of this *great workshop*.

In its first ten years of life, before Victorian seriousness got the better of the reckless spirit of gambling extravagance in London, Crockford's 'workshop' made him a millionaire. Gronow's summing-up was that, thanks in part to the 'excellent tone' of his club, Crockford

won the whole of the ready money of the then existing generation. As is often the case at Lord's cricket ground, the great match of the gentlemen of England against the professional players was won by the latter.

'Who that ever entered that dangerous little room', he asked,

can ever forget the large green table, with the croupiers, Page, Darking, and Bacon, with their suave manners, sleek appearance, stiff white neck cloths, and the almost miraculous quickness and dexterity with which they swept away the money of the unfortunate punters?

But his most vivid impression was of 'the old fishmonger himself, seated snug and sly . . . in the corner of the room, watchful as the dragon that guarded the golden apples of the Hesperides'.

SEVEN

SOME REGENCY ROGUES AND CHARACTERS

The early nineteenth century produced a quite remarkable assortment of rogues and malefactors – law-breakers, cheats, and sexual adventurers. In an age of immense national wealth unevenly distributed, of conspicuous personal consumption, and of decidedly lax policing, an ever-increasing number of urban criminals ruthlessly exploited the opportunities which presented themselves; and by no means all of them came from the long-established families of the rookeries.

Some of the factors making for a breakdown of law and morality can be readily identified. The quickening flow of population from country to city caused social stress and unrest, as did far-reaching changes in patterns of work, leisure and unemployment. War and the aftermath of the French Revolution also played a part in bringing about the conditions in which crime could flourish. There had been a time when everyone had 'known his station', and only the riotous and the truly desperate had dared to challenge the rules which kept them bound in a condition of toil, poverty, obedience and limited expectation. Now all that was changing. The poor were still poor – in the years of famine after 1815, abjectly so – but ideas about a need for radical redistribution in the ownership of property, and about the rights of the common man, had lodged in many minds. And instead of finding expression in political activity, a rebellious spirit combined with the sense of material deprivation might sometimes lead men to steal from or in other ways to prey upon their neighbours.

It would be misleading to suggest that any single explanation accounts for the multiple subversive energies of the London underworld at this time; but certain kinds of crime and vice were so common as to be strongly characteristic of the period. These involved fraud, theft and deception. At a time when social identities were no longer as clear as once they had been, opportunists of every kind could thrive on the chance to pass themselves off as better – morally and otherwise – than they actually were. Law-abiding citizens who had not learned to be on their guard against trickery were easily cheated by fair-spoken individuals – who might be of either sex – practised in the art of dissimulation. No less typical of Regency criminal behaviour was an unrestrained love of swagger and show. It was not enough to rob and then live in quiet comfort, although this was what many criminals persuaded themselves that they would do. The late Georgian law-breaker could seldom resist letting the signs of his wealth appear, for it mattered greatly to him that he should be seen to have prospered. He was a worshipper of display, and display as often as not became the means of his downfall.

The four different characters whose careers are recounted here can perhaps be taken to speak for themselves, and for the period. One man whose career illustrates both the habit of deceiving and an addiction to stylish living was John Hatfield, swindler, forger and bigamist. Born in 1759, he had already committed a long string of offences before the nineteenth century opened; but it is for his final and most daring exploits in sustained criminal deception that he has a place in the *Dictionary of National Biography*. Hatfield came from the village of Mottram in Cheshire, not far from Stockport. After receiving a 'fair education', he became an apprentice in the wool trade, and served as a traveller for a linen draper in the north of England. This employment gave him an early opportunity to develop a persuasive line of talk; but he disliked the drudgery of regular work. The next phase of his life saw him in the Army, probably as a private, fighting along with the Hanoverian forces sent to put down the rebellious American colonies. He gained from the experience a certain air of mystery and of a man widely travelled, which was to be turned to advantage. On returning to England, he courted the illegitimate daughter of Lord Robert Manners-Sutton, a previous Duke of Rutland. She had the promise of £1,000 in dowry if her father approved of her choice of husband. Hatfield had taken pains to impress Lord Manners, and in the event was presented with £1,500 on his wedding day.

Thereafter he moved to London, and, letting it be known that he was 'a near relation of the Rutland family', proceeded to spend his wife's dowry on luxurious living. The money went quickly, creditors became importunate, and he decided to decamp, abandoning his wife and infant family. Shortly afterwards his wife died, reputedly from a broken heart. Hatfield now began to specialize in a particular kind of confidence trick involving the use of his considerable ability to charm impressionable or lonely women. More than once he came close to marrying women of means, but his debts had been widely reported, and in 1782 he was imprisoned in the King's Bench Jail for a debt of £160. Ingeniously he managed to make a visiting clergyman take pity on him and describe his plight to the present Duke of Rutland, who lent him £200 and secured his release. Two years later the Duke went to Ireland as Lord Lieutenant and Viceroy, whereupon Hatfield promptly crossed to Dublin also, claiming relationship with the most powerful man in the land. The brogue he picked up at this time proved a useful professional acquirement back in London, but before long he was again arrested for debt and placed in the Marshalsea. Again the long-suffering Duke of Rutland came to his rescue, but only on the strict understanding that he would now leave England for good.

Instead, Hatfield went to Scarborough on the coast of Yorkshire. Its bracing atmosphere suited his health, but on 25 April 1792 he was arrested for not paying a hotel bill. No longer having any excuse to turn for help to the Rutland family, he spent the next seven years as an inmate of Scarborough Jail. Then fate intervened in a way which must have surprised even so arrogant a man as Hatfield. A young woman from Devonshire called Michelli Nation came to Scarborough for a spring holiday and chanced to lodge in rooms opposite the prison. Every day she saw a tall and military-looking man, with ruddy cheeks and contrasting fair hair and thick black brows, who seemed too distinguished and altogether too much of a gentleman to be behind bars. Without exchanging a word with Hatfield, she fell in love with him, and intervened with the prison authorities to pay his debts. When the two met, he placed his hand over his heart, in a favourite gesture. He was released on 13 September 1800, and the next morning married Michelli Nation by licence in St Mary's Church, Scarborough.

So romantic a start to the new century perhaps caused Hatfield to think seriously for a while about turning over a new leaf, but before long he was up to his old tricks – or rather to bold new ones. He and his new bride had gone to live at Hele Bridge, near Dulverton, on the Devon–Somerset border, where his father-in-law was steward to a landowner. When they had been there for barely a year, Hatfield succeeded in having himself made a partner in a reputable firm of merchants in the neighbouring town of Tiverton. He did this by offering a deposit of £3,000, obtained on the security of the partnership from a Mr Nucella in London. Quite possibly he genuinely intended to repay Nucella in due course, but his high style of living soon made it inconvenient for him to do so. In 1802, with the express idea of obtaining an MP's immunity from arrest, he stood as a parliamentary candidate for Queensborough, but without success. The promissory drafts he had written to Nucella now became due, and he was obliged to quit Devon altogether, once more leaving behind him a distraught wife and young family.

When he felt footloose, Hatfield tended to gravitate to London, but Nucella's duns made it dangerous for him to linger in the capital at this time. He decided therefore to make for a part of the country which attracted well-to-do people of fashion, but where he would be unknown. He chose the Lake District, which in 1802 was enjoying considerable fame and popularity both for the splendour of its scenery and the eloquence of those – like the traveller Gilpin and the poet Wordsworth – who had written in its praise.

Hatfield had assumed a variety of false names in his time, and had more than once passed for a sporting Irish gentleman. He had that gift for entering into the part which helps actors and confidence men alike; an expansive sense of fantasy went along with shrewdness and much cunning. Arriving at the Queen's Head Hotel in Keswick in the second half of July 1802, he let it be known that he was going to make a long stay. His name was Colonel the Honourable Alexander Augustus Hope, he was MP for Linlithgowshire, and brother of the third Earl of Hopetoun. He had his own fine carriage with him, and the best hired horses available. A servant, he explained, was not necessary while he was away from home.

Before many days had passed, the handsome newcomer to Keswick was being discussed eagerly, and as warmly welcomed. Hatfield certainly knew how to charm, and the genteel community of the better private houses and hotels of the area around Keswick took him into their midst. One person who had slight misgivings about him was the poet Coleridge, who – for all his growing addiction to opium – was a highly intelligent observer. It struck Coleridge that there was something a little vulgar and ungrammatical about Colonel Hope's speech. This thought found its way into one of the poet's letters, but his adverse impression did not interfere with Hatfield's successful progress.

Hatfield had always liked to have more than one base, and it was natural to him to make contact with well-to-do visitors in Grasmere, to the south, as well as with the people in Keswick. His fine horse took him there in the course of a morning's ride; yet conveniently, Grasmere was just too far from Keswick for there to be many daily comings and goings among the natives. In the same way, Buttermere, nine miles to the west of Keswick, was a little too far away for everyday business; but for an active man with a spirited horse and time on his hands it was within easy reach.

Hatfield's chief companion in Grasmere was a Liverpool businessman, John Gregory Crump. Crump was so impressed by his new friend's vivacity and winning ways that when his wife had a baby son, Crump decided he should be christened 'Augustus Hope'. In Keswick, Hatfield became intimate with the family of Colonel Nathaniel Moore, a fellow tourist who had represented the town of Strabane in the recently extinct Irish Parliament. Colonel Moore's party included a pretty young woman to whom he was a guardian. Hatfield was all attentiveness and gallantry; after a week or two he made an offer of marriage. She was ready to accept him, and Colonel Moore was pleased that she would be marrying a man of rank and wealth. He suggested, however, that 'Hope' should inform Lord Hopetoun, so that the betrothal might receive formal approval from the head of the family. When after several weeks there was still no word from Scotland, Moore began to be suspicious. His friend had not ceased to urge an early wedding, yet seemed to be spending long spells most days away from the side of his fiancée. Moore could only guess that Colonel Hope was in the habit of joining Mr Crump on excursions from Grasmere.

Hatfield, in fact, was now playing a different game. On his first visit to Buttermere some weeks before, he had called in, as most travellers did, at the unromantically named Fish Inn, and set eyes on the landlord's daughter, Mary. Now in her mid-twenties, extremely attractive, and still unmarried, Mary Robinson had been the most celebrated landlord's daughter in the north of England ever since she had been enthusiastically described in a travel book by Joseph Budworth in 1792 as 'Sally of Buttermere'. She was the subject of eulogistic verses by admiring visitors to the district, and the names 'Maid of Buttermere' and 'Beauty of Buttermere' were on many lips; but her head had not been turned, and she remained unspoiled. It did not take Hatfield long to discover that, thanks to their daughter's looks and their own skilled inn-keeping, Mr and Mrs Robinson of the Fish Inn had quietly prospered. With things in Keswick temporarily at a stand, he decided to lay siege to Mary.

Like Michelli Nation (and others) before her, Mary Robinson was completely captivated by Hatfield. In addition, of course, she believed him to be the Honourable Alexander Augustus Hope, MP, and the way in which he used the parliamentary privilege of franking letters confirmed his social standing. His personal charm, along with talk about his titled family and noble prospects, succeeded in dazzling her, as none of the poetic tributes of earlier visitors had done. She agreed to run away with him to what she believed to be his ancestral estate in Scotland. The first inkling Colonel Moore had of this turn of events came on Saturday 2 October. The day before, he had been surprised to receive a letter from Hope in Buttermere, explaining that business called him to Scotland, and enclosing a draft for £30, drawn on Mr Crump, which he was asked to cash. Moore had met this request at once, and had forwarded an additional £10 so that Hope would not lack funds during his journey. What he now learned to his dismay and astonishment – it was the talk of the place – was that Hope had been married by special licence on Friday morning at the church of Loweswater, to Mary Robinson of Buttermere.

The man who had married the runaway couple was the Reverend John Nicholson, the chaplain of Loweswater. As it happened, Nicholson had himself lent money to the bridegroom, and this perhaps helps to explain why, a few days after the ceremony, he sent a friendly letter to await Colonel Hope in a Border Scottish town, informing him of a rumour carried from Keswick that he, Hope, was an impostor. Hope could easily put an end to such malicious talk, Nicholson pointed out, simply by returning for a short visit. It might be thought that Hope/Hatfield would not now dare to be seen in the Lake District again, but at times like this he tended to believe that reality could be bent to his will. Besides, he needed access to a sum of £200 saved up by Mary's parents. Immediately after receiving Nicholson's letter, therefore, he travelled south with Mary, and on Tuesday 12 October was once more in Buttermere, the suitably contrite and devoted son-in-law looking for Mr Robinson's sign of approval.

His pockets would probably have been lined with 'dowry' according to plan – for Mary was clearly very much in love with him – but the next day he pushed his luck too far. With the idea that his physical presence would stop false and damaging rumours at their source, he and Nicholson rode over to Keswick. A casual social visit to the Queen's Head Hotel passed pleasantly enough, until a new visitor to Keswick named George Hardinge asked him if he would care to carry on the conversation in his private room. There Hatfield found himself confronted with a sort of judicial inquiry. Hardinge turned out to be an eminent Welsh magistrate on holiday, and a friend of the Earl of Hopetoun. He bluntly told Hatfield that he was not the real Colonel Hope, whom he knew well. When Hatfield tried to brazen things out by stating that he was another member of the same family, Colonel Moore and the local postmaster were called in to give 'evidence' that Hatfield had always posed as Lord Hopetoun's brother, and had franked letters as a Member of Parliament. On the strength of this information Hardinge obtained a warrant of arrest from a neighbouring magistrate, and Hatfield was placed in charge of a Keswick constable.

His response to this crisis was characteristically inventive. Claiming that the whole affair was a matter of mistaken identity and something to be treated lightly, he ordered dinner to be prepared at the Queen's Head for Nicholson and himself, then obtained permission from the rather bemused constable in whose charge he was to go fishing on Derwentwater. Outside the hotel, a sympathetic crowd of country people listened and watched, unable to believe that the fine-looking man who had married Mary Robinson was an impostor. Soon, Hatfield was sitting in a small fishing-boat, the oars of which were taken by a local man-of-all-work called Birkett, whom he had treated generously during his period in Keswick. Birkett rowed the boat away from the lake's edge towards where the best fish were said to be – and on Hatfield's instructions kept rowing. When night fell, the two men were far south on Derwentwater. No boat could reach them now, but in view of the nature of the surrounding terrain, Hatfield's escape was by no means assured. Under cover of darkness, Birkett guided him through the gorge of Borrowdale and up the Langstrath valley, close to Langdale Pike. The journey must have been exhausting and difficult, for it involved climbing and scrambling over high rocky ground.

When he had emerged from the Stake, 'a fearful Alpine pass' dividing the northern lakeland from less precipitous slopes to the south, Hatfield parted company with Birkett, no doubt after promising him a liberal reward, and struck west towards the coast. Reaching the seaport of Ravenglass on the Esk estuary, he managed to get hold of a seaman's coat and boots. For some days, he took refuge in a sloop moored near the shore, but, finding no possibility of getting away by sea without arousing suspicion, headed back inland. Early in November he was spotted by an acquaintance at a theatre in Chester. By this time, a reward of £50 had been offered for his arrest; advertisements were printed in newspapers throughout the country. The hunted man continued to elude capture for another fortnight. Eventually, he was run to earth in south Wales, while staying at an old coaching inn, the Lamb and Flag, about sixteen miles from Swansea. He was placed in Brecon gaol, and was then taken to Bow Street, where he appeared before Sir Richard Ford on 6 December.

Hatfield was by now a celebrity. Whenever he appeared in public, large crowds formed to get a sight of him. He enjoyed playing to the gallery, but took the chance to demand a private room at Tothill Fields' Bridewell, on the grounds that he objected to being confined 'along with common pickpockets'. His long-suffering wife Michelli travelled all the way from Devonshire – the journey at this time took more than thirty hours – to spend Christmas Day with him in prison. She won some pity from those who followed the story in the Press, but as was inevitable in the circumstances, attention and sympathy were largely focused on Mary of Buttermere, who, it was now learnt, was going to have a child. A subscription was started to raise money on her own and her parents' behalf, since her father had been reduced almost to ruin by loans he had advanced to Hatfield.

Early in the new year Hatfield was transferred to Newgate. However, since his recent crimes had been committed in the north of England, it was decided that he should be tried at Carlisle Assizes, and a long delay occurred. On 15 August, he was arraigned in Carlisle before Sir Alexander Thompson, a stern judge known as the 'staymaker' from his habit of checking witnesses; a few years later, he would show little mercy towards the Luddite rioters of Yorkshire and Lancashire. Hatfield faced charges of impersonation and forgery, which were punishable by death, and a third – fraud – carrying a possible sentence of transportation for seven years. After a trial lasting for six hours, it took the jury only ten minutes to return a verdict of guilty. The next morning, Hatfield was brought back to court and condemned to death.

He had aged so much during his months in prison that someone described him now as 'looking at least fifty'. But despite the harsh sentence, his courage held out. On Saturday 3 September 1803, the day fixed for his execution, he behaved with cool dignity. When he appeared before the large crowd who gathered beside the River Eden outside Carlisle, it was remarked that he was neatly dressed and still had an air of distinction. Just before he was turned off he was heard to murmur, 'My spirit is strong though my body is weak.' During the hanging, the rope slipped twice by accident so that his feet almost touched the ground, but Hatfield died in an instant and without a struggle.

Mary of Buttermere's child, born in June 1803, did not survive. A few years later, having recovered from this traumatic episode, she quietly married a Cumbrian farmer, Richard Harrison, and moved to his family home at Caldbeck, beyond Skiddaw, where in the course of time two sons and three daughters were born to her. But the story of her first marriage, which had been the subject of several ballads and plays in 1803, was not forgotten. After her death in 1837 her old schoolfellow William Wordsworth, who had visited Hatfield while he was a prisoner in Carlisle, recalled going to a London theatre when the events were fresh in public memory and seeing a play with

> Story drawn
> From our own ground, the Maid of Buttermere,
> And how the Spoiler came, 'a bold bad Man'
> To God unfaithful, Children, Wife, and Home,
> And wooed the artless Daughter of the hills,
> And wedded her, in cruel mockery
> Of love and marriage bonds.

Hatfield had been an exceptionally plausible deceiver and betrayer of women, but there were many others like him in the Regency. The social customs and prejudices of the time put women at a disadvantage, and tales of broken promises of marriage made to pretty serving-girls were common. Occasionally it came about, however, that the boot was on the other foot, and that the one to exploit a lover's gullibility, quite without scruple, for financial gain was not a man but a woman. A married man who indulged in an illicit affair was liable to the threat of blackmail, especially if he was wealthy or titled and had strayed beneath his social class. When this happened, journalists and satirically minded cartoonists were very quick to turn the ensuing scandal to advantage. In the normal run of events, the public interest created in this way spent itself in a week or two, but any hint of possible corruption in high places gave an additional point to every scrap of gossip. Such was the case when, a few years after the runaway wedding of poor Mary of Buttermere, the whole nation was set talking about the reported association of a lady by the name of Mary Anne Clarke with no less a person than the Duke of York.

Frederick, Duke of York, the second and favourite son of

George III and next in line of succession to the throne after Prince George, was a bluff and uncomplicated man of large natural appetites. He enjoyed to the full the masculine pursuits of hunting and gambling, and was, besides, an experienced professional soldier. At his father's insistence, he had been made Commander-in-Chief of the Army in 1798 at the age of twenty-nine. He discharged his reponsibilities enthusiastically, winning the respect of many officers by the keen personal interest he took in their careers, and by common consent made up by sheer hard work for a lack of military flair. Thus he was able to live down a series of notably unsuccessful engagements with the enemy on the Continent –

> Ch the Grand Old Duke of York,
>   He had ten thousand men,
> He marched them up to the top of the hill,
>   And he marched them down again

– and the powers of strategic recovery of his fellow generals Sir Ralph Abercromby and Henry Edward Fox covered up for his mistakes and made his record in the field appear more distinguished than it actually was. The Duke of York's special contribution was to the morale and social standing of the fighting men under his command; he understood their needs and was able to argue on the Army's behalf at Court and so influence those who controlled the national exchequer.

In many ways very different from his elder brother (Frederick for instance had little interest in painting or literature), he nevertheless shared with George one characteristic tendency. Where women were concerned, he had a larger capacity for admiration than cool judgement, and at various points in his career showed himself to be 'a fool in love'. It is true that he had pleased his father by making a thoroughly prudent dynastic marriage in Berlin with the Princess Frederica Charlotte Ulrike, great-niece to Frederick the Great, and eldest daughter of King Frederick

William II of Prussia. His unassuming duchess, however, lacked the requisite vitality to captivate a man of his robust temperament. After a short time in the public eye, she retreated into a life of quiet retirement at their country seat near Weybridge, chiefly diversified by the presence of a large number of pet dogs, on which she lavished her affection. She also enjoyed the respect and goodwill of a curious circle of acquaintances, including Beau Brummell; it was as if her gentle tolerance of marital misfortune made her the natural ally of those who suffered from other kinds of adversity. Her husband brought house-guests to Weybridge for noisy weekend parties, when he would sit up until four in the morning over whisky and cards – but he looked elsewhere for the pleasures of the bed. In the early years of the century his name was linked with those of several women, from society hostesses anxious to be seen with a royal duke to the more expensive kind of prostitute. Then for several years he displayed single-minded, weather-all devotion to one remarkable woman, Mary Anne Clarke.

Mary Anne Clarke, many years his junior, was dark-eyed, attractive, and well versed in the ways of men. Born in 1776 into a poor family living in Ball and Pin Alley, Chancery Lane, she had contrived to prosper after her father's death and her mother's remarriage to a composer called Farquhar. One story had it that she owed her education to the son of his employer, who fell in love with her and taught her to read. In due course, she married an ambitious young stonemason from Golden Lane, and when he came into some money, migrated with him to the West End of town. Mr Clarke unfortunately turned out to be a spendthrift. He and his brother both took to gambling, and the brother amassed such large debts that he committed suicide. After bearing two children, Mary Anne began to eke out her meagre allowance by keeping company with gentlemen, with, she later claimed, Mr Clarke's full knowledge and compliance. How exactly she met the Duke of York is a matter of some dispute. One source states that he saw her at the theatre, and was immediately enraptured, another that she had joined the parade of promiscuous fashionables in Hyde Park with the specific purpose of attracting a man of substance. At any rate, they began to see each other regularly in a clandestine sort of way. The Duke was like a horse in clover: his friends noticed a decided change for the better in his prevailing mood and temper.

Mary Anne Clarke, though, was not the kind of woman likely to be content for long with a stowaway role like that of the pale-cheeked Duchess. She soon insisted on, and got, the full rights of a great lady with a town house. The Duke probably reckoned that this was preferable to having her interfere, as on occasion she had threatened to do, in the canine domesticities of Weybridge. (When he found her a weekend cottage near Weybridge, she intensely embarrassed him by tripping into Sunday morning service and watching the family at their prayers.) In any case, he was at this stage too anxious to please her to be able to resist with any success her personal wishes. Thus it came about that he set up house in Gloucester Place, off Portman Square, with Mary Anne Clarke in residence. Whenever he was called away on duty, as frequently happened, he would write to her in terms which expressed unfaltering passion – for example:

How can I sufficiently express to my darling love my thanks for her dear dear letter or the delight which the assurances of her love give me? Oh, my angel, do me justice and be convinced that there never was woman adored as you are. . . Ten thousand thanks, my love, for the handkerchiefs which are delightful: and I need not, I trust, assure you of the pleasure I feel in wearing them, and thinking of the dear hands who made them for me. . . Adieu, therefore, my sweetest, dearest love, till the day after to-morrow and be assured that I shall ever remain yours and yours alone.

In the early days of their relationship, the Duke would appear to have been completely blind or indifferent to his mistress's besetting weakness, a love of extravagance. She spent very large sums of his money, and he took no notice. That this should have happened is perhaps not really surprising, for he had been brought up to be careless about money matters, and found it easy enough to turn to his advisers or to his father when – as invariably happened – his annual expenditure exceeded his allowance of £70,000. His tutor put it succinctly and truthfully: 'though the Royal Brothers received instructions in Latin and Greek with ease, yet they could never be taught to understand the value of money.' To the Duke, it appeared quite in order for Mrs Clarke to have a staff of more than twenty servants, including two butlers and six footmen. He enjoyed being entertained in a setting of sumptuous splendour, and was ready to let her pay £500 for a dinner service which had belonged to Louis XVI's nephew, the Duc de Berri. Until love cooled, he liked to sip his wine from glasses costing two guineas apiece. A stable with a splendid coach and eight or ten horses was what he had always known. Why should he now object to his dearest friend tasting that pleasure?

The Duke's delightful liaison lasted for more than three years. Eventually, he tired of Mary Anne Clarke, and found a fresh source of consolation in a Mrs Cary of Fulham, a lady with rather less expensive tastes. His change of habit was satirized in a newspaper verse of the time:

> Mighty as Mars, as Venus soft in mien,
> At our Horse Guards plump Frederick is seen,
> To eat, drink, chat and call his Fulham groom.

But Mrs Clarke was unwilling to be dropped without some suitable financial arrangement being made, and her debts, which stood at more than £2,000, compelled her to ask outright for due recompense. Had this request been dealt with by the Duke alone, she would probably have been paid off quietly. He had already promised her an annual allowance of several hundred pounds, as well as seeing to the payment of her large-scale purchases of furniture and trappings for the Gloucester Place house. But because the Duke's chief interest now lay in another quarter, he passed the request instead to the Prince of Wales's Attorney-General, who kept a friendly eye on his affairs. This was William Adam, MP for Kincardineshire and a Scot with a zealous sense of the need for economy in the royal household. Adam refused point-blank to consider the idea that Mrs Clarke's £2,000 debt should be paid. Increasingly hostile and unyielding letters passed between the two. When she protested afresh and began to threaten that she would take appropriate action to secure the repayment, he acted on the belief that a long silence would at last force her to acquiesce. A cast-off mistress, in his scale of values, had no lasting claims. He already had troubles enough of that kind through the indiscretions of the Prince of Wales, who with much smugness remarked about the affair: 'I have been no party to my brother's irregularities. I have never been connected with the women with whom my brother has been connected. Indeed I dislike such society.'

Mary Anne Clarke, however, was in genuine distress, for she now had to support the children of her marriage single-handed, while contending with her many creditors. More than once she was on the point of being placed in prison for debt. In some desperation, she formed the idea of disclosing to the public what had taken place between the Duke and herself. Not only so, but she decided that it would add point to the case if she revealed that during the period of their affair, the Duke had often listened to her recommendations about which officers in the Army he ought to promote. She knew that 'corruption in high places' was a charge which even the flinty William Adam and neglectful Duke of York could not ignore for long.

Two men egged her on. One was the discontented confidential secretary of the Duke of Kent, Major Dodd, who had grown tired of serving an unemployed Field-Marshal and seems to have believed that his master's military career had been blighted by the interventions of his royal brother, the Commander-in-Chief. (It is true that the

Duke of York had refrained from helping Kent, but the criticism that he had spoiled his chances was misplaced.) The other was a needy and ambitious Welshman, Colonel Gwyllym Lloyd Wardle, an opposition MP for Okehampton with a keen interest in Army reform. Wardle was eager to take up the cudgels on Mrs Clarke's behalf partly because his party, the Whigs, was at this time looking for every opportunity to accuse the government of misconduct in the running of the war. For a long while the Whigs had argued that the country ought not to be at war at all. Recently, however, they had reluctantly accepted the need for continued warfare against Napoleon, and had begun to make much instead of the theme of governmental corruption and inefficiency. Wardle also had other more personal motives for wanting to see the Duke of York discomfited – he was himself a recent lover of Mary Anne Clarke – but for the time being these were not known to his parliamentary colleagues or to the nation.

It was with considerable shock that the House of Commons heard him propose on 27 January 1809 that

> a committee be appointed to investigate the conduct of His Royal Highness the Duke of York, in his capacity of Commander-in-Chief, with regard to appoint-ments, promotions, exchanges, the raising of new levies and the general state of the Army.

There were loud Whig cheers of support for Wardle, and Spencer Perceval, Leader of the House and Chancellor of the Exchequer, found himself faced with a difficult decision. As he saw it, if he agreed merely to the idea of a Select Committee inquiry – which was what Wardle demanded – it might be thought that the government had something to hide. He therefore took the view that something more open was called for, and his Cabinet colleague, Lord Castlereagh, Secretary for War, was able to announce confidently in the Lords:

I think the greatest possible publicity should be given to this examination, and that every step of it should be in the face of day. I am, therefore, not leaving it to any select committee, nor even to the Twelve Judges, nor to anything short of that full and open examination, which may be had at the bar of the House.

The subsequent inquiry, therefore, took place before the whole House, with witnesses of all kinds – including Mary Anne Clarke herself – appearing there. The proceedings lasted for seven weeks, and newspaper reports (which were almost as detailed as the seven hundred closely printed pages of parliamentary proceedings) drove every other scandal of the period into the shade.

It soon became clear that Mrs Clarke had indeed schemed to win promotions for persons whose names were known to her. These included ecclesiastics as well as members of the armed forces seeking to jump the queue for the purchase of coveted commissions. Her tale of how she had tried without success to obtain a bishopric for a certain Dr O'Meara raised much mirth. She had persuaded the Duke of York to bring his authority to bear to have O'Meara invited to preach before the King. The 'trial' preaching took place according to plan at Weymouth, but the Duke later reported to her that there was no chance for O'Meara, 'as the King did not like the great O in his Name'. Mrs Clarke did not long disguise from the House that her motives for bringing these names to the attention of her royal lover had been mercenary. She had grossly overspent during the early days at Gloucester Place; and the only way she could think of to get back on a stable footing had been to use her influence with the Duke and charge well for the service. On the military side in particular, she had seen to it that the operation was smoothly organized. At one stage, for example, she had given notice through an intermediary that her terms for recommending men for promotion were:

	Full pay Price	Half pay Price
Majority	£2,600	£900
Company	1,500	700
Lieutenancy	550	400
Ensigncy	400	200

Unabashed, she gave details of some of the 'numerous' occasions when, she alleged, she had urged the Duke to see to it that Mr X or Lieutenant Y would have the door to a bright military career opened from within. Why, she remarked to the House, it had happened so often that she had even pinned the names that she needed to remember on to the costly bed-curtains at Gloucester Place.

Mary Anne Clarke greatly impressed the all-male assembly with her beauty, courage and sauciness. On at least one occasion in the House a note was thrust into her hand saying '300 guineas and supper with me tonight'. When the cross-questioning became too embarrassing, she would look down modestly and reply in a soft voice, 'I cannot tell you because it was indelicate'. Many members on the opposition side accepted the truth of every word she spoke; Colonel Wardle for the time being was looked on as a fearless champion of national liberty and purity, a sort of latter-day John Wilkes. But of course it was one thing for the House as a whole to believe that a lovely woman stooping to folly had sought to pay for her extravagances by whispering details of possible lieutenancies or colonelcies in her lover's ear, quite another for members to be convinced that the Duke of York had known all that was going on, as a party to actual corruption. Mrs Clarke's main witness in this connection was a Miss Taylor, who admitted to keeping an establishment for women off the King's Road in Chelsea, though she declined to give its address. Miss Taylor swore that she was present in her friend's house when the question of promotion for a certain Colonel French was discussed between the Duke and Mrs Clarke. According to Miss Taylor, the Duke had remarked, 'I am continually worried by Colonel French – he worries me continually about the levy business and is always wanting something more in his favour.' Then he had turned to Mrs Clarke and asked, 'How does French behave to darling?' Mrs Clarke had replied, 'only middling, not very well'; whereupon the Duke had said with some irritation, 'Master French must mind what he is about or I shall cut up him and his levy too.' This story caught the fancy of the town, so that when the poor tossed up half-pence in the streets they began to cry 'Duke and Darling' instead of 'heads and tails'. Clearly, though, Miss Taylor was not the most reliable of witnesses. The issue of the Duke's complicity was far from clear-cut.

The Duke himself had decided that his best course was to write to Spencer Perceval declaring his complete innocence. This he did early in February 1809, and the text of his letter, in which he denied 'not only all corrupt participation in any of the infamous transactions which have appeared in evidence at the Bar of the House of Commons, or any connivance at their existence, but also the slightest knowledge or suspicion that they existed at all', swung the government benches behind him. The House of Commons, however, was still troubled by some of the evidence amassed against him. There was, for instance, one love-letter, less vacuous than some of the others, in which he had written,

> What a time it appears to be since we parted and with what impatience do I look forward to the day after to-morrow; here are still however two whole nights before I shall clasp my darling in my arms! . . . Clavering is mistaken, my angel, in thinking that any new regiments are to be raised; it is not intended; only second battalion to the existing corps; you had better therefore tell him so and that you were sure there would be no use in applying for him.

Nevertheless, Spencer Perceval was able to win a majority of 82 for a resolution stating that the Duke of York was innocent. But no fewer than 196 MPs had voted against the motion, and as a result the Duke at once resigned as Commander-in-

Chief. Many observers remarked that the Prince of Wales, who had considerable influence with Whig parliamentarians when he cared to use it, had not lifted a finger on his brother's behalf. Fortunately for the harmony of the royal family perhaps, the Duke was restored as Commander when George became Regent.

The Duke of York spent two miserable years in unemployment and disgrace, but could take the view thereafter that he who laughs last, laughs longest. In April 1809 Colonel Wardle was so popular as to be voted a freeman of the City of London; medals were struck, portraits were painted, and he received illuminated addresses from all over the kingdom. By the following summer, however, the bubble of his popularity had burst. An upholsterer called Wright, who had furnished Mary Anne Clarke's house, sued Wardle, casting him for damages, and suddenly it came out that Wardle had himself lived for a time with Mrs Clarke, and that so far from being a disinterested patriot he was a dissolute hypocrite motivated by common jealousy. The cartoonists enjoyed a field-day at his expense. Then Wardle indicted Mrs Clarke and the upholsterer, and somewhat absurdly writs began to fly in every direction. In the end, Wardle lost his seat in Parliament, and after 'selling milk about Tunbridge' for a time, fled to the Continent. He dragged out the rest of his life in Italy, while Mrs Clarke, after publishing a number of indignant and self-contradictory pamphlets, took herself off to exile in Boulogne.

Presumably simply because it was there, most people accepted the harsh penal code of early nineteenth-century Britain as inevitable and at least approximately just. But there was one feature of the law which consistently provoked widespread criticism – the continuing use of the death penalty to punish forgery. In trying to save the life of a civilized but hapless forger called William Dodd, Dr Johnson had argued eloquently against this practice, but to no avail. In his *Letters from England* Robert Southey shrewdly noted that forgery remained a capital crime because it struck at 'the holy of holies' of the country, the Bank of England. Merchants, bankers and large-scale property owners made up a formidable lobby, opposed to any change in the law. In Southey's view, it would have made better sense to transport forgers than to hang them. He slipped in a plea to this effect in his book:

Of all crimes, there should seem to be none for which change of climate is so effectual a cure as for forgery; and as there is none which involves in itself so little moral depravity, nor which is so frequently committed, it is evident that these needless executions deprive New South Wales of those who would be its most useful members, men of ingenuity, less depraved, and better educated in general, than any other convicts.

But thirty years were to pass before forgery ceased to be an offence punishable by death, and during that time, a large number of 'men of ingenuity' went to the scaffold.

The most daring and inventive of these was a banker called Henry Fauntleroy. A Jekyll-and-Hyde character, with a strict Nonconformist upbringing and a string of expensive mistresses, he devised a system of fraud which was more successful and lucrative than anything previously recorded in the annals of English crime. When he was caught in 1824, after nine years of embezzlement, he was found to have misappropriated the best part of half a million pounds – the property of unsuspecting customers who had banked with him, and of the Bank of England. Like Dr Johnson's friend Dodd, Fauntleroy was a well educated man. There was a wave of sympathy and protest when he was sentenced to death at the Old Bailey; but the spectacular nature of his crime was one reason why reform in this part of the penal code was so slow in coming.

Fauntleroy was the eldest son of one of the founders of Marsh, Sibbald and Company, a bank of solid and respected reputation established in Berners Street since 1782. He became a clerk in the bank in 1800, and on his father's death in 1807 was at once made a partner. His father had been the partner most closely involved in the day-to-day running of affairs; and Sir James Sibbald, who was elderly, and William Marsh, a victualler with business interests elsewhere, were delighted that young Fauntleroy showed from the beginning that he had the same natural aptitude and keenness for figures as his father. If it sometimes seemed a little hard to Fauntleroy that as a mere twenty-two-year-old he should have to shoulder such a burden, he made no complaint. Living next to the bank with his widowed mother during the week, he formed the habit of arriving at work before the clerks in the morning and staying on until they had left. He was the kind of man who could carry a great deal of statistical information in his head: Sibbald and Marsh were always impressed, when they came to Berners Street for board meetings, that he appeared to know the exact position of the accounts of all their main investors.

Fauntleroy at work was a model of quiet concentration and assiduity, but in the late evenings and at weekends he sought quite other kinds of satisfaction. He had a strong sensual side to his nature, which in time affected the direction of his entire life. In 1809 he seduced, on promise of marriage, Susannah Young, a spirited girl, the daughter of a Captain in the Royal Navy. When he was about to abandon her, her brother challenged Fauntleroy to a duel to protect her honour, and Fauntleroy was obliged to go through with the marriage. A child was born, but he and his wife soon parted; he made scant provision for her thereafter. This episode left him embittered and restless. Before long, he began to keep company with women of doubtful reputation, and to spend quite large sums of money on their temporary upkeep. His boldest liaison was with Mary Bertram or Kent, whom he installed for some years in Hampton Lodge, an imposing villa in Brighton. She was a notorious woman of pleasure, sometimes known as 'Mrs Bang', and was the original of Pierce Egan's Corinthian Kate. Then, tiring of her fondness for gin and display, he turned to a younger generation, and got with child a girl called Maria Forbes, who was still at boarding-school when they met. Maria was devoted to Fauntleroy from the first. When he suggested that she should move into a house in South Lambeth, she readily agreed. He settled £6,000 on her, and before long a second child was born. His life was always discreetly compartmentalized, so that certain nights of the week were spent in South Lambeth, where in everything but name he was a devoted family man. Fauntleroy, however, had other mistresses, including a Mrs Disney, wife of the Somerset herald, who happened to be one of his customers at the bank; he liked to visit the theatre frequently, and to relax in his club; and it pleased him to invite his more raffish acquaintances to join him for weekend house-parties in Brighton.

Short-sighted, and of less than average height, Fauntleroy was greatly obsessed with power. He kept a bust of Napoleon on his drawing-room mantelpiece at all times, and the billiard-room of the Brighton villa, where Mary Bertram had an awkward habit of throwing tantrums, was decorated 'in facsimile of Napoleon's travelling tent'. Coincidentally, it was in 1815, when his hero was finally stripped of an Emperor's power, that Fauntleroy took to embezzling funds. The immediate cause was a sudden embarrassment brought about because the bank had lent a large sum of money to a speculative builder, who had failed. Fauntleroy was faced with the choice of admitting Marsh, Sibbald and Company's serious loss, which would almost certainly have resulted in the bank's failure, or somehow concealing it. He chose the second course, and contrived to make things appear normal to the Bank of England by forging documents which authorized transference of a client's stocks to the Marsh, Sibbald and Company accounts.

Once begun on a career of fraud, Fauntleroy carried the practice to extraordinary lengths. The sale of stocks required signatures of clerks and of others. Fauntleroy mastered everything which was needed, and concealed the deception from stockholders by continuing to pay dividends on the sums which they believed they still owned; the correct figures were in every instance entered in their pass-books. At this date, stockholders were not automatically informed when their holdings were transferred. Fauntleroy, having spotted a major weakness in the way banks conducted their business, turned it ruthlessly to his own advantage.

On several occasions Fauntleroy was chosen as an executor of wealthy men's estates. The affairs of Benjamin West, for instance, who as President of the Royal Academy had enjoyed a lucrative career as a portrait-painter, were administered by the Berners Street banker both during and after his lifetime. Such a role gave Fauntleroy scope, for in the normal run of events one executor was charged with looking after investments, which involved buying and selling stocks. It was, however, a trusteeship of this kind which led to Fauntleroy's undoing. In January 1824 a Lieutenant-Colonel Frank Bellis died, leaving £46,000 invested in 3 per cent Imperial annuities for the benefit of his widow and family. Fauntleroy's fellow-executors, John Goodchild and John Deacon Hume, not wanting to be saddled with a continuing responsibility, were anxious to have the estate managed by the Court of Chancery. In the early autumn Fauntleroy surprised them by protesting strongly that this was unnecessary. He presented them with plausible reasons, but the truth was that he had embezzled all but £6,000 of the stock, and a move to terminate the executorship would cause this to be revealed. While he was considering how to handle this acute difficulty, his co-trustees chanced to pay a visit to the Bank of England. There they learned that Fauntleroy had sold the greater part of the Bellis stock under power of attorney. Astonished by this discovery, which went far beyond any suspicions they might have had, they at once consulted the solicitor of the Bank of England, and on his advice went to see Conant, the Marlborough Street magistrate, who issued a warrant for the arrest of Fauntleroy.

On the morning of Friday 10 September, Fauntleroy was confronted at the bank by a police officer, Samuel Plank, who had in fact spent the entire night outside, waiting for the banker to return to Maria Forbes's house in South Lambeth. When he heard Plank's official words of arrest,

Fauntleroy went very pale and exclaimed, 'Good God! cannot this business be settled?' According to more than one contemporary source, he immediately offered Plank a bribe of £10,000 if he would allow him to escape; but Plank would have none of it.

In the course of the next day-and-a-half, rumours began to circulate that a prominent and respected banker would shortly be placed on trial. The negligent Marsh and Sibbald, along with other hitherto inactive partners, made a frenzied search of Fauntleroy's office and security boxes in the bank. This showed them that crimes on the scale of that committed against Colonel Bellis's estate had been taking place ever since Waterloo. Recognizing that the bank faced ruin, the self-indulgent Marsh – who had become rich through three marriages to wealthy women – let his daughter draw out £5,000 from his own account; but this action was later detected and disallowed. On Monday 13 September, the *Morning Chronicle* carried a cryptic announcement from the partners:

> The very unexpected situation in which we suddenly find our House placed by the extraordinary conduct of our partner, Mr Fauntleroy, has determined us, for the present, to suspend our payments, as most just and becoming to our friends generally.

An angry crowd formed outside the bank when this news went round. Marsh, Sibbald and Company numbered among their clients many tradesmen and small investors who rapidly realized that their life savings had been put in jeopardy. At one point, police had to be summoned to prevent a riot from breaking out in Berners Street.

Fauntleroy's papers yielded more than enough evidence to hang him. Most clearly incriminating of all was a document listing no less than £170,000 of stolen securities, followed by a note in Fauntleroy's hand dated 7 May 1816, which stated:

In order to keep up the credit of our house I have forged powers of attorney and have thereupon sold out all these sums without the knowledge of any of my partners. I have given credit in the accounts for the interest when it became due. The bank [i.e. Bank of England] began first to refuse our acceptances and thereby destroy the credit of our house; they shall smart for it.

In prosecuting Fauntleroy at the Old Bailey six weeks after his arrest, the Attorney General expressed his astonishment that the embezzler had not destroyed such an explicitly compromising document. Perhaps the explanation was that in 1816, when several banking houses collapsed, there had indeed been a feeling on Fauntleroy's part that he wanted to make the mighty Bank of England smart for daring to act disdainfully towards Marsh, Sibbald and Company; then the original motive had given way to personal greed and corruption. Here, at any rate, was a signed admission of guilt. Fauntleroy's protestations in court that he had acted solely to help the bank, eschewing personal gain, fell on deaf ears. It was already known, through the investigations of *The Times*, that he had 'kept up several establishments' and spent very large sums on his mistresses. The Attorney General hinted briefly at this side of things, but based his case on a detailed examination of Fauntleroy's manipulation of stocks entrusted to his care, which he proved to have been dishonest. The clerks at Berners Street were summoned to testify that Fauntleroy had knowingly and on many occasions forged their signatures on documents which were produced in court. There was also much detailed and irrefutable evidence from long-serving staff of the Bank of England, among them one Robert Browning, father of an exceptionally clever twelve-year-old boy who would one day write poems showing insight into the psychology of just such highly individual criminals as Henry Fauntleroy.

The outcome of the trial was inevitable: the law of the land dictated that Fauntleroy must die. To those who had lost their life savings, the verdict no doubt brought a certain sense of just retribution. (Litigation on behalf of some of his victims was to last for twelve years.) But the tide of popular feeling ran strongly in Fauntleroy's favour once his fate was known. He was, after all, a gentleman, and his weaknesses had been those of humanity writ large. Newspaper readers learned that his wife had more than once been to see him, while Maria Forbes brought him pigeon pie in the condemned cell at Newgate. Surely it said something for him that both women remained loyal even in the glare of publicity during his last days on earth? It was recalled that he had been able to persuade a score of respected men in the City to testify to his general integrity. Could it be that in condemning Fauntleroy, a terrible mistake was being made?

Appeals were considered, and more than one attempt was made to have the verdict reversed on technical legal grounds. There were repeated demands for the sentence to be commuted, and a certain crazed teacher of languages, Edmund Angelini, even begged to be allowed to go to the gallows instead of Fauntleroy and when he was turned away took to hammering desperately on the gate of Newgate.

Despite all these protests, the sentence of the court was carried out, before a huge crowd numbering 100,000. Fauntleroy dressed neatly for the occasion, and in the style the underworld loved, 'died game'. By doing so, he became a popular hero. A rumour got about on Ludgate Hill that he had escaped death by having a silver pipe inserted in his wind-pipe. Small boys told each other that he had begun a new life abroad, where the rich were less spiteful than in England.

The story of Fauntleroy's many acts of embezzlement and fraud sent shock-waves through the City, which suddenly felt itself to be insecure and vulnerable. Large-scale speculation on the stock market in 1824 and 1825 compounded the mood of uncertainty and jitteriness in financial circles, and many bankruptcies took place. Soon, however, it was the turn of another section of London society – the fast-living demi-monde – to become worried and apprehensive. The reason was an event of a quite different kind from the arrest of a prosperous banker. Harriette Wilson, the most successful society prostitute of Regency London, had decided in her forty-first year to prepare for a comfortable retirement in Paris by publishing her memoirs. Not only so, but in defiance of the accepted convention governing such matters, she was bent on naming names throughout. Her purpose was strictly mercenary. The instalments of her story were published serially, by Joseph Stockdale, 'bookseller and coalmerchant', who kept a shop at 24 Opera Colonnade selling books and prints of a doubtful kind. (Among his best-selling lines was a print, unobtainable elsewhere, of 'a Magnificent Painting of the Redemption of Coventry by the Countess Godiva'.) Harriette Wilson's practice was to give warning at the end of each episode of her memoirs of what was likely to come next. Thus it was open to dukes, earls and the numerous others with whom she had been on terms of intimacy to 'buy themselves out' of her work. She wrote in blunt terms to the aristocratic members of the *ton* formerly in her life. A typical approach culminated in ungentle blackmail:

. . . if you like to forward £200 directly to me, else it will be too late. Mind I have no time to write again as what with writing books, & then altering them for those who pay out, I am done up – frappé en mort.

Some paid up at once, thus saving themselves and their families from unwanted publicity and scandal.

Others, however, scorned to do any such thing. Ever firm in a crisis, the Duke of Wellington was reported to have sent the reply 'publish and be damned'. Harriette published, with the result that the Duke's extra-marital adventures became the talk of the town. People queued ten deep outside Stockdale's shop to buy an early instalment of the memoirs which related how Harriette first met the Duke through the agency of Mrs Porter, a procuress. They relished especially the cheeky way in which Harriette mimicked Wellington's laconic speech and direct manner:

The next morning I received another visit from Mrs Porter, who informed me that she had just had an interview with my new lover, and had reported to him all I had desired her to say.

'Since you object to meet a stranger', continued Mrs Porter, 'His Grace desires me to say, he hopes you can keep a secret, and to inform you, that it is the Duke of Wellington who so anxiously desires to make your acquaintance.' . . .

Well, thought I, with a sigh; I suppose he must come. I do not understand economy, and am frightened to death at debts. Argyle is going to Scotland; and I shall want a steady sort of friend, of some kind, in case a bailiff should get hold of me.

. . . most punctual to my appointment, at three on the following day, Wellington made his appearance. He bowed first, then said –

'How do you do?' then thanked me for having given him permission to call on me; and then wanted to take hold of my hand.

'Really,' said I, withdrawing my hand, 'for such a renowned hero you have very little to say for yourself.'

'Beautiful creature!' uttered Wellington, 'where is Lorne?'

'Good gracious,' said I, out of all patience at his stupidity – 'what came you here for, Duke?'

'Beautiful eyes, yours!' reiterated Wellington.

'Aye, man! they are greater conquerors than ever Wellington shall be; but, to be serious, I understand you came here to try to make yourself agreeable?'

'What, child! do you think I have nothing better to do than to make speeches to please ladies?' said Wellington.

'*Après avoir depeuplé la terre, vous devez faire tout pour la repeupler,*' I replied.

'You should see me where I shine,' Wellington observed, laughing.

'Where's that, in God's name?'

'In a field of battle,' answered the hero.

'*Battez-vous, donc, et qu'un autre me fasse la cour!*' said I.

But love scenes, or even love quarrels, seldom tend to

amuse the reader, so, to be brief, what was a mere man, even though it were the handsome Duke of Argyle, to a Wellington!!!

In one sense, Harriette Wilson's autobiography was remarkably reticent. Her explicitness in identifying her lovers did not extend to what she wrote about their love-making, much of which was all coyness and cliché. But those who knew the individuals involved agreed that, so far as it went, her written record showed her to be a clever mimic of the conversation of the famous men with whom she had kept company. Sir Walter Scott paid her a novelist's tribute. Recalling that he had met her once many years before at a supper-party in London – 'a smart saucy girl with good eyes and dark hair and the manners of a wild schoolboy' – he wrote in his Journal in December 1825:

The gay world has been kept in hot water lately by the impudent publication of the celebrated Harriet Wilson. W——n from earliest possibility I suppose lived with half the gay world at hack and manger; and now obliges such as will not pay hush-money with a history of whatever she knows or can invent about them. She must have been assisted in the stile spelling and diction though the attempt at wit is poor – that at pathos is sickening. But there is some good retailing of conversations in which the stile of the speakers so far as known to me is exactly imitated.

Some of the liveliest and most natural writing in Harriette Wilson's memoirs is not about the famous at all. In describing the behaviour of lesser men with whom she had dealings over the years, she displays a gift for satire and a keen sense of the absurd. A typically disrespectful passage introduces 'Smith, the haberdasher of Oxford Street', who found himself torn between lust and anxiety over Harriette's unpaid bills:

I guessed at the motive for his visiting me on this occasion; for I knew that two of my promissory notes of hand, for fifty pounds each, had been returned to him on that morning, as they had also been three months before, when I made him renew them. Not that I was in any sort of difficulty during the whole period I remained with Lord Ponsonby, who always took care of me, and for me; but Smith's scolding furnished me with so much entertainment, that I purposely neglected his bills, knowing his high charges, and how well he could afford to give long credit. He came into the room with a firmer step than usual, and his bow was more stately.

'Your sarvant, Miss.'

'Smith,' said I, 'those bills were paid today, I hope?'

Smith shook his head. 'Too bad, too bad, Miss, upon my word!'

I laughed.

'You are a pretty creature!' said Smith, drawing in his breath, his amorous feelings, for an instant, driving the bills out of his head, and then added hastily, with an altered expression of countenance, 'But you really must pay your bills!'

'You don't say so?'

'If,' continued Smith earnestly, 'if you had but ha' let me ha knode, you see; but, in this way, you hurt my credit in the city.'

'What signifies having credit, in such a vulgar place as that?'

'You talk like a child,' exclaimed Smith, impatiently.

'Come,' said I, 'Smith, hand out your stamps.'

'And Miss, do you expect me to find you in stamps too –'

I laughed.

'But,' continued Smith, growing enthusiastic all at once, 'you look so beautiful and charming, in your little blue satin dress. You bought that satin of me, I think? Ah, yes, I remember – you do look so pretty, and so tempting, and so, so – oh Lord.'

'Mr Smith, I really will speak to Mrs Smith, if you will go into these sort of raptures.' . . .

'Beg pardon – thousands of pardons – it's the worst of me, I'm so imperdent, you see! – can't help it – been so from a child – never could keep my hands off a fine woman! and Mrs Smith is confined, you see: that's one thing! hay? hay? but it shan't happen again. Now, about these here bills? If I draw you up two more, now, will you really give me your word they shall be paid?'

'No,' answered I.

'You won't?'

'No!'

'Then I'll tell you what, Miss! I can't say as you treat me exactly like a lady, and – now don't laugh – oh, you sly, pretty rogue! – hay? hay? beg pardon – it's my only fault, you see. So very imperdent! Come, I'll draw up these here bills.'

He began writing, and I laughed at him again. He shook his head at me. 'Sad doings, Miss, these here bills being returned.'

'It's the worst of me,' said I, mimicking his manner. 'It's the worst of me, that I never do pay my bills. Have been so from a child!'

Lord Ponsonby's well-known rap at the door occasioned Smith to be bundled into the street, bills and all, without the slightest ceremony.

Clearly, Harriette was capable of winding Smith round her little finger. In that quarter, at least, credit gave her no serious problem, and the haberdasher's amorous inclinations merely amused her. But one occasion when she did actually have to call for her servant was during what was ostensibly a medical visit from a Dr Bankhead, while Harriette was living at Brighton.

Dr Bankhead came into my bedroom, with the air and freedom of a very old acquaintance.

'What is the matter, my sweet young lady?' said he, 'and what can I do for you?'

'I see! I hear!' said he, interrupting me, observing that I

had spoken with difficulty. 'Fever? Yes', feeling my pulse.

'Oppression? ah! Cough? hey? Do not speak, my sweet creature. Do not speak! You have been exposing that sweet bosom!' endeavouring to lay his hand upon it, and which I resisted with all my strength of hand.

'Nay! nay! nay! stop! stop! hush! hush! You'll increase your fever, my charming young lady; and then what will our friend Fred Bentinck say? quiet! quiet! There, don't speak; can you swallow a saline draught? and I'm thinking, too, of James's powders; but it is absolutely necessary for me to press my hand on that part of your chest, or side, which is most painful to you.'

'Dr Bankhead, excuse me. This is by no means my first attack of the kind, and I pretty well know how to treat it.'

'There! there! then! be quiet, my dear young lady. I give you my honour, you have already increased your fever. Hush! you will take your draught tonight?'

'Dr Bankhead, I must –'

'Nay! nay! there! keep yourself quiet, I entreat. Quietness is everything, in these inflammatory fevers, you know, my sweet.' . . .

'Dr Bankhead, I'll ring the bell'; and I tried to reach it.

'You shall have just as much, or as little of me as you please. Be still! pray! pray! and this is an offer I never before made to any woman; not even to my dear friend, Lady Heathcote.'

Dr Bankhead laid his giant-hand on my bosom, to demonstrate one of his former feats. My passions were now roused in a peculiar manner, and, catching hold of my bell, I never ceased ringing it till my maid appeared.

I desired her to show Dr Bankhead out of my house, 'and, above all things, do not leave my room without him'.

'Good morning, to you, my sweet, comical lady,' said Bankhead, and left the house.

The combination of saucy anecdotes of this kind with scandalous gossip about the Marquis of Worcester, the Earl of Craven, the Duke of Argyle and many others, made Stockdale's publication extremely popular. He claimed at one point tht thirty editions had been sold within a year. Although this was a deliberately misleading statement – there were instead numerous impressions of a single edition – it is certain that more than twenty thousand copies of the *Memoirs* were in circulation. Harriette's reaction on becoming a best-selling writer was one of delight. 'Now', she exclaimed, 'we are the two greatest people in Europe! Scott in his way, I in mine! Everything which comes after us will be but base copies.' In one sense at least she spoke more truly than she knew. Before long, two pirated editions of her work were on sale, and the craze for the *Memoirs* threatened to become a public nuisance. Harriette was read by people of all classes. Sir Richard Birnie, the chief magistrate at Bow Street, gave orders for the arrest of hawkers caught selling a broadsheet version, *The Adventures of Harriette*. On 14 March 1825 his officers brought in a half-starved apprentice shoemaker, who had been found hawking penny pamphlets inside the gateway of New Inn; round his neck was a placard advertising 'the whole of the amorous letters from Harriette Wilson to the King, the Duke of Wellington and other noblemen'. Taking his cue from such incidents, and from a report that Stockdale the publisher, not content with advertising 'the moral effects on society and manners throughout the civilized world' of the *Memoirs*, had gone so far as to join the Society for the Suppression of Vice, a wit sent the following announcement to the newspapers:

TO HEADS OF FAMILIES AND OTHER SUPPRESSION PEOPLE.

We are delighted to be able to inform our readers on the most undoubted authority, that an edition of the moral and instructive *Memoirs of Harriette Wilson* adapted for families and young persons, by the omission of all objectionable passages, which cannot with propriety be read aloud, by the Reverend Thomas Bowdler, FRS, &c, author of the Family Shakespeare, is in the press.

A 'Family Harriette Wilson' was too large a contradiction in terms even for the self-righteous Stockdale! That summer two lawsuits were successfully brought against him, and he was forced to spend some months in the Fleet prison. Harriette herself had recently 'made a Fleet marriage' with an impecunious Irish man-about-town called 'Moustaches' Rochfort – 'homme très inconnu', in the words of the *Biographie des Contemporains*.

The months of notoriety which followed publication of her *Memoirs* exposed Harriette to more than verbal attack. On her return from one trip to France, a certain Mrs Graham Campbell met her at Dover Pier, knocked her down and pulled her hair out. When the fuss died down, Harriette settled permanently in Paris, and lived for another twenty years. With the passage of time, she grew pious, like the century itself.

EPILOGUE

Investigative writings about London's underworld by Henry Mayhew, tellingly illustrated by Gustave Doré, have fathered the illusion that the nineteenth-century underworld came into being only in the Victorian period. Mayhew himself knew better: the life he describes in *London Labour and the London Poor* (1851–64) is in most essential respects a direct continuation into Victorian times – and often a pale imitation at that – of the street experience of the Regency. Mayhew's most eloquent informants are survivors, leftover victims of the appalling social conditions and urban overcrowding of the earlier part of the century. As his work shows, memories of the unreformed and unpoliced rookeries of the old days were extinguished only with life itself. The generation which came of age between Waterloo and the introduction of the Metropolitan Police had seen the most colourful incidents and the worst horrors of all, and were tradition-bearers of an extraordinary kind. In their youth, crime and poverty had a firmer hold in large areas of London than at any subsequent date: if there were no Police, there were few soup kitchens either. It was before 1820, rather than later, that London's forgotten thousands ran the greatest risks, whether of hanging or of starving.

Someone who instinctively understood their bold and dangerous way of living was Joe Grimaldi, the greatest of all English clowns. He learned his art from the life of the backstreets adjoining Drury Lane and Covent Garden, and from his father, a hard taskmaster familiar with the insecurity of theatre employment. From the beginning of the century until well into the 1820s Grimaldi delighted and captivated people of all ages, degrees of sobriety, and social backgrounds. He did it partly by the expressiveness of his face, which was painted with patches to look comical, and especially of his large dark eyes; partly by the sheer agility with which he flung himself about the stage – before his career was over, he had broken nearly every bone in his body; and partly by his quicksilver combination of clever words, often in rhyme, with accurate miming. Grimaldi, or 'Joey' as children lovingly called him, was able to eat links of sausages or a tray of tarts faster than any Dogberry or Verges of the Watch could say Jack Robinson. In this, he simply carried to its high point of absurd parody the Georgian habit of guzzling: like Rowlandson, he drew from life. No less significantly, he created endless laughter out of the comedy of stealing – in which he specialized. A contemporary wrote of him in 1827:

> He was the very *beau idéal* of thieves – robbery became a science in his hands – you forgave the larceny, for the humour with which it was perpetrated. He abstracted a leg of mutton from a butcher's tray with such a delightful assumption of nonchalance – he threw such plump stupidity into his countenance, whilst the slyness of observation lurked in his half-closed eyes – he extracted a watch, or a handkerchief, with such a bewitching eagerness – with such a devotion to the task – and yet kept a wary eye upon the victim of his trickery – seemed so imbued with the spirit of peculation that you saw it in him, merely as a portion of his nature, and for which he was neither blameable nor accountable.

Richard Findlater, Grimaldi's biographer, comments acutely on this passage: 'everyone laughed at Clown, the master-thief, when petty larceny was punishable by death. The greater the danger, the better the joke.' In the Regency, everyone thought they knew about stealing, whether as victims or practitioners. Grimaldi pleased them by proving, with his innocence intact, that they knew less than he. Playing with a deftness which the young Charles Dickens was to remember all his life, he mimicked the amorality of underworld London, and made it a source not of fear but of comedy. His successor, the naughty clown in modern pantomime or circus, can perhaps be seen as a continuation of the Regency spirit.

Aspects of the Regency underworld live on, too, in the visual satires of Rowlandson and Cruikshank, and in novels by Dickens and Thackeray. Dickens, who became so successful and prosperous, never lost his memories of childhood wretchedness in the shabby purlieus of the Marshalsea, in which his father was imprisoned for debt. Desolating images of that prison haunt the pages of *Little Dorrit*; while in *Bleak House* he demonstrates a connection between a decadent aristocracy and the terrible poverty of London's outcast children by means of the interlinked stories of Lady Dedlock, who once lost her heart to a Regency gambler, and of poor Jo, the penniless crossing-sweeper of 'Tom-all-alone's'. Jo, who is constantly being told to 'move on', has nowhere to lay his head but a miserable corner of one of the worst rookeries in London. Dickens wrote in indignation that old wrongs had not been righted by the mid-century; Thackeray's tone was one of amused resignation tinged with cynicism. In *Vanity Fair* he creates a splendidly apt image for life in London during his youth: a perpetual fairground exhibition 'in which all is vanity'. *Vanity Fair* is described by its author as a novel without a hero, but it does have a heroine, or rather an anti-heroine, who comes from and in spirit belongs to the urban underworld. Her name, Sharp, is taken from Regency slang, and in her later career she resembles at certain moments the bold Harriette Wilson of London and Paris.

Becky Sharp is an opportunist and a parasite – 'people in Vanity Fair', writes Thackeray, 'fasten on to rich folks quite naturally' – resourceful, materialistic, self-interested and calculating in everything that she does, but never spineless or passive beneath life's onslaughts. She is a natural survivor, and her response to any situation is to exploit it in whatever ways she can while her luck holds out. All this recalls the real-life background of the London streets and of the salons and gambling hells opening off them. In Regency London, as we have seen, countless individuals actually tried – as Becky Sharp seeks to do in *Vanity Fair* – to survive by their wits in a dishonest city. A large number succeeded. Some, driven by envy of the wealth all about them or by sheer necessity, not only bent morality but broke the law. When they did this, they announced themselves to their own kind as heirs of the underworld, natural citizens of the largest thieves' kitchen in Europe.

BOOK LIST

London

Two volumes in the Secker and Warburg History of London overlap in our period: George Rudé, *Hanoverian London 1714–1808*, and Francis Sheppard, *London 1808–1870: The Infernal Wen* (both 1971). Evidence of continuity, as well as of change, is to be found in R.J. Mitchell and M.D.R. Leys, *A History of London Life* (1958), Gamini Salgado, *The Elizabethan Underworld* (1977), Dorothy George, *London Life in the Eighteenth Century* (1925), Henry Mayhew, *London Labour and the London Poor* (1851–64), and Kellow Chesney, *The Victorian Underworld* (1972). Robert Southey's *Letters from England*, published anonymously in 1807, have been edited by Jack Simmons (1951).

Crime, Police and Punishment

Parliamentary Papers consulted in the course of research for this book include Select Committee reports on Gaols (P.P. 1813–14, iv; 1814–15, iv; 1818, viii; 1819, vii), Mendicity (P.P. 1814–15, iii; 1816, v), Police (P.P. 1812, ii; 1816, v; 1817, vii; 1818, viii; 1822, iv; 1828, vi), and Transportation (P.P. 1812, ii). The evidence accompanying these reports is often of very great interest. The best general book on criminal behaviour and its causes in nineteenth-century London is J.J. Tobias, *Crime and Industrial Society in the Nineteenth Century* (1967). The same author's *Prince of Fences: The Life and Crimes of Ikey Solomons* (1974) is a detailed biography of a notorious receiver. John Wade's highly informative *Treatise on the Police and Crimes of the Metropolis*, published in 1829, has been reprinted with an introduction by J.J. Tobias (1972). T.A. Critchley is the author of *A History of Police in England and Wales* (1967), and with P.D.

James of *The Maul and the Pear Tree: The Ratcliffe Highway Murders 1811* (1971). Donald Rumbelow's *I Spy Blue* (1971) offers a good account of the policing of the city of London. A wealth of material on nearly every aspect of crime and punishment will be found in Leon Radzinowicz's magisterial *A History of English Criminal Law* (4 volumes, 1948–68). Books on body-snatchers include J.M. Ball, *The Sack-'Em-Up Men* (1928), Hubert Cole, *Things for the Surgeon* (1964), and Owen Dudley Edwards, *Burke and Hare* (1980). On punishment, see Michael Ignatieff, *A Just Measure of Pain: The Penitentiary in the Industrial Revolution* (1978), and W. Branch-Johnson, *The English Prison Hulks* (1957). On the Poor Law and vagrancy, see Sydney and Beatrice Webb, *English Poor Law History* (1929, reissued 1963); J.D. Marshall, *The Old Poor Law, 1795–1834* (1968); and *The Poor Law Report of 1834*, eds S.G. and E.O.A. Checkland (1974).

Entertainment

Robert W. Malcolmson's *Popular Recreations in English Society 1700–1850* (1973) is a wide-ranging survey. Most forms of entertainment were lubricated by drink. On this subject, see Brian Harrison's exhaustive and fascinating *Drink and the Victorians* (1971). Richard D. Altick is the author of a richly annotated study of *The Shows of London* (1978). On theatre, see Joseph Donohue, *Theatre in the Age of Kean* (1975), and Michael Booth *et al.*, *The Revels History of Drama in English*, volume vi, 1750–1880 (1975), which includes an extremely useful list of minor London theatres. Richard Findlater's excellent *Joe Grimaldi: His Life and Theatre* is available in a second edition (1978). There is no modern reprint of *Life in London; Or, the Day and Night Scenes of Jerry Hawthorn, Esq. and His Elegant Friend Corinthian Tom, Accompanied by Bob Logic, the Oxonian, in their Rambles and Sprees through the Metropolis* (1821): but Pierce Egan is the subject of J.C. Reid's valuable *Bucks and Bruisers* (1971), while J. Ford has written *Prizefighting: The Age of Regency Boxomania* (1971), as well as an introduction to selections from Egan's *Boxiana* (1976). Especially useful on gambling are Henry Blyth, *Hell and*

Hazard: Or William Crockford versus the Gentlemen of England (1969) and Peter Arnold, *The Encyclopedia of Gambling* (1978). Much may also be learned from a number of older books, including Andrew Steinmetz's *The Gamblers* (1870), and John Ashton's *A History of English Lotteries* (1893) and *The History of Gambling in England* (1898). Early nineteenth-century newspapers contain much information about popular recreations, including gambling. One of the richest sources is *Bell's Life in London and Sporting Chronicle*, a weekly which started in March 1822 and continued into the Victorian period.

Memoirs

The Memoirs of James Hardy Vaux: Including His Vocabulary of the Flash Language has been edited by Noel McLachlan (1964). *The Reminiscences and Recollections of Captain Gronow* were published in 1892. There have been various reprints of Harriette Wilson's *Memoirs*, including that of the Folio Society (1964).

Some Additional Sources on 1800–1830

Baer, Marc, *Theatre and Disorder in Late Georgian London* (Oxford: Clarendon Press, 1992)

Barr, John, *Britain Portrayed: A Regency Album 1780–1830* (London: British Library, 1989)

Burford, E. J., and Joy Wotton, *Private Vices – Public Virtues: Bawdy in London from Elizabethan Times to the Regency* (London: Robert Hale, 1995)

Clark, J. C. D., *English Society 1688–1832: Ideology, Social Structure and Political Practice during the Ancien Regime* (Cambridge University Press, 1985)

Colley, Linda, *Forging the Nation, 1707–1837* (New Haven, CT: Yale University Press, 1992)

Fox, Celina, *London – World City, 1800–1940* (New Haven, CT: Yale University Press, 1992)

Garner, Lawrence, *The Georgian and Regency Legacy, 1730–1840* (Shrewsbury: Swan Hill, 1990)

Gatrell, V. A. C., *The Hanging Tree: Execution and the English People, 1770–1868* (Oxford: Clarendon Press, 1994)

Graham, Peter W., *Don Juan and Regency England* (Charlottesville: University Press of Virginia, 1992)

Klancher, Jon P., *The Making of English Reading Audiences, 1790–1832* (Madison, WI: University of Wisconsin Press, 1987)

Laudermilk, Sharon H., and Teresa L. Hamlin, *The Regency Companion* (New York: Garland, 1989)

Linebaugh, Peter, *The London Hanged: Crime and Civil Society in the Eighteenth Century* (London: Allen Lane, 1991)

McCalman, Iain, *Radical Underworld: Prophets, Revolutionaries, and Pornographers in London, 1795–1840* (Cambridge University Press, 1988)

Monaghan, David, ed., *Jane Austen in a Social Context* (New York: Macmillan, 1981)

Morley, John, *Regency Design 1790–1840: Gardens, Buildings, Interiors, Furniture* (New York: Harry N. Abrams, 1993)

Newman, Gerald, ed., *Britain in the Hanoverian Age, 1714–1837: An Encyclopaedia* (Hamden, CT: Garland, 1997)

Newman, Gerald, *The Rise of English Nationalism: A Cultural History 1740–1830* (New York: St Martins Press, 1987)

Parissien, Steven, *Regency Style* (London: Phaidon Press, 1992)

Patten, Robert L., *George Cruikshank's Life, Times, & Art*, 2 vols, 1792–1835 (Cambridge: Lutterworth Press, 1996)

Porter, Roy, *London: A Social History* (London: Hamish Hamilton, 1994)

Porter, Roy, *Mind-forg'd Manacles: A History of Madness in England from the Restoration to the Regency* (London: The Athlone Press, 1987)

Richardson, Ruth, *Death, Dissection and the Destitute* (London: Penguin, 1989)

Rudé, George, *Criminal and Victim: Crime and Society in Early Nineteenth-century England* (Oxford: Clarendon Press, 1985)

Sales, Roger, *English Literature in History 1780–1830: Pastoral and Politics* (New York: St Martins Press, 1985)

Sales, Roger, *Jane Austen and Representations of Regency England* (London: Routledge, 1994)

Schwartz, L. D., *London in the Age of Industrialisation:*

Entrepreneurs, Labour Force and Living Conditions, 1700–1850 (Cambridge University Press, 1992)

Smith, Robert A., *Late Georgian and Regency England 1760–1837* (Cambridge University Press, 1984)

Wainwright, Clive, *The Romantic Interior: The British Collector at Home 1750–1830* (New Haven, CT: Yale University Press, 1989)

Walker, Richard, *Regency Portraits*, 2 vols (London: The Stationery Office Books, 1985)

Worsley, Giles, *Architectural Drawings of the Regency Period* (London: Andre Deutsch Ltd. 1991)

Xavier, Baron, ed., *London, 1066–1914: Literary Sources and Documents*, II: Regency and Early Victorian London, 1800–1870 (Mountfield: Helm Information, 1997)

INDEX

Plates are indicated by bold print